T0304083

ROUTLEDGE LIBRARY EDITIONS:
ACCOUNTING

Volume 8

PERSPECTIVES ON ACCOUNTING AND FINANCE IN CHINA

PERSPECTIVES ON ACCOUNTING AND FINANCE IN CHINA

Edited by
JOHN BLAKE AND SIMON GAO

LONDON AND NEW YORK

First published in 1995

This edition first published in 2014
by Routledge
2 Park Square, Milton Park, Abingdon, Oxon, OX14 4RN

and by Routledge
711 Third Avenue, New York, NY 10017

Routledge is an imprint of the Taylor & Francis Group, an informa business

British Library Cataloguing in Publication Data
A catalogue record for this book is available from the British Library

ISBN: 978-0-415-53081-1 (Set)
eISBN: 978-1-315-88628-2 (Set)
ISBN: 978-0-415-83457-5 (Volume 8)
eISBN: 978-1-315-88651-0 (Volume 8)

Publisher's Note
The publisher has gone to great lengths to ensure the quality of this reprint but points out that some imperfections in the original copies may be apparent.

Disclaimer
The publisher has made every effort to trace copyright holders and would welcome correspondence from those they have been unable to trace.

Perspectives on accounting and finance in China

Edited by John Blake and Simon Gao

London and New York

First published 1995
by Routledge
11 New Fetter Lane, London EC4P 4EE

Simultaneously published in the USA and Canada
by Routledge
29 West 35th Street, New York, NY 10001

Typeset in Times by Florencetype, Stoodleigh, Devon
Printed and bound in Great Britain by TJ Press Ltd, Padstow, Cornwall

British Library Cataloguing in Publication Data
A catalogue record for this book is available from the British Library

Library of Congress Cataloging in Publication Data

Perspectives on accounting and finance in China / edited by John Blake
and Simon Gao.
    p. cm.
  Includes bibliographical references and index.
  ISBN 0–415–11812–3
  1. Accounting — China. 2. Finance — China. I. Blake, John, 1950–.
  II. Gao, Simon, 1962–.
HF5616.C5A33 1992   94–39780
657′.0951–dc20   CIP

ISBN 0–415–11812–3

Contents

Figures

Tables

Part I

Introduction

One approach to explaining international variations in accounting practice is to identify the environmental features that explain such variations. In Chapter 1, Blake reviews the environmental factors that have been identified as explaining national accounting variations in the West, considers their relevance to the Chinese experience, and identifies the strong explicit recognition of ideology as a factor explaining the distinctive Chinese accounting tradition. In Chapter 2, Tang, Cooper and Leung focus on the recent and continuing pattern of development in Chinese accounting. Their review embraces the influence of equity joint ventures in bringing international accounting practices to China, the recognition of domestic share capital enterprises, the issue of the first Chinese accounting standard in 1993, and the fast development of both a national accounting profession and the presence of the international accounting firms. They also give guidance on the issues to address for accounting firms.

Chapter 1

A Chinese perspective on international variations in accounting

J. D. Blake

INTRODUCTION

This Chapter reviews the literature on the reasons for international variations in accounting regulations and practices, identifying a failure of that literature to cite Chinese examples. Based on a review of English language literature on accounting in China, we cite Chinese examples for each type of explanation for the emergence of distinctive national practices. On the basis of this analysis it is argued that:

1 The distinctive experience of issues in accounting in China adds useful examples to enhance our understanding of national accounting variations.
2 The Chinese example illustrates the importance of ideology as a factor underlying national patterns of accounting in a particularly explicit way.
3 Aspects of Chinese accounting where research would offer particularly interesting insights into the study of international accounting can be identified.

FUND MANAGEMENT ACCOUNTING

Following the foundation of the People's Republic of China in 1949 a 'uniform accounting system' (UAS), based on control through the identification of 'funds', developed. A brief description of this system is given here because many of the examples presented below refer to the nature and workings of 'funds accounting', although in 1989 revised accounting regulations removed the obligation to analyse the balance sheet into three separate 'funds'.

Under the UAS the basic accounting equation can be expressed as:

Fund applications [=] Fund sources.

Tang and Fang (1987) observe that:

> Fund application is the state of existence of fund. Fund source is the source where fund is obtained. Technically speaking, fund applications and fund sources equate respectively to assets and equities in Western accounting, but since fund sources incarnate socialist public ownership, the term cannot simply be used interchangeably with the term equities.
>
> (Tang and Fang 1987: 145)

Under the UAS a balance sheet showed three separate 'funds', each of which should show an equal balance of applications and sources. Table 1.1 shows a summary of a 'funds' based balance sheet as it would appear before the 1989 reforms. More detailed explanations can be seen in Tang *et al.* (1992: 18–23) and Wang and Qian (1987: 9–16).

The three funds were:

1 The 'Fixed Fund' employed for the acquisition of various kinds of fixed asset such as buildings, plant, machinery, and equipment.

2 The 'Current Fund' being items continuously circulated in the process of production and operation. Those items involved in the production cycle such as raw materials, work in progress, deferred charges, and finished goods had specified 'norms' on which state financing was based. There were no fixed norms for the trading items of receivable and cash balances.

3 The 'Special Fund', relating to special purpose funds of the enterprise allocated to specific objectives outside the operating cycle such as the renewal and renovation of assets, production development, and employees' welfare. Applications of this fund would be to related specific assets or bank deposits accumulated to meet objectives.

Financing for each fund can come from four sources.

1 State investment. A specific amount is allocated to the enterprise for application under each of the three headings. There has been a move away from this type of direct investment by

Table 1.1 Summary of a 'funds' based balance sheet prior to the 1989 reforms

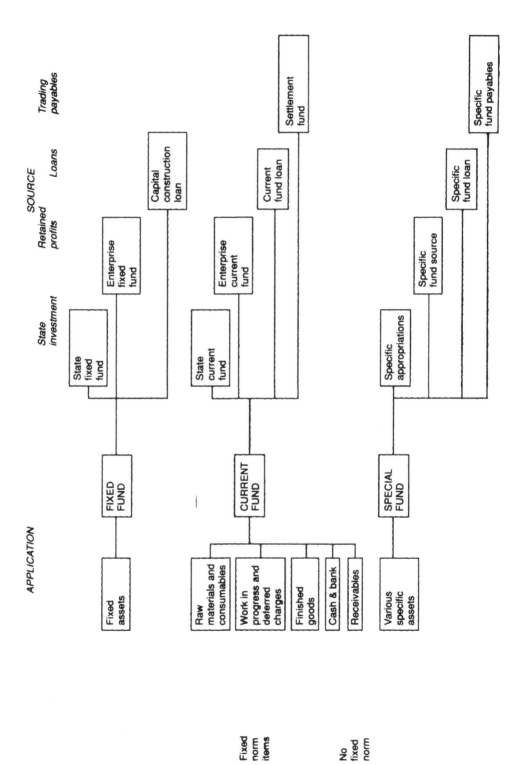

the state to loan finance during the 1980s. Thus Wen–Zheng (1987) reports on a key change in 1985:

Recent economic structure reforms have abandoned State appropriation of fixed fund for bank loans and have changed the single interest rates of bank loans of the past to compound interest rates. As a result, capital cost becomes an essential factor in project evaluation.

(Wen–Zheng 1987: 35)

Similarly the state current fund, computed by reference to the 'norms' referred to above, ceased to be advanced in 1983. Since then increases in working capital needs have had to be financed by interest bearing loans.

2 Various appropriations of profit have been permitted. For example, amounts provided as depreciation are accumulated as a specific fund source which should be applied in cash balance until these are utilized for renovation and replacement.

Until 1979 all profits of the enterprise were remitted to the state. Since 1979 a system of income tax on state enterprises has been developed (see Zhou 1988), applying fully since 1983, so that profit after tax has been available for reinvestment in the business.

3 Loans. As we have seen above, there has been a move away from direct state provision of funds to a requirement that enterprises arrange loan facilities as required.

4 Various forms of outstanding amounts due as a result of the business activities, such as trade creditors and taxation outstanding, constitute the 'trading payables'.

INTERNATIONAL VARIATIONS IN ACCOUNTING

Analyses of the reasons for variations in national accounting practices are offered by a range of authorities including Nobes and Parker (1991), Zeff (cited in Choi and Mueller 1984: 473), Pomeranz (1984: 484–7), Busse von Colbe (1984), and Samuels and Piper (1985: 100–109). Drawing on these authorities a list is considered:

1 Sources of finance.
2 Economic environment.

3 Economic consequences.
4 Nationalism.
5 Other country influences.
6 Tax accounting link.
7 Different user groups.
8 Legal context.
9 Language.
10 Influence of theorists and professional bodies.
11 History.

In addition to the above, one extra item, ideology, is based on the Chinese example.

Sources of finance

A major reason for national variations in accounting practice is that in different countries different sources of finance predominate. In particular, in countries where the stock exchange is a major form of finance, such as the UK and the USA, there is a demand for fuller disclosure in the accounts than in countries where banks are the main source of finance, such as Germany. This proposition is supported by studies in a number of countries that show more extensive disclosures by stock exchange listed companies, such as the USA (Cerf 1961, Singhvi and Desai 1971), the UK (Firth 1979), Sweden (Cooke 1989) and Italy (Hagigi and Sponza 1990).

In China the development of the 'funds' approach to accounting, as described above, illustrates how a particular financing system leads to a distinctive approach to accounting. The point is emphasized by the special accounting rules that have been created for joint ventures with foreign investors, where the 'funds' system does not apply. Zhou (1988) explains the reasons for this separate system:

> The principle of equality and mutual benefit is to be enforced. As joint ventures are enterprises operated by both the Chinese and foreigners, it would be unfair for one side to ask the other to accept its own accounting method and conventions without due regard to the other.
>
> (Zhou 1988: 102)

On the one hand the published accounting regulations for joint ventures have drawn heavily on International Accounting Standards. On the other hand, because the joint ventures have substantial business transactions with state or collective enterprises, some element of Chinese accounting practices also appears in the regulations. The result is that, as Tang *et al.* (1992: 52) observe, 'accounting for joint ventures is a hybrid of Chinese and Western practices'.

Thus China illustrates in two ways how accounting methods develop in response to the source of finance:

1   The development of the 'funds' system to reflect state financing.
2   The existence of a completely separate accounting system for joint ventures to accommodate foreign providers of finance.

Economic environment

Differences in national accounting environments can lead to variations in national accounting practices. A commonly cited example is that some Latin American countries with high inflation rates have responded with inflation accounting systems (see, for example, Tweedie and Whittington 1984: 234–6).

The emergence of inflation in China during the 1980s has led to some discussion of inflation accounting approaches, including a specific proposal to revalue and depreciate fixed assets at replacement cost (He Wei 1987, cited in Tang *et al.* 1992). However, no inflation accounting system has yet emerged.

China offers an example of major accounting changes following on from changes in the economic environment. Thus, following the economic reforms of 1979, 'a series of reforming steps or measures are being adopted for planning, finance, costing or pricing and profit distribution, all of which require more sophisticated and complicated accounting procedures and methods' (Lin 1988: 101).

Lefebvre and Lin (1990) describe the procedures developed by accountants in China to circumvent the constraints of the 'funds' system in a decentralized economy. Managers, frustrated by the legal requirement to borrow at high interest rates to balance one fund while cash balances were held in another fund, would engage in creative accounting to transfer balances between funds. They conclude:

All the above examples of creative manipulations are not rare in China. These kinds of manipulation cause the financial information users, except (maybe) the government, to disregard the accounting information as 'inaccurate and irrelevant'. The costly uniform regulations cannot stop manipulations.

(Lefebyre and Lin 1990: 179)

Thus the new economic environment has forced the demise of the accounting separation of funds.

Economic consequences

In the West, particularly in the USA, 'economic consequences' have been perceived as a significant factor in the development of accounting regulation. Published accounts can give rise to 'economic consequences' in two ways:

1 Users of the accounts may make decisions based on them. For example, shareholders may buy or sell shares, or trade unions may target wage claims at a level they believe is within the company's capacity to pay.

2 Contractual obligations of the company may be monitored or quantified by reference to the published accounts. For example, a company is commonly subject to 'debt covenants' or restricted 'borrowing powers' which limit the total amount of money the company can borrow to a multiple of the shareholders' equity as reported in the accounts.

Blake (1992) has suggested the terms 'judgemental' for the first type and 'mechanistic' for the second type of economic consequences issue.

An awareness of 'economic consequences' issues explains why accounting rules are sometimes hotly debated with a range of interested parties, particularly company management, lobbying for what they perceive as a desirable outcome. This leads to national variations in accounting practices because in different countries both different regulations and different patterns of decision-making are to be found.

An awareness of these 'economic consequences' issues has arisen in the West because it explains the pressures to which private sector accounting regulators can be subject (see, for example, Horngren 1972, 1973, and 1976). Thus we would not expect similar issues to be a major factor in China. One example can be identified in an argument that the use of historic cost accounts in times of inflation, with consequent overstated profit figures, leads to erosion of operating capability because of excessive taxation and distribution of profit to employees.

A major reason for choice of equity boosting accounting measures in the West has been that company borrowing limits are commonly expressed as a multiple of the equity shown in the accounts. A recent UK study identified this as the most common reason for creative accounting schemes (Naser 1993). In China the Bank of China prescribes that:

> the amount of a loan cannot exceed 200 per cent of a joint venture's *registered capital*.
>
> These limits generate problems when a joint venture reinvests earnings. The capacity to borrow remains the same. Thus, the debt-to-equity ratio declines. As a result, the joint venture may not be able to take full advantage of its financial leverage.
>
> (Simyar 1988: 183; emphasis added)

If prescribed borrowing limits in China continue to be based on registered capital rather than reported equity then one of the major factors that underline creative accounting in the West will be avoided.

Nationalism

Arpan and Radebaugh (1985: 346) observe that 'nationalism, egotism and pride also impede progress [towards international harmonization]'. As an example, Zeff (1984) reports that some Latin American countries find it politically unacceptable to follow the lead of the 'imperialist' USA. Instead, Mexico will adopt a US approach then other countries will follow the 'Mexican' example.

As discussed below, China has deliberately explored a range of foreign examples with a view to developing accounting thought. However, the break with the Russian example did demonstrate a deliberate rejection of an over-dominant foreign influence: 'the ideological confrontation of the Sino-Soviet relationship led to a "free-of-Soviet-influence" attitude. This accounting reform resulted in some adjustments in Chinese accounting education programmes' (Lin and Deng 1992: 166).

Other country influences

For a variety of reasons one country can find its accounting system influenced by another. As an example, in 1973 the Spanish government adopted an accounting 'plan' based on the French model.

From 1949 to 1957 China adopted a Soviet style accounting system. Thus Kwang (1966: 74–5) observes: 'The Chinese concept of "economic accounting" originated from the Soviet Union. In fact, the measures adopted in China to establish the "economic accounting system" are largely identical to their Soviet counterparts.'

This influence underlay scholarship: 'Accounting research concentrated on the translation of Soviet accounting literature and textbooks or the interpretation of Soviet accounting regulations or standards' (Lin and Deng 1992: 166). All students of accountancy were obliged to learn Russian, and many faculty members were sent to study in the Soviet Union. This intellectual background continues to be reflected among China's senior academics:

> At present, a large number of Soviet-trained accounting faculty members still teach accounting courses in Chinese universities and colleges. We find, by way of surveying accounting faculty members from five Chinese institutes/universities of economics and finance in 1991, that 54 per cent of accounting professors and associate professors in those institutes/universities were formally re-educated or trained in the Soviet institutes/universities, and that 67 per cent of the rest were trained by Soviet accounting experts in China.
>
> (Gao 1992a: 397)

From 1978 the 'open to the outside world' policy has involved the use of published materials from the West (see Skousen and Yang 1988). At the same time Chinese scholars have worked in various Western countries, both spreading understanding of the Chinese situation and acquiring knowledge of Western methods. Thus Tang and Fang (1987) report:

> Many Chinese accounting educators have been to the United States, Continental Europe, Britain, Australia, and other nations to engage in advanced study as visiting scholars. Thus, knowledge of the features of Chinese accounting is gradually being extended to foreign colleagues and potential investors.
>
> (Tang and Fang 1987: 147)

Gao (1992b: 15) points out that the cultivation of contacts with accountants in the West is an explicit role of the Accounting Society of China: 'More importantly, the Society was made responsible for co-ordinating relations with similar bodies in the Western world.'

The Chinese attitude is summarized by Yang (1981: 17): 'In management, and in accounting work as well, we are doing our best to absorb advanced experiences from foreign countries, and, at the same time, to restore and carry forward the fine traditions we cultivated.'

Tax accounting link

In some countries the law effectively requires published accounts to be prepared on the same basis as the tax accounts. Germany is generally cited as the leading country to take this approach, termed the '*massgeblichkeitsprinzip*' and translated as the 'principle of congruency' (Haller 1992) or the 'principle of bindingess' (Nobes 1989).

By contrast the UK has traditionally been cited as a country where the computation of taxable profits does not influence published accounts. However a recent survey has concluded:

> In the UK the tax-accounting relationship . . . is strong both in principle and in practice ... We observe a number of accounting standards that have been formulated in response to tax considerations, and we find the tax authorities adapting their approach in response to accounting standards.
>
> Blake and Fortes 1993: 24)

In virtually every country in the world national tax law has at least some impact on national accounting practice. In China the introduction of an income tax system in place of the original system of full profit remittance to the state gave rise to the identification of retained profits in the 'source of funds' part of the balance sheet, as discussed above. The principle in China that financial and tax accounts should be on the same basis has exposed some interesting problems of principle during the period of economic reform. Tang et al. (1992–41) cite the example of bad debt provisions. Under the new economic system an enterprise now faces the possibility that some customers who receive commercial credit will become insolvent. Sound accounting practice would lead to a system of

provision for bad debts but this has been resisted by the government because of the consequent reduction in taxable profit.

Different user groups

Accounting regulations and practices vary from country to country
because they aim to satisfy different user groups. Thus Gray *et al.*
(1987: 37), in a comparative study of corporate social reporting,
comment on the 'diversity of aims, target audiences, and practices' that they find between different countries.

In China the development of the funds system, as described
above, illustrates how a distinctive national accounting pattern has
emerged to meet the needs of government as a user of the
accounts in a centrally planned economy. Farag (1988: 148)
observes: 'Enterprise accountants will have a dual position: to
represent the state to strengthen financial position in order to
protect the interest of the national economy and to serve the
enterprise to increase its operational economic benefits'.

The adaptation of requirements to meet user needs is illustrated
in the regulations on the audit of joint ventures. Formerly the
auditor had to be a Chinese CPA. Recognizing that a foreign
partner might see such an auditor as lacking independence from
the Chinese government, appointment of a non-Chinese CPA firm
is now permitted (Lefebvre and Lin 1990: 180).

In the context of management accounting Yang (1981) describes
the development of a system of analysing performance designed
to serve workers as a user group:

> The performance of each group is calculated accordingly and
> is itemized daily on a billboard at the common entrance to the
> department so that every employee on his way to work the
> next day can see the results of a previous day's work for all
> the groups.
>
> (Yang 1981: 16)

Legal context

The national legal system can impact on the accounting system in
various ways. For example:

1 Countries with a common law tradition, such as England, tend
   to legislate on broad principles of accounting rules rather than

laying down detailed requirement. By contrast countries with a Roman law tradition, such as Germany, are likely to have a codified set of accounting rules laying out required disclosures and practices in detail.

2 The USA offers a distinctive example of a country where an intensely litigious environment has caused auditors to seek detailed guidance from the accounting regulators so as to provide unambiguous evidence of good practice to cite in court.

The Chinese legal environment is developing fast. However, Tang *et al.* (1992) observe:

> It is taking time to establish the idea of the 'rule of law' in China, a country without common legal concepts, which is being transformed into one in which laws and regulations play an increasing part in the ordering of economic and social intercourse.
>
> (Tang *et al.* 1992: 5)

Accounting regulation in China applies within a framework of 'uniform regulation and flexible application' whereby local finance bureaux may adapt national regulations to local conditions.

The regulations on the conduct of government audits indicate the limitations of the Chinese legal system: 'this set of regulations on auditors' legal authority indirectly reveals the weakness of the legal system in China, i.e. for the defending party the only appeal is to the higher-ranked audit bureau, which is within the auditing organizational structure' (Lau and Yang 1990: 60).

Language

Differences in language can give rise to variations in national accounting practice even where there is an intention to take a common approach. To give two examples:

1 Hussein (1981) reports on an experiment using a 'back translation' approach which identified a number of differences in meaning between the English and Spanish language versions of IAS 3 on consolidated accounts.

2 Translation of the EC fourth directive requirement that accounts should give a 'true and fair view' into other European languages produced a variety of approaches with a variety of meanings (see Nobes 1993).

Given the distinct character of the Chinese alphabet and language, problems of relating to other national practices exist at the most basic level. Thus development of computerization of accounting in China has had to wait for standardization of programs with Chinese character inputs (Lin 1988: 103).

Influence of theorists and professional bodies

A country sometimes adopts particular national accounting practices under the influence of a lending theorist or professional body. An example of the former is the influence of Theodore Limperg in promoting value-based accounting in the Netherlands (see Van Seventer 1984: 348–56). An example of the latter is the success of the Institute of Chartered Accountants in England and Wales in promoting the 'true and fair view' requirement first in the UK then in the European Community (see Higson and Blake 1993).

In China two professional bodies have been established to promote accounting development:

1 The Accounting Society of China, reorganized in China in 1980, fosters research on accounting theory, practice and education.
2 The Chinese Institute of Certified Public Accountants was founded in 1988 to organize the accounting profession, although administration of examinations and certification is still vested in the Ministry of Finance.

Gao (1992b) reviews the structure of the accounting profession in China.

History

Nobes and Parker (1991) cite 'historical accident' as a factor in determining national accounting practice. One example given is that the German occupation of France in the early 1940's gave rise to the adoption in France of a 'plan' system based on the work of the German scholar Schmalenbach.

An important factor in the understanding of the Chinese intellectual environment is that there is a tradition of accounting stretching back over 4000 years. Thus Fu (1971) notes an elaborate form of 'funds' system designed to control imperial finances in the first millennium BC. One interesting parallel is that in the West accountants take a pride in the author of the first text on double entry bookkeeping, Luca Pacioli; a prominent renaissance scholar who was Italy's first professor of Mathematics and co-author of a book with Leonardo da Vinci (see, for example, Hatfield 1924). In China it has similarly been observed that at one stage of his career Confucius was an accountant, and included accounting in his teaching. (Zhao 1987: 166).

As we have seen above, recent Chinese history has had a major impact on accounting developments. A major disruption of accounting practice came with the ten years of chaos, beginning in 1966, of the 'Cultural Revolution' (Z. L. Zhao (1988) observes:

> Many accountants later complained that during this period they could not do their routine bookkeeping during office hours because that time was supposed to be used for the 'unprece-dented revolution'! Many accounting measures designed to aid management, such as the regular comparison of major ratios among enterprises of the same industry and of similar size, were denounced as running contrary to the 'revolutionary line' and were dropped.
>
> (Z. L. Zhao 1988: 28)

The impact of the Cultural Revolution on accounting educa-tion was even more disruptive:

> During the 'Cultural Revolution' of 1966–76, accounting educa-tion completely vanished at the college level as a result of radical views towards management education and the intellec-tual class at large. . . . Faculty members were obliged to receive 're-education' or 'ideological remoulding' in factories or on farms. Accounting education, and higher education as a whole, became the target of a bloody political battle which resulted in a ten year void in China's education history.
>
> (Lin and Deng 1992: 166–7)

Ideology

Lin and Deng (1992: 173) observe: 'The nature of accounting is defined as something that is intrinsically ideological.' Bromwich and Wang (1991: 53) contrast this explicit recognition of the cen-tral role of an ideological perspective with the tradition of Western accounting: 'somewhat surprisingly from a Western perspective, the philosophical view in China required theoretical and political

justification of these techniques before they could be applied.'
They see one result of this ideological emphasis being to enhance
the importance of the academic accounting community and its representative body, the Accounting Society of China, reorganized in
1980: 'Its reconstitution facilitated achieving the necessary theoretical justification for management accounting and greatly
contributed to the further popularization of this subject' (ibid.).

Lou (1987) explains:

> Both accounting and auditing theories are deeply rooted in the
> ideological foundation of Marxism–Leninism. Marxist–Leninist
> political economics have far reaching effects on the formation
> and development of accounting and auditing theory. Definitions
> of some basic accounting terms are directly linked to the
> nations elaborated in Marxist–Leninist political economic. . . .
> It is explicitly recognized that Marxism–Leninism is the guiding
> philosophy which should be employed to judge whether a
> particular theory is acceptable in accounting.
>
> (Lou 1987: 4)

The importance of ideology is emphasized in university
accounting education and in admission to the accounting profession. Thus Winkle *et al.* (1992: 181) report that 'The candidate
sitting for the national examination, administered by a national
body approved by the ministry of finance, must be "a Chinese
citizen who loves the People's Republic of China and supports
the socialist system".' Tang *et al.* (1992) give an example of one
university course in accounting where Political Theory accounts
for 17 per cent of teaching hours. Watne and Baldwin (1988)
describe such a course at Xianen university:

> The political study class is actually a political indoctrination
> class that is held every Saturday afternoon for two years. . . .
> The class is often taught by those faculty assigned to do polit-
> ical work and consists largely of learning about recent policies
> and documents approved by the Chinese Communist Party. It
> is somewhat of a current events study.
>
> (Watne and Baldwin 1988: 149)

The ideological basis of the current willingness to revive
Chinese accounting practice has its root in the economic structure reforms launched in 1979 and described by Yu (1988) as
follows:

According to the decision to build socialism in a country such as China, whose economy is comparatively backward, we can overstep the fully developed stage of capitalism but not that of commodity production. Without the full development of commodity production, it is impossible to have the full development of socially productive forces and an extremely ample supply of material products, and, without these products, it is impossible to create a highly developed socialistic society and, finally, to enter into a communistic social structure.

(Yu 1988: 55)

Yu argues that China 'should adhere to the principle of drawing widely on the strengths of numerous schools of thought, merging and refining them, and finally developing its own style of management under the guidance of the principles of Marx, Lenin and Mao Tse–Tung' and that 'Critical examination of Western modern management accounting indicates that, to develop this Chinese system, it is necessary to assimilate some of its principles and methods'. (Yu 1988: 56). Thus the adoption of Western accounting methods responds to a development in Chinese political theory and takes place within the context of socialist principles.

CONCLUSION

Y. Zhao (1987) points out that there is very little awareness of Chinese accounting in Western countries and identifies a number of international accounting texts that fail even to mention China. Our analysis above shows that the Chinese experience offers a range of insights into Western perceptions of the international environment and, in explicit recognition of the role of ideology in the development of accounting practice, adds a dimension to that perception.

REFERENCES

Arpan, J. S. and Radebaugh, L. H. (1985) *International Accounting and Multinational Enterprises*, New York: John Wiley.

Blake, J. D. (1992) 'A classification system for economic consequences issues in accounting regulation', *Accounting and Business Research* 22(88): 305–21.

Blake, J. D. and Fortes, H. (1993) 'The relationship between tax regulations and financial accounting: a comparison of Germany and the United Kingdom', paper to the International Accounting Workshop,

University of Portsmouth, September.

Bromwich, M. and Wang, G.-Q. (1991) 'Management accounting in China: a current Evaluation', *International Journal of Accounting* 26(1): 51–66.

Busse von Colbe, W. (1984) 'A discussion of international issues in accounting standard setting', in M. Bromwich and A. Hopwood (eds) *Accounting Standards Setting: An International Perspective*, London: Pitman, pp. 121–6.

Cerf, A. R. (1961) *Corporate Reporting and Investment Decisions*, University of California, Berkeley.

Choi, F. D. S. and Mueller, G. G. (1984) *International Accounting*, Englewood Cliffs, N. J: Prentice Hall.

Cooke, T. E. (1989) 'Disclosure in the corporate annual reports of Swedish companies', *Accounting and Business Research* 19(74): 113–24.

Farag, S. M. (1988) 'Accounting developments in the People's Republic of China: a commentary', *International Journal of Accounting* 23(2): 145–9.

Firth, M. A. (1979) 'The impact of size, stock market listing and auditors on voluntary disclosure in corporate annual reports', *Accounting and Business Research* 9(36): 273–80.

Fu, P. (1971) 'Governmental accounting in China during the Chou Dynasty (1122 BC — 256 BC)', *Journal of Accounting Research*, 9(1): 40–51.

Gao, S. (1992a) 'Accounting education under the economic reforms: the Chinese case study', in M. P. B. Bonnet *et al.* (eds) *FMA Kroniek*, The Netherlands: Samsom, pp. 395–415.

(1992b) 'The accounting profession in the People's Republic of China', *Pacioli Journal*, October, pp. 15–18.

Gray, R. Owen, D. and Maunders, K. (1987) *Corporate Social Accounting*, Englewood Cliffs, NJ: Prentice Hall.

Hagigi, M. and Sponza, A. (1990) 'Financial statement analysis of Italian companies: accounting practices, environmental factors and international corporate performance comparison', *International Journal of Accounting* 25(4): 234–51.

Haller, A. (1992) 'The relationship of financial and tax Accounting in Germany: a major reason for accounting disharmony in Europe', *International Journal of Accounting* 27(4): 310–23.

Hatfield, H. R. (1924) 'An historical defense of bookkeeping', *Journal of Accountancy*, April, pp. 241–53.

He Wei (1987) 'A discussion of revaluation of fixed assets of the textile industry', *Shanghai Accounting* (in Chinese), March.

Higson, A. and Blake, J. (1993) 'The true and fair view concept: a formula for international disharmony — some empirical evidence', *International Journal of Accounting* 28(2): 104–115.

Horngren C. T. (1972) 'Accounting principles: private or public sector?', *Journal of Accountancy*, May, pp. 37–41.

—— (1973) 'The marketing of accounting standards', *Journal of Accountancy*, October, pp. 61–6.

—— (1976) 'Will the FASB be here in the 1980s?', *Journal of Accountancy*, November, pp. 90–6.

Hussein, M. E. (1981) 'Translation problems of international accounting standards', *International Journal of Accounting* 17(1): 147–55.

Kwang, C. W. (1966) 'The economic accounting system of state enterprises in mainland China', *International Journal of Accounting* 1(2): 61–99.

Lau, A. H. -L. and Yang, J. -L. (1990) 'Auditing in China: historical perspectives and current developments', *International Journal of Accounting* 25, (1): 53–62.

Lefebvre, C. and Lin, L. -Q. (1990) 'Internationalization of financial accounting standards in the People's Republic of China', *International Journal of Accounting* 25(3): 170–83.

Lin, Z. (1988) 'A survey of current developments in Chinese accounting', *Advances in International Accounting*, vol. 2, pp. 99–110.

Lin, Z. and Deng, S. (1992) 'Educating accounting in China: current experiences and future prospects', *International Journal of Auditing* 27(2): 164–77.

Lou, E.-Y. (1987) 'Introduction and outline', in Shanghai University of Finance and Economics and the University of Texas at Dallas (E.-Y. Lou, S. N. Wang and A. J. H. Enthoven [eds]), *Accounting and Auditing in the People's Republic of China: A Review of its Practice, System, Education and Development*, Dallas: Centre for International Accounting Development, University of Texas, pp. 1–6.

Naser, K. H. M. (1993) *Creative Financial Accounting: Its Nature and Use*, London: Prentice Hall.

Nobes, C. W. (1989) *Interpreting European Financial Statements: Towards 1992*, London: Butterworth.

—— (1993) 'The true and fair view requirement on and of the fourth directive', *Accounting and Business Research* 24(3): 35–48.

Nobes, C. W. and Parker, R. H. (eds) (1991) *Comparative International Accounting* (3rd edn), London: Prentice Hall International.

Pomeranz, F. (1984) 'International accounting organizations', in H. P. Holzer (ed.) *International Accounting*, New York: Harper & Row, pp. 483–501.

Samuels, J. M. and Piper, A. L. (1985) *International Accounting: A Survey*, London: Croom Helm.

Simyar, F. (1988) 'Joint ventures in the People's Republic of China', in *Recent Accounting and Economic Developments in the Far East*, Centre for International Education and Research in Accounting, University of Illinois.

Singhvi, S. S. and Desai, H. (1971) 'An empirical analysis of the quality of corporate financial disclosure', *Accounting Review*, vol. 46.

Skousen, C. R. and Yang, J. L. (1988) 'Western management accounting and the economic reforms of China', *Accounting, Organizations, and Society* 13(2): 129–38.

Tang, Q.-L. and Fang, Z.-L. (1987) 'Accounting and auditing organizations and research', in Shanghai University of Finance and Economics and the University of Texas at Dallas (E.-Y. Lou, S. N. Wang and A. J. H. Enthoven [eds]), *Accounting and Auditing in the People's Republic of China: A Review of its Practice, System, Education and Development*,

Dallas: Centre for International Accounting Development, University of Texas, pp. 139–53.

Tang, Y. W., Chow, L. and Cooper, B. J. (1992) *Accounting and Finance in China: A review of current practice*, Hong Kong: Longman.

Tweedie, D. and Whittington G. (1984) *The Debate on Inflation Accounting*, Cambridge: Cambridge University Press.

Van Seventer, A. (1984) 'Accounting in the Netherlands', in H. P. Holzer (ed.) *International Accounting*, New York: Harper & Row, pp. 345–68.

Wang, S. N. and Qian, J. F. (1987) 'Financial accounting and reporting' in Shanghai University of Finance and Economics and the University of Texas at Dallas (E.-Y. Lou, S. N. Wang and A. J. H. Enthoven [eds]), *Accounting and Auditing in the People's Republic of China: A Review of its Practice, System, Education and Development*, Dallas: Centre for International Accounting Development, University of Texas, pp. 9–29.

Watne, D. A. and Baldwin, B. A. (1988) 'University-level education of accountants in the People's Republic of China', *Issues in Accounting Education*, 3(1): 139–55.

Wen–Zheng, L. (1987) 'System of cost and management accounting' in Shanghai University of Finance and Economics and the University of Texas at Dallas (E.-Y. Lou, S. N. Wang and A. J. H. Enthoven [eds]), *Accounting and Auditing in the People's Republic of China: A Review of its Practice, System, Education and Development*, Dallas: Centre for International Accounting Development, University of Texas, pp. 31–51.

Winkle, G. M., Huss, F. H. and Tang, Q. (1992) 'Accounting education in the People's Republic of China: an update' *Issues in Accounting Education*, 7(2): 179–92.

Yang, C. (1981) 'Mass line accounting in China', *Management Accounting*, May, pp. 13–16.

Yu, X.-Y. (1988) 'The general character of Chinese and US management accounting and an analysis of the new Chinese management accounting style', in *Recent Accounting and Economic Developments in the Far East*, Centre for International Education and Research in Accounting, University of Illinois, pp. 51–64.

Zeff, S. A. (1984) 'Promoting international harmony', *Accountant's Journal*, August, p. 291.

Zhao, Y. (1987) 'A brief history of accounting and auditing in China', in Shanghai University of Finance and Economics and the University of Texas at Dallas (E.-Y. Lou, S. N. Wang and A. J. H. Enthoven [eds]), *Accounting and Auditing in the People's Republic of China: A Review of its Practice, System, Education and Development*, Dallas: Centre for International Accounting Development, University of Texas, pp. 165–91.

Zhao, Z. L. (1988) 'Accounting in the People's Republic of China: contemporary situations and issues', in *Recent Accounting and Economic Developments in the Far East*, Centre for International Education and Research in Accounting, University of Illinois, pp. 12,28.

Zhao, Z. W. (1987) 'Investment laws and regulations for foreign entities', in Shanghai University of Finance and Economics and the University of Texas at Dallas (E.-Y. Lou, S. N. Wang and A. J. H. Enthoven [eds]),

Accounting and Auditing in the People's Republic of China: A Review of its Practice, System, Education and Development, Dallas: Centre for International Accounting Development, University of Texas, pp. 95–108.

Zhou, Z. H. (1988) 'Chinese accounting systems and practices', *Accounting, Organizations, and Society* 13(2): 207–24.

Chapter 2

Accounting in China

Developments and opportunities

Y. W. Tang, B. J. Cooper and P. Leung

INTRODUCTION

China is a huge country, where an estimated ten million people currently work in accounting-related occupations. China is also a fast developing country and its accounting profession is going through a period of rapid development. Accounting in China is very much influenced by the socio-economic environment in which enterprises operate, and, being a centrally controlled economy, accounting practices in China differ to a considerable extent from those of Western countries. Since the late 1980s, however, China has recognized the need for accounting reform. The uniform accounting regulations were no longer sufficient to meet the needs of investors and users of financial information. Some of the critical factors which have influenced accounting reform have been the diversification of business operations and ownership, the increasing complexity of business transactions, internationalization of economic activities, and the development of the accounting profession (Chow *et al.* 1994).

The accounting reform launched in 1985 embraces a wide range of areas, including the regulatory framework of financial reporting, accounting theory, accounting education and the accounting profession. During the last decade, the major achievement of the reform was mainly in the area of regulation of financial reporting. The current task is to develop a new regulatory framework which is adaptable to China's unique socialist market economy, with maximum harmonization with international accounting practices (Chow *et al.* 1994). This Chapter discusses the background of accounting in China, the factors which have triggered accounting reform, the new regulatory framework for financial reporting, the accounting standards setting process, and the latest development in the accounting profession in China. The latter part of the Chapter focuses on the impact of Western accounting bodies and their role in accounting development in China.

AN OVERVIEW OF THE TRADITIONAL ACCOUNTING SYSTEM IN CHINA

The background

Financial reporting in China has been governed by three levels of legislative framework. The National People's Congress, which enacted the Accounting Law of the People's Republic of China in 1985, promulgated the top level legislation for accounting. Below this level, the State Council provides regulatory support, with, for example, the issue of the 'Regulation on Cost Management for State-Owned Enterprises' (1984), and the 'Tentative Regulation on Fixed Asset Depreciation for State-Owned Enterprises' (1985). At the third level, that is, the operational level, the Ministry of Finance is empowered to administer all accounting affairs (Tang *et al.* 1992).

The Ministry of Finance (MOF) has in the past issued a number of accounting regulations for specific industries and various types of enterprises. These regulations prescribed a set of all-embracing technical guidelines, which included charts of accounts, formats of accounting statements, and detailed rules for the recording of transactions. Although some accounting principles, such as consistency, objectivity and matching were implicitly embodied in these regulations, no accounting principles or standards were explicitly established.

All accounting regulations issued by the MOF were mandatory. The uniform reporting system and detailed regulations facilitated the hierarchical financial reporting system essential for central planning. Enterprises were established on a system of fund allocation, and each source of fund from the government had a specific application. Accounting was uniform and rigid, characterized by its close link with public finance and taxation. Rules for measuring accounting profit were the same as those for measuring taxable profit.

Impact of economic reform

The economic reform has resulted in a series of changes in the government's role in macro-economic management. These changes include the introduction of diversification of business operations and ownership and the globalization of capital markets, which in turn led to increasing complexity of business transactions and rapid internationalization of economic activities. In an attempt to separate ownership from the management of enterprises, various business operating systems, including the business contract system and share capital system, have been introduced. Enterprises have been delegated with autonomy of business operations and finance, with the objective of alleviating reliance on central fund allocations (Cooper and Leung 1993).

As economic reform has progressed, it has become difficult to adopt the uniform accounting regulations previously promulgated by the MOF. Moreover, new types of business transactions and financing activities have become common with advances in technologies, investment by international interests, and the growth of the capital markets. These activities include transferring rights of land use, equipment leasing, hire purchase, securities listing and trading, and an influx of foreign investment. Although the uniform accounting regulations have been revised in recent years, the process has been too slow and rigid to cope with the increasing complexity of business transactions.

PHASES OF THE ACCOUNTING REFORM

There have been three main phases in the reform of the accounting system in China.

Phase 1: recognition of equity joint ventures

The first phase commenced in March 1985 with the promulgation of the 'Accounting Regulations for Joint Ventures Using Chinese and Foreign Investment'. These Regulations were used to provide more flexibility for Sino-foreign joint ventures which employ foreign capital. Similar to international accounting practices, the Regulations departed from the fund-based accounting approach and established the concept of accounting elements, such as assets, liabilities, capital, revenue and expenses. The concept of financial statements (i.e. the balance sheet, the income statement and the statement of changes in financial position) was adopted. The principles of historical cost, matching, consistency, and distinction between revenue expenditure and capital expenditure were explicitly required. The Regulations also established revenue recognition principles and accounting measurement for intangible assets, land use rights, organization costs and long-term investments. The long-standing practice of absorbing general administrative expenses into product costs was removed.

The Regulations were the first attempt in harmonizing Chinese accounting practices with international practices. Until recently, two distinct streams of accounting regulations have coexisted, one for domestic enterprises based on the traditional fund management approach, the other for Sino-foreign joint ventures. Although the issue of the Regulations marked a significant breakthrough in China's accounting reform, some issues remained unresolved. While the Regulations applied to equity joint ventures, which share profits/losses in proportion to equity contribution of partners to the ventures, there were no accounting regulations established for other types of foreign investments, such as co-operative joint ventures and wholly foreign-owned enterprises. Also, there were still some requirements in the Regulations which did not conform to international practices, such as the prohibition of provision for bad and doubtful debts or for possible inventory losses. The accounting treatment for foreign currency transactions was also significantly different from international practices.

Since the promulgation of the Regulations, a series of tax laws relating to foreign investments have been enacted. In particular, the Income Tax Law for Enterprises with Foreign Investment and Foreign Enterprises, effective from 1 July 1991, brought all forms of foreign investments under one umbrella of tax laws. The unification of tax requirements has laid a foundation for unifying the accounting requirements for various types of foreign investment and joint ventures. In 1992, the 'Accounting Regulations for Enterprises with Foreign Investment', applicable for all types of foreign investment, was issued to replace the 1985 Regulations.

The 1992 Regulations took another step further in bringing Chinese accounting practices more in line with international practices. The 1992 Regulations recognize differences between accounting and taxation treatments, and accept that provisions in accounting regulations might be different from those in tax laws. The accounting treatment for foreign currency transactions, provisions for doubtful debts and inventory losses are considered and revised to conform to international practices. Also, for long-term investment which accounts for more than 25 per cent of the investee company's capital, the equity method of accounting is required. Where there is a controlling interest in an investee company, the investing company must prepare consolidated financial statements. Exclusion of a subsidiary from consolidation is allowed if the business activities carried out by the subsidiary are dissimilar from other companies in the group. The new regulation stipulates that, in normal circumstances, revenue recognition should be at the time of sale. For long-term contracts with work in progress, the degree of completion method is adopted for measuring profit/loss.

Phase 2: recognition of domestic share capital enterprises

The second phase of the reform was marked by the promulgation of the 'Accounting Regulations for Share Enterprises' in 1992. To ensure smooth operation of the share capital system, the government has since 1984 developed a comprehensive set of laws in taxation, finance, labour management and personnel, state property management, and auditing of share enterprises. A share enterprise is a separate legal entity, and has full autonomy of operations. The management is accountable to the investors for stewardship and management of the funds entrusted. In this sense, the accounting requirements and functions are similar to those in Western countries. The 'Accounting Regulations for Share Capital Enterprises', which became effective on 1 January 1992, is thus the first set of regulations which adopts international practices for domestic enterprises. These regulations were also similar in many respects to those for enterprises with foreign investment.

Phase 3: issue of accounting standards

The reform entered its third phase when the first accounting standard, entitled 'Accounting Standards for Business Enterprises', was issued by the MOF and became effective on 1 July 1993. The Accounting Standard has introduced major changes to the traditional accounting practices in China. These changes are as follows:

1 The Standard is applicable to all enterprises in China. It changes the long-standing approach of setting accounting regulations for specific types of ownership and industries.

2 The Standard brings changes in the function of accounting. It addresses the needs of different users of accounting information. Traditionally, accounting in China has been used to provide information for the government's decision-making for macro-economic management. The Standard broadens the user groups of accounting information to include external users, such as investors and creditors, and internal users such as management. It states that accounting information must be designed to meet the requirements of national macro-economic control, the needs of all concerned external users who wish to assess an enterprise's financial position and operating results, and the needs of management of enterprises to assist them to strengthen their financial management.

3 The Standard incorporates fundamental accounting assumptions, namely, going concern, business entity, the accounting period and money measurement. It also stipulates the general principles for accounting measurement, including true presentation, consistency, comparability, timeliness, understandability, matching, prudence, materiality, historical cost, and a distinction between revenue expenditure and capital expenditure.

4 The Standard introduces accounting elements, namely, assets, liabilities, owner's equity, revenue and expenses, and adopts the accounting equation

$$\text{Assets} = \text{Liabilities} + \text{Owner's equity.}$$

5 Other provisions relating to possible losses of inventory and doubtful debts, and requirements of consolidations, are similar to those for share enterprises and enterprises with foreign investment.

To incorporate the requirements of the accounting standard into the industry-based accounting regulations, the MOF issued new accounting regulations for fourteen industries, all being effective on 1 July 1993. In other words, accounting practices for all types of enterprises established in China are now being standardized and brought in line as closely as possible to international practices.

The next phase of reform will be the establishment of a full set of accounting standards covering operational aspects of business activities. The MOF plans to complete this task in about three years. The Accounting Standards aim to address the following three major aspects:

1 Accounting Standards relating to measurement of individual accounting elements, including fixed assets, inventory, receivables, payables, and equity;
2 Accounting Standards relating to financial statements, including the balance sheet, income statement, funds statement, and consolidated financial statements;
3 Accounting Standards relating to specific business activities, such as foreign currency transactions and translations, research and development, long-term contracts, post-balance date events, accounting for changing prices, and segmental reporting.

It appears that on completion of the above Accounting Standards, the accounting reform for regulating financial reporting will be accomplished.

THE STANDARDS SETTING PROCESS

The Accounting Society of China (ASC), a national organization in which the majority of members are accounting academics, first initiated the process of accounting standards setting in the late 1980s, by forming the Research Group on Accounting Theory and Standards and by organizing symposia on accounting standards. Soon after this initiative, the Department of Administration of Accounting Affairs (DAAA) of the Ministry of Finance (MOF), the official accounting administration body, formed a working group and formulated a plan for the establishment of accounting standards, with input from the ASC.

After the promulgation of the first accounting standard in 1992, the DAAA formulated a three-year plan of standards setting. Several working groups on specific topics were organized and led by a core team in charge of overall planning and decision-making. Two groups of consultants were formed, one consisting of local accounting academics and practitioners, the other being Deloitte Touche Tohmatsu International (Deloitte) which was successful in the bid for an accounting standard setting project funded by the World Bank.

The consultants from Deloitte are producing reports on comparative studies for each accounting area, which lays down relevant accounting standards adopted by different countries, mainly the USA, UK, Canada, Hong Kong, Australia, Germany, Japan and France. These reports will provide a basis for the MOF working groups to prepare a draft. These drafts will become discussion papers to be circulated nationally for comment, among local consultants, accounting academics, and practitioners. By this process, the MOF aims to formulate the accounting standards in the context of China's existing legal framework and socio-economic environment, which are also comparable with international practices.

THE ACCOUNTING PROFESSION IN CHINA

After the suspension of CPA services for more than three decades, the 'Detailed Rules and Regulations for the Implementation of Income Tax Law Concerning Sino-foreign Joint Ventures', which was issued on 14 December 1980, first stipulated that an audit report by a CPA registered in China is required for a tax return. On 23 December 1980, the MOF issued the first 'Tentative Regulations Concerning Establishing Public Accounting Firms'. One week later, the Shanghai Certified Public Accountants (firm) was set up, being the first CPA firm after the revival of the CPA system. Before the regulations on the CPA profession were published in 1986, there were already over eighty public accounting firms established all over China.

The 'Regulations of the People's Republic of China on Certified Public Accountants' was issued by the State Council in July 1986. The regulations contain provisions in regard to examination and registration, scope of business of CPAs, professional rules, and registration of CPA firms. It designates the Ministry of Finance as the regulatory body at the national level and the finance bureaux at the provincial level, with the responsibility to administer affairs relating to the CPAs and public accounting firms. The establishment of local public accounting firms is administered by the provincial finance bureaux, which file with the Ministry of Finance the articles of association and name of the persons in charge of the firms established.

The qualification of CPA is awarded through an examination and evaluation system. College graduates who have worked in the field of accounting and auditing for three years can apply to sit for the professional examination. However, if evaluation shows that a person meets the 'required standard', exemption can be granted to those who are senior accountants, professors or research fellows and who possess appropriate accounting experience (Cooper and Leung 1994).

Although a publicly owned enterprise may engage a public accounting firm to perform accounting and auditing services, the major clients of public accounting firms are Sino-foreign joint ventures and wholly foreign-owned enterprises. Public accounting firms may carry out feasibility studies, act as a consultant in lodging a tax return, apply for business licences, establish accounting systems, negotiate a joint venture, audit financial statements, certify capital contributions for joint ventures, and so on.

Each public accounting firm is attached to an administering agency. For example, the public accounting firm of China International Economic Consultants Inc. is under the direction and supervision of the China International Trust and Investment Corporation (CITIC) (*South China Morning Post*, 8 June 1993). The MOF and finance bureaux also sponsor some CPA firms. It is also noteworthy that some universities of finance and economics or the departments of accountancy in other universities have also established public accounting firms, and second their professors to work in them part-time or full-time. The public accounting firms attached to universities provide opportunities for both teaching staff and students to acquire practical experience and are also a valuable source of revenue (Tang *et al.* 1992).

The Chinese Institute of Certified Public Accountants (CICPA) was established in November 1988. The setting up of the CICPA was a landmark event in the development of the CPA profession in China. The CICPA is a professional body with independent status. It has some administrative responsibility delegated by the Ministry of Finance in respect of registration of CPAs and public accounting firms. It also serves as a bridge between practising accountants and the government.

The CICPA's plans include the organization and conduct of professional examinations, developing the code of professional conduct and regulations concerning the CPA firms, and organizing training courses to provide continuous professional education for CPAs.

The preliminary objective of the CICPA was to formulate a uniform examination structure, and to conduct examinations in different areas throughout the nation on a uniform time schedule.

The examination structure was to cover subject areas such as accounting, financial management, auditing and law. The first examination was held in December 1991. The membership of the CICPA includes individual and corporate members. All public accounting firms are corporate members and are required to contribute 1 per cent of their annual gross revenue as subscription fees.

CO-OPERATION BETWEEN CHINESE AND FOREIGN CPA FIRMS

The establishment of foreign public accounting firms in China

Foreign public accounting firms began to explore a commercial future in China in early 1978, when China launched its modernization initiatives. During the years 1981–3, all the then Big Eight firms established representative offices in major cities. Registration of these offices is administered by the MOF. Business licences were not issued, however, as technically they do not carry on business in China. Nevertheless, their profits are subject to income tax.

According to regulations, statutory audits for Sino-foreign joint ventures and wholly foreign-owned enterprises are to be performed by Chinese CPAs. However, on approval of the board of directors, foreign investors may also appoint a foreign CPA firm to audit the accounts. In this case, all costs incurred are borne by the foreign investors. The foreign CPA firms provide services mainly to their multinational clients who invest in China. Services rendered cover auditing, tax consultancy, business and management consultancy, accounting, and financial management.

Normally, a common approach is to collaborate with Chinese CPA firms for joint audits. A team which consists of both Chinese and foreign CPAs is formed to plan a division of responsibilities and auditing procedures are agreed. A cross-review may be done after the completion of the audit and the audit report is signed by both parties. For Chinese CPAs, these joint audits provide an opportunity to work with foreign CPAs who have internationally recognized experience and professional qualifications.

Another form of co-operation are the joint corporations formed between Chinese and foreign CPA firms, to provide consultancy services to foreigners who are interested in investing in China.

Through Hong Kong, a number of joint ventures of this kind have been formed, staffed by both Chinese and foreign CPAs. Also, foreign CPA firms have established close links with the Ministries. They provide extensive consultancy services for the Chinese government in the drafting of tax laws, training CPAs, and sponsoring university Professors to be trained abroad. Foreign CPA firms in China also adopt a localization policy, so that they can gradually train local people to achieve international standards. They realize that developing this market demands an investment which is unlikely to be paid back for years. Nevertheless, they generally are positive about the long-term development of the accounting profession and related opportunities in China.

To date, all Big Six firms have offices in cities such as Beijing, Shanghai and Guangzhou. Each of these firms operates with up to fifty local staff in each city. There has also been an upsurge in the demand for financial services owing to the development of the Share Enterprise system and the Stock Exchange. Additional financial services include financial reporting for Share Listing Requirements, consultancy services for takeovers and mergers, and trade advice and reporting for international aid agencies such as the World Bank and the International Monetary Fund. Moreover, firms have also participated in the accounting reform process in the form of tendering to the Ministry of Finance for the design of accounting standards for industries and financial institutions.

The work of the international accounting bodies

Western accounting bodies are also assisting China by offering various training opportunities for China's accountants. The most active of these accounting bodies is the Chartered Association of Certified Accountants (ACCA), which commenced its professional training programmes in China in 1989, to meet the increasing demand from the accounting firms, the universities, the Ministries and other sectors of the economy. Currently, the ACCA has around 200 registered students in its mainstream professional qualification programme, and about 100 undertaking its Certified Diploma in Accounting and Finance programme. In 1993, the ACCA also received sponsorship from the European Commission, to conduct accountancy and financial management training in China. The programme included short courses in accounting, auditing, stock market operations, management accounting, and financial management, conducted for over 700 participants from all over China. The ACCA training programmes have become a major source of recognized Western professional accounting education in China.

Other professional accounting bodies which have shown an interest in China include those from the USA, Canada, Hong Kong and Australia. With the increasing business opportunities and the development of accounting reforms, there is also an increasing interest from other institutions wishing to provide short and long-term training for the Chinese. Training and consultancy in education and business have become very timely services that the Chinese urgently need. For example, the Australian govern- ment has recently announced a $A15 million management training programme for Chinese enterprises. The demand for training is extensive, from the ministries, individual enterprises and private firms. Also, universities and academics have become heavily involved in the whole process of transformation of the economy and the associated services including accounting (Cooper and Leung 1994).

THE RISKS AND REWARDS

Before the Shanghai Vacuum Company was listed on the Shanghai Stock Exchange in 1992, a team of Arthur Andersen staff spent 6,000 hours rewriting the accounts of the company, the first state- owned Chinese enterprise to make shares available to foreigners. The task of bringing three years of accounts to international stan- dard carried a fee of approximately $US1.2 million, but even this assignment was regarded as small compared with the potential for future work (Lyons 1993).

The rush of entrepreneurial activities in China is opening up great opportunities for accounting firms (Way 1992). But they need to be aware of the pitfalls. The scope of the work may be enormous, such as developing accounting standards, but the finan- cial returns are not immediate, or even medium-term. Many of the assignments are funded by the World Bank or the Asian Development Bank, and are therefore short-term or single projects.

Still, the Chinese market offers considerable opportunities because of its sheer size and diversity. A number of state-owned enterprises are now listed in Hong Kong, New York, and Canada, as well as within China. Most joint venture accounting firms now offer a full range of services and employ Chinese staff on local wages. Deloitte Touche Tohmatsu, for example, signed a joint-venture agreement with a Shanghaiese firm to form Deloitte Touche Tohmatsu Shanghai CPAs, Ernst & Young Hua Ming has an office in Beijing, and Arthur Andersen performs audits under a joint venture agreement as Arthur Andersen Hua Qiang. KPMG Peat Marwick has teamed up with the MOF to form KPMG Peat Marwick Huazhen and Price Waterhouse Da Hua was recently established in Shanghai.

The MOF is actively seeking foreign support in its process of accounting reform. For example, the ACCA has co-operated closely with the MOF in training initiatives and other technical support. DAAA officials have been given opportunities to visit the UK to learn about procedures and techniques used for professional examinations and the administration of professional matters.

China also took a decisive step in 1993 towards full convertibility of the yuan, by allowing the value of the currency to float at its fifteen foreign exchange swap centres. Such convertibility of China's currency is a prerequisite for entry to GATT. As the black market previously handled more than 70 per cent of exchange business on a daily basis, Chinese authorities were determined to eliminate its influence. However, the move to float the currency could lead to even higher inflation (currently around 20 per cent), as import prices rise. It is anticipated that there could be a period of uncertainty in exchange rates at the swap markets (Fluendy 1993).

There are also problems of poor infrastructure. An infrastructure of good roads, railways, communications, power supply and so on, which most business people take for granted, is generally below standard in China. The concepts of maintenance of quality control and of security of services do not generally exist in China in the Western sense. However it is true that some headway is being made in tackling China's infrastructure problems. For example, Shanghai is currently undertaking a large elevated roadway project. Also, the Construction Bank of China recently announced the approval of a 2.6 billion yuan project to construct a Beijing–Hong Kong railway, which will be a vital artery in opening up China's heartland to the booming areas of the south (Chan 1993).

From a social and business viewpoint, corruption is a problem in China, and is recognized as such by the Government which is attempting to curb the problem. Both Chinese and foreign business people complain endlessly about how much their deals cost in bribes. The difficulties for business are further compounded by traditional cultural values. The success of any business done in China depends very much on a proper appreciation of factors such as the perceived omnipotence of authority and the concept of 'guanxi'. 'Guanxi' means relationships, or more accurately, connections, and without them, it is difficult to operate any type of business in China.

Any foreigners doing business in China should be aware of the magnitude of these infrastructure and cultural problems. It is easy to be carried away by the seemingly endless banquets and numerous toasts to good friendship. There have been examples where busineses have gone sour and projects failed after substantial investments have been made following positive signals to foreign investors. Also, government intervention and sudden change of personnel are quite common, even after 'contracts' are signed.

Patience and perseverance are essential when operating in China. Western concepts of urgency and time management are not the same there. Developing trust and friendship is also very important in doing business, and in fact more important than long legal contract documents which are not readily understood in a country that does not have Western concepts of law. The foreign accounting firms that operate in China find their senior Mandarin-speaking Chinese staff indispensable in developing the right contacts and securing business.

CONCLUSION

As the economic reforms in China continue to gather pace, many of the changes in Chinese society are now probably irreversible, particularly in the eastern seaboard provinces where the affluence of the Chinese is growing rapidly. In keeping with these reforms and the growing sophistication and profit-orientation of Chinese businesses, accounting practice has become a major part of China's transformation process. There is a general recognition of the need for accounting reform, as evidenced by the modification to regulations covering equity joint ventures and domestic share capital enterprises, and the issue of the first accounting standard in July 1993. In addition, an accounting standard-setting process has been established and the accounting profession itself is undergoing a period of reform. Despite the many difficulties, the opportunities for business in China are considerable; there are risks but also rewards.

REFERENCES

'Business Post Guide to China Securities Rules' (1993) Hong Kong: *South China Morning Post*, 8 June, Business pp. 4–5.
Chan, P. (1993) 'Beijing — HK rail to bring boom towns along route', Hong Kong: *Standard*, 3 June, p. 23.
Chow, L., Tang, Y. W. and Cooper, B. J. (1994) 'Accounting reform in China' (unpublished), Hong Kong Polytechnic.
Cooper, B. J. and Leung, P. (1993) 'Business opportunities in China', *Australian Accountant*, October.
——P. (1994) 'China: opening up to business', *Certified Accountant*, February.
Fluendy, S. (1993) 'Mainland to float yuan on market', *Hong Kong Standard*, 3 June, 1993, p. 21.
Lyons, M. (1993) 'The numbers are adding up in China', *Business Review Weekly*, 3 September.
Tang, Y. W., Chow, L. and Cooper, B. J. (1992) *Accounting and Finance in China: A Review of Current Practice*, Hong Kong: Longman.
Way, N. (1992) 'Profits and perils in the rush to China', *Business Review Weekly*, 19 June.

Chinese publications

Regulations on Cost Management for State–Owned Enterprises (1984).
Accounting Law of the People's Republic of China (1985).
Accounting Regulations for Joint Ventures Using Chinese and Foreign Investment (1985).
Tentative Regulation on Fixed Asset Depreciation for State–Owned Enterprises (1985).
Accounting Regulations for Enterprises with Foreign Investment (1992).
Accounting Regulations for Share Enterprises (1992).
Accounting Standards for Business Enterprises (1992).

Part II

Business and financial structure

The joint venture has been the form of business enterprise that has led China both in developing international commercial links and in opening up the economy. In Chapter 3, Shi, Woodward and Fretwell-Downing consider the major legal developments in this field from 1979 onwards. Their analysis of Chinese practice compared to other countries highlights a number of areas where foreign investors need to be cautious and where further reform in China will be necessary if foreign investment is to be encouraged. Chapter 4 looks at a broader range of types of foreign direct investment, and the range of incentives on offer; they also explain the potential problems.

Two chapters explore the re-emergence of the Chinese stock market. In Chapter 5, Ayling and Jiang explore the issues that will need to be addressed to develop China's stock market to a position comparable with the West. In Chapter 6, Brayshaw and Teng offer a detailed review of progress up to the current time, and identify a number of issues that still need to be resolved.

In Chapter 7, Hwang and Tang offer a broad overview of the economic and financial problems that have led to the current reforms in China.

Part II

Business and financial structure

Chapter 3

Joint venture legislation in China

B. Z. Shi, D. G. Woodward and
F. A. Fretwell-Downing

INTRODUCTION

A joint venture has been described as an economic co-operative endeavour based on capital contributions from two or more partners from different countries, which are independent of each other economically, legally and administratively, but who co-operate in joint business undertakings within set legal agreements (Bojar 1994: 1).

Joint venture regulation has been an important legislative activity in China since that country's 'open door policy' was adopted in 1979, and several commentators have discussed and offered quite different interpretations of that legislation (Frankenstein 1990, Nyaw 1990, Pomfret 1991, Webb 1993). Given that the major industrialized countries appear to have no specific laws relating to joint ventures (Herzfeld 1989), the success that China has experienced in attracting this type of investment may perhaps be explained. Sornarajah (1992) attributes some of this success also to the romantic notion of trading in a hitherto relatively unknown area, and the attraction of a vast market of a billion people.

However, to date little attention has been paid in the literature to an international comparison of China's joint venture legislation. This chapter describes joint venture legislative practices in China and, based on an international comparison, discusses some proposals for further improvement.

THE LEGISLATIVE FRAMEWORK

Recent developments

Potential investors in China have been held to fear the murkiness of that country's legal system (Anon. 1992a). In order to improve the Chinese investment environment, one aspect that has received considerable attention has been the development of a set of laws governing joint ventures. An indication of the major developments that have taken place in Chinese joint venture legislation appears in Table 3.1.

In addition, further laws have been drafted (or are pending), and will be submitted during 1994 to the National People's Congress for verification and adoption. They are (*China Daily*, 16 July 1993):

1 Company Law.
2 Anti-unfairness Law.
3 Foreign Trade Law.
4 Bank Law.
5 Advertisement Law.
6 Arbitration Law.
7 Auditing Law.
8 Negotiable Instruments Law.
9 Insurance Law.

Progress has already been recorded in respect of at least one of these areas (Xiao and Pan 1994), whilst a further 2,300 local laws and provisions, many of them concerning joint ventures, had been enacted by provincial governments by the end of 1992 (*China's Scholars Abroad*, no. 11, 1993).

Three types of joint venture in China are recognized by the legislation:

1 Equity joint ventures.
2 Contractual joint ventures.
3 Wholly foreign-owned ventures.

In addition, Sino-foreign business alliances may take other recognized forms, such as:

1 Co-operative exploration and development (e.g. offshore oil drilling).
2 Process/assembly-buyback agreements.

Table 3.1   The major developments in Chinese joint venture
legislation

Year	Developments in legislation
1979	Law on Equity Joint Ventures which permits foreign investment and defines 'equity joint venture'.
1980	The Income Tax Law concerning joint ventures provides detailed taxation regulation including tax incentives. China becomes a part of the World Intellectual Property Organization. China joins the World Bank and International Monetary Fund.
1981	China becomes a party to the United Nations Convention on Contracts for the International Sale of Goods.
1982	Trademark Law. New Constitution adopted, which provides clear protection for foreign investment (Article 18 of the Constitution). China is elected a member of the United Nations Commission on international trade law.
1983	Joint venture regulations implemented, which further clarify the legal environment for joint ventures.
1984	Patents Law. China becomes a party to the Paris Convention for the Protection of Industrial Property.
1985	Foreign Economic Contract Law, and Provisions for the Management of Technology Transfer Contract.
1986	Provisions for Joint Venture Foreign Exchange Balance. Provisions for the Encouragement of Foreign Investment. Law on Wholly Foreign-owned Enterprises.
1987	China becomes a party to the New York Convention on the Recognition and Enforcement of Foreign Arbitration Awards. Application to rejoin GATT.
1988	Law on Contractual Joint Ventures.
1989	Law on Inspection of Import and Export Goods. New rules governing arbitration are issued, which bring Chinese arbitration procedures into closer conformity with international practices.
1990	Amendment to the Law on Equity Joint Ventures adopted, which announces: 'The State will not nationalize or expropriate any equity joint venture.' The chairman of the board shall be chosen through consultation by the parties or elected by the board of directors. Wholly Foreign-owned Enterprise Implementation Regulations provide detailed operating regulations for wholly foreign-owned enterprises.
1991	Law on Equity and Provisions for Protection of Computer Software. Both the income tax law concerning joint ventures and the income tax law concerning foreign enterprises cease and are replaced by the Income Tax Law Concerning Foreign Enterprises and Foreign Investment Enterprises. The new law retains the principles of previous laws and provides more tax concessions.

3 Licensing agreements.
4 Technology transfer agreements.
5 Compensation trade agreements.

These activities are generally regulated by a separate set of laws and regulations, but the joint venture laws are suitable if these activities take a joint venture form (Wang 1991). From 1979 to 1992, $US 98.83 billion of foreign business capital was invested in China, including $US 38.18 billion in direct foreign investment. By the end of 1992, there were 84,000 equity joint ventures, contractual joint ventures and wholly foreign-owned enterprises in China (Qin 1993).

The legal characteristics of equity joint ventures

Sometimes the expression 'joint venture' is encountered rather than 'equity joint venture'. The former signifies corporate entities owned partly by foreigners and partly by Chinese, established and operating in China, whose main legal characteristics may be summarized as follows:

1 Established by bilateral or multilateral part-owners of whom one at least must be Chinese.
2 Authorized by the Chinese government and established within the territory of China.
3 Enjoying the status of an independent and separate legal personality under Chinese Law.
4 Taking the form of a limited liability company.
5 The foreign contribution should in general be at least 25 per cent of the capital assets of the joint venture, with no upper limit. Each party may contribute cash, capital goods, industrial property, etc. as its investment in the venture.
6 Parties share the profits, risks and losses in proportion to their contributions.

Contractual joint ventures (which may also be called co-operative joint ventures) take the form of joint operations within the territory of China between one or more foreign entities and one or more Chinese entities. In some of their features, contractual joint ventures are similar to equity joint ventures. Thus, in order to eliminate potential investors' concerns regarding unlimited liability, and to stimulate their enthusiasm for projects, contractual joint ventures in China may, under Chinese joint venture and contract legislation, also take the form of limited liability companies. This is different to the situation in other countries that have joint venture enabling legislation. In the Chinese case, with both joint ventures and contractual joint ventures, the domestic partners normally supply land, plant, labour, infrastructure and some machinery, as well as materials. Foreign partners are expected to provide technology, capital, marketing and management expertise, and possibly some raw materials also. The main legal characteristics may be differentiated as shown in Table 3.2.

As is obvious from Table 3.2, contractual joint venture participants enjoy greater flexibility compared with those engaged in equity joint ventures, in that the parties share greater freedom to regulate many matters by contract.

The legal characteristics of wholly foreign-owned enterprises

Wholly foreign-owned enterprises are those businesses which are established within the territory of China in accordance with the relevant Chinese legislation, and which have their entire capital subscribed by foreign investors. This category does not include mere branches of foreign enterprises and other economic organizations established within the territory of China. The main legal characteristics may by summarized as follows:

1 The capital is exclusively invested by foreign investors (this is the fundamental difference between this type of venture and the two categories previously discussed).
2 Registered in China in accordance with the relevant Chinese laws and thereby enjoying the status of a legal entity (it is this feature which differentiates the type from branches of foreign enterprises and other economic organizations established within the territory of China).
3 Established and operating in China.

Other general provisions for joint ventures

1 The contract must be submitted for examination and approval to the relevant authorities.
2 A feasibility study and written contract are required for approval according to the Foreign Economic Contract Law.

Table 3.2   Comparison of equity joint ventures and contractual joint ventures

Dimension	Equity joint ventures	Contractual joint ventures
Legal status	Must be an independent economic entity. Possesses legal personality under Chinese law.	May or may not be an independent economic entity. Can also possess or not possess legal personality under Chinese law.
Capitalization mode	Non-cash contributions (capital goods, property rights, etc.) must be valued to determine the partners' relative contributions.	Non-cash contributions by the partners are not valued, and are merely made as a condition of co-operation.
Organization form	All take the form of a limited liability company.	If negotiated and embodied in the contract, each partner can assume joint liability.
Profits and risks distribution	In proportion to the capital contributions..	As stipulated in the contract.
Investment regulation	The foreign contribution should not be less than 25 per cent of the registered capital assets. Technology (*qua* investment) should not be more than 20 per cent of the registered capital.	As stipulated in the contract.
Liquidation method	In general, pay-off should be made in proportion to the capital	The foreign participant can recover its share of the investment first. Any outstanding income tax comes from the Chinese partner's share.
Management system	Shared management and the administration of the general manager is the responsibility of the board of directors.	Management and administration can be shared by the partners or conducted by one partner – who could also entrust a third party to be responsible for its share of the management.

3 Special tax and other incentives are given to some joint ventures, as shown in Table 3.3.
4 Net profits may be remitted through the Bank of China 'in accordance with the foreign exchange regulations and in the currency specified in the joint venture contract' (Article 10, Equity Joint Venture Law).
5 In principle, the joint venture should be for a variable period of between 10 and 30 years, but joint ventures in the specific areas of service provision, land development and natural resources must operate for a fixed term.
6 The right of autonomy of the joint venture in its operation and management shall not be subject to interference (Article 11, Law of Contractual Joint Venture).

Table 3.3 Special tax and other incentives

Enterprises type	*Incentive items*
General enterprises	30% enterprise income tax and 3% local income tax.
Export-oriented and technologically/advanced enterprises	Enterprise income tax exemption in the first profit-making year. 15% enterprise income tax for the next two years, local income tax exemption for 8–20 years subject to the local legislation. Priority in approval procedure: receiving loans, obtaining raw materials.
Enterprises which reinvest profits in China	40% of the taxes paid can be refunded.
Enterprises which have operated for a period in excess of 10 years	Enterprise income tax exemption for 2 years and 50% deduction for 3 years.
Enterprises involving energy, transportation or infrastructure and those located in underdeveloped areas of China	After the exemption and deduction period expires, 15–30% tax deduction in the following 10 years. Local taxes also may by waived by the local authorities.

AN INTERNATIONAL COMPARISON

The joint venture legislation already in place in China demonstrates that the country has altered its erstwhile aversion attitudes and policies to foreign investment after an extended period of isolation. The joint venture form itself was borrowed from capitalist legal systems (Sornarajah 1992) but, with the growing importance of joint ventures in China, the requisite legal structure concerning joint ventures has been created quickly since 1979. The main trends in this legislative development are as follows.

Simultaneous liberation and decentralization

A feature of joint venture legislation is that much of it has rapidly undergone amendment in the light of experience. Both liberation and decentralization can be found in the on-going development of China's legislative activities. For example, the initial joint venture legislation required that 51 per cent of investment should be controlled by the Chinese partner, and that both the chairman of the board of directors as well as the chief executive officer of the joint venture be Chinese citizens. These restrictions have been removed by subsequent amendments. Meanwhile, as indicated above, decentralization of legislation has led to a large number of local laws and provisions being created, with much of the legislation offering considerable flexibility to the parties involved.

Devoting more attention to investment incentives

Pomfret (1991: 67) makes reference to the US-China Business Council's assessment that China's legislated investment incentives compare favourably with such incentives available elsewhere in Asia. Such a comparison is carried out in Table 3.4.

Harmonizing with international practices

Most of the legislation concerning joint ventures in China is increasingly coming into line with international standards in respect of such areas as the protection of intellectual property rights (Bangsberg 1992). The Foreign Economic Contract Law also provides that international customs and practices should be applicable in areas in which Chinese Laws are absent or unclear

Table 3.4   A comparison of investment incentives available in various Asian countries

Country	Income tax rate %	Income tax exemption deduction period	Site use fees (per year)	Foreign investment proportion (min/max %)
China (general enterprises)	30	Exemption for 1–2 years and 50% deduction for 3–6 years	1–15 yuan/m^2	25 min.
China (SEZs and special enterprises)	15	Free of local tax and preferential treatment to some industries	Preferential treatments to some industries	25 min.
South Korea	30	Exemption for 5 years and 50% deduction for 3 years	$0.65/$m^2$	50 max. in some industries
Malaysia	40	Free export promotion	N/A	30 max. in some industries
Thailand	35	Exemption for 3–8 years for some industries	N/A	50 max. in some industries
Singapore	31	Exemption for 5–15 years for some industries	$428.8/$m^2$	49 max. in some industries
India	38	Exemption for 5–10 years for some industries	N/A	40 max. in some industries

Sources: Wang 1991, Sornarajah 1992
Note: SEZ = Special Economic Zone

Table 3.5   Differences between China's joint venture operations and
                international practices

International practices	*Real practices in China*
Joint ventures have the right to set up affiliated agencies	Joint ventures setting up affiliated agencies abroad need approval by the authorities.
Negotiating time less than three months usually.	The process of negotiating and approval is usually longer than three months.
Host countries generally guarantee to meet foreign infrastructure needs	Infrastructure problems existed to varying degrees.
Negotiators have the right to sign the contract.	Negotiators on the Chinese side sometimes are not the representatives of enterprises but the officers of authorities. Sometimes the negotiators are changed during the discussions. Contracts must be approved by the authorities.
Joint ventures have the right to determine their personnel system, including the right to employ or dismiss staff and workers.	Recruitment is usually only on a regional basis and there is a need to report to the labour authorities (for the record). Cannot employ or dismiss foreign senior management personnel without approval by the authorities.
Joint ventures' products may be distributed on both domestic and foreign markets.	The proportion of products distributed on the domestic market may be varied subject to the approval of the authorities.
Joint ventures have the right to price their products.	Joint ventures have export product pricing rights, but the pricing of some products distributed on the domestic market must be approved by the authorities.
Joint ventures may go bankrupt.	China's law on bankruptcy is suitable only to State enterprises. Joint ventures may be dissolved under certain conditions and the liquidation is conducted in accordance with legal procedures.

(Article 22). Thus, owing to both economic and political influences, much progress has been made, even though further improvements are still required in China's joint venture legislation.

An investigation of eighteen joint ventures in the Yunnan province, during June and July 1992, uncovered many differences still existing in the operation of joint ventures in China when compared with international practices. The main differences revealed are shown in Table 3.5.

DIFFERENCES BETWEEN INTENTION AND PRACTICE

Opening up trade to the outside world is a basic policy of the Chinese government. Absorbing direct foreign investment, and thereby introducing advanced technology in order to develop the national economy, is an important part of that policy. The joint venture legislation in China complements this objective.

Like other developing countries, export-orientation and technology-transfer are the outstanding objectives of China's joint venture legislation.

As is well known, over a long period in China the state centrally controlled the economy via a 'public ownership' (state ownership) planned economy model copied from the former Soviet Union, and modified to Chinese requirements. Under that system, the private sector was limited in scope, and state enterprises were not treated as independent accounting units, bearing responsibility for their own profits and losses. The state controlled all of the revenues and expenditures of public enterprises and dictated all material purchases and output distributions. These state enterprises were frustrated by a lack of autonomous authority, ranging from decisions regarding production planning, employment, management and raw material supplies, to concern for the distribution and marketing of their outputs. The situation has been gradually improving with the economic reform that shifting from a planned economy to a market economy since 1979 has engendered. However, the situation has not been changed completely, and another important feature of China's joint venture legislation has been the state acting as a third party, as an agent and also as a management approval body, in the absence of any other party having the requisite authority.

Ideologically, joint ventures have been considered 'state capitalist enterprises', with the activities and operations of a joint venture being subject to regulation by the state. Guided by the theories of a planned economy and 'state capitalism', joint venture legislative activities in China have relatively stressed the administrative function of the State. The situation has been changed to a certain extent in the latest legislation, but remains a fundamental doctrine. 'Despite the proliferation of laws,' one commentator opined, 'the state is the final arbiter' (Frankenstein 1990). Another observer commented that 'law and politics are never far apart in China' (*Economist*, 19 October 1991). Indeed, experience has shown that over-centralized administration of the state will inevitably lead to cumbersome bureaucracy and inefficiency. This is a limiting factor to the actual effect of China's joint venture legislation. This point is supported by the following evidence.

1 Actual foreign investment in China is much less than the amount of foreign capital pledged. For example, by June 1985, of $8.5 billion pledged foreign investment only $2.4 billion had been actually invested (World Bank 1988: 254). By September 1989, of $32.2 billion pledged foreign investment only $14.1 billion had been actually invested (*China Daily*, 4 December 1989).

2 The amount of foreign investment following the 'open door' policy was uneven. During the early 1980s, growth occurred very slowly, with the first foreign investment boom being in 1985. Things then slipped back in 1986, until the second boom of 1988. This pattern was repeated yet again in 1989–91, following which continuous growth appears to have been maintained.

3 Given recent political developments in China, many foreign firms have adopted a 'wait and see' approach before committing themselves. Foreign firms have also entered into some form of limited arrangement to test the Chinese waters before committing substantial capital (Pomfret 1991). One encouraging feature is that currently there seems little prospect of expropriation of foreign-owned assets. 'The probability of nationalization, already small, is diminishing as economic reform grows and China becomes involved in the international marketplace' (Anon. 1992b).

It should also be noticed that South-east Asian and Eastern

European nations have also become major pursuers of foreign investment capital. So, to remain competitive, China will have to take further steps to improve its investment environment.

IMPLICATIONS AND SUGGESTIONS

The experience of China's joint venture legislation indicates that joint ventures are China's favoured vehicle for attracting foreign investment. They are also an important mechanism for multinationals expanding into the Chinese marketplace.

The analyses of China's joint venture legislative practices, as previously discussed, demonstrate that legislation is an important aspect in the encouragement of an appropriate investment environment, but this is not the only relevant issue. In spite of China having offered favourable investment incentives when compared with other Asian countries, as was indicated in Tables 3.3 and 3.4, there are still a number of factors limiting the attractiveness of investing in China. Hence, not as much foreign investment has occurred as was both expected and hoped for by the Chinese authorities. Factors which have contributed to this situation may be summarized as follows:

1 Higher political risk level.
2 Difficulties in dealing with the state bureaucracy.
3 Chinese officials' low level of technical and international experience (Vogel 1989).
4 A generally poorly developed legal framework.
5 Inadequate specific rules or guidelines to follow (Nyaw 1990).
6 A lack of reliable and comprehensive statistical and market information (Woodward and Liu 1993).
7 The difficulty of negotiating with Chinese partners (Pomfret 1991).
8 Poor infrastructure.
9 Market protectionism (Woodward and Liu 1993).
10 Cultural differences and language problems.
11 Inconvertibility and overvaluation of the Chinese currency (Pomfret 1991).

It becomes obvious from this that, in order to improve the investment environment and to facilitate the absorption of foreign investment, China not only will have to offer better incentives and higher returns to foreign investors but also will have to pay greater attention to improve its other deficiencies.

In addition, in order that further improvement of the joint venture legal environment might occur, it is proposed that the following steps will need to be enacted via the legal framework:

1 Improvement of the joint venture laws such as to encourage operation of the market economy, following adoption of this model by the Chinese. This will mean that legislative activities should shift control of businesses away from the state and more towards the businesses themselves. The actual joint venture legislation enacted should aim to be in harmony with international practices and to follow international standards.

2 Again, following from market economy concerns, the formulation of a composite set of laws, especially including company law (currently absent in China) and other laws relating to joint ventures. This legislation should be promulgated and come into force as soon as possible.

3 Strict enforcement of all laws. It is essential to get rid of the present situation of the rule of man rather than the rule of law, and of the ability to circumvent the law.

4 More attention devoted to the propagation of the joint venture legislation both at home and abroad. It is necessary to give wide publicity to the significance of conducting operations in accordance with the law.

5 The training of large numbers of domestic lawyers and the opening of Chinese legal practice to overseas law firms.

REFERENCES

Anon. (1992a) 'China approves dozen legal firms to open first foreign law offices', *Journal of Commerce*, 14 October.

(1992b) 'Nationalization and privatization policy', *Investing, Licensing & Trading Conditions Abroad*, 1 February.

Bangsberg, P. T. (1992) 'Chinese mission purchases $400 million in British goods; more investment by Italy sought', *Journal of Commerce*, 16 July.

Bojar, E. (1994) *Joint Ventures in the Polish and Russian Economies*, discussion paper released through Telford College, Edinburgh.

Frankenstein, J. (1990) 'The Chinese foreign trade environment', *International Studies of Management and Organisation* 20 (1/2) 135–48.

Herzfeld, E. O. (1989) *Joint Ventures*, Bristol: Jordan and Sons.

Nyaw, M.-K. (1990) 'The significance and managerial roles of trade unions in joint ventures with China', *International Studies of Management and Organisation* 20 (1/2): 109–]24.

Pomfret, R. (1991) *Investing in China: Ten Years of the 'Open Door'*

Policy, Hemel Hempstead: Harvester Wheatsheaf.

Qin, S. (1993) *China 1992*, Beijing: New Star Publishing House.

Sornarajah, M. (1992) *Law of International Joint Ventures*, Singapore: Longman.

Vogel, E. F. (1989) *One Step Ahead in China: Guangdong Under Reform*, Cambridge, Mass: Harvard University Press.

Wang, H. (1991) *Management of Foreign Economy and Trade Law in China*, Beijing: Law Publishing House.

Webb, E. (1993) 'Firm facing up to a Chinese practice', *Independent*, 8 January.

Woodward, D. G. and Liu, B. C. F. (1993) 'Investing in China: guidelines for success', *Long Range Planning Journal*, April, pp. 83–9.

World Bank (1988) *A World Bank Country Report — China: External Trade and Capital*, Baltimore, Md: Johns Hopkins University Press.

Xiao, J. and Pan, X. (1994) 'The Chinese Approach to Accounting Standards and Conceptual Framework', paper presented to the International Symposium on Chinese Accounting and Financial Management, University of Central Lancashire, Preston, 21 March.

Chapter 4

Corporate investment in China

More problems than solutions?

B. C. F. Liu and D. G. Woodward

INTRODUCTION

The 'open door' policy instituted by the Chinese government in 1978 was one aspect of its modernization programme, the aim of which was to attract investment to a country whose commercial doors had been closed to the outside world for many years. It was intended that much of the technology, both hardware and software, which China needed to attract in order to advance itself economically, should come through the medium of joint ventures entered into in partnership with overseas companies (Yu 1988: 176).

The laws and regulations on joint ventures first published in 1979 incorporated some of the negotiating and operating experience gained from Sino–Soviet joint ventures, and offered a number of incentives to investors. In return, China expected foreign partners not only to offer technology, manufacturing know-how, and capital investment but also to assume responsibility for marketing the hoped-for products on an international basis.

The response of Western businesses to the opportunities presented by the new policies has not been as enthusiastic as the Chinese had hoped (the cumulative total to the end of October 1991 has been estimated at $22 billion [Anon. 1992a]); a fact which is openly acknowledged. Apart from a fear that policies to encourage investment might be reversed, another problem has been the cumbersome and complex bureaucracy with which the foreign investor must deal.

Efforts are being made by the Chinese to reassure Western business people that the days of sudden shifts of policy are over, to reduce the bureaucratic element somewhat, and to create a business environment more familiar to those from capitalist countries. New legislation is continually being enacted (see Chapter 3) further to improve the environment for foreign businesses. The Chinese have also demonstrated their willingness to submit to internationally accepted adjudication procedures in the event of disputes or defaults on foreign debt.

What success has been recorded is largely a result of China's low labour costs, huge and underdeveloped domestic market, abundant material reserves and, not least, because of the overall enthusiasm displayed by the Chinese themselves.

However, investors have encountered numerous problems such as infrastructure deficiencies; obtaining a share of the domestic market; getting assistance from the relevant authorities; and over-coming the managerial style differences involved. There is also no doubt that the recent political power struggle in China, and the Tiananmen Square bloodshed in 1989 — following which most Western countries and multilateral agencies froze aid and investment (Bangsberg 1991) — have shaken confidence among investors. In addition, given the length of time China was cut off from international markets, there has been a severe underestimation of 'how much they would have to improve their infrastructure, upgrade cadre training, and fundamentally alter their way of thinking to be competitive with other countries' (Vogel 1989: 126).

CHINESE ENCOURAGEMENT OF FOREIGN INVESTMENT

To some extent, absorption of foreign direct investment may be seen as a fairly obvious solution to what the Chinese identified for themselves as:

1 Lack of investment funds.
2 Low level of domestically available technology.
3 Low product quality.
4 Lack of international trading experience.

Indeed, it is has been suggested that it was the *only* solution available (Vogel 1989: 125). The intention was primarily to bring in (Woodward and Liu 1993: 83):

1 Foreign capital.
2 Advanced technology.
3 Management skills.
4 Urban construction.

Tourism and expanding exports were considered secondary objectives, but nevertheless complementary to the primary ones (Lockett 1987). In addition, it was anticipated that selling exported products in competitive international markets would cause investors to try their best to raise the quality and lower the cost of their products. This should introduce more advanced techniques and better management systems into China, so as to improve efficiency and productivity.

The year 1979 saw the announcement of the Law on Joint Ventures Using Chinese and Foreign Investment, as a way of encouraging foreign investment in China. Under the joint venture arrangements, the Chinese provide the things that they have in abundance, principally land and labour (infrastructure support is also promised, although that can be a meaningless gesture), whilst the overseas partner contributes:

1 'Hard' technology (equipment).
2 'Soft' technology (management expertise, especially
   marketing).
3 Capital.
4 (Possibly) raw materials.

One significant part of the 'open door' policy was the establishment of special economic zones (SEZs) — initially in the four areas of Shenzhen, Zhuhai, Shantou and Xiamen. The SEZs offer various tax and other incentives to investors (Woodward and Liu 1993: 83–4).

In 1984, an additional fourteen cities along the east coast and Hainan Island were opened to foreign investors (Chu 1988). These coastal cities have the same purposes as the SEZs and are planned to upgrade their existing enterprises with foreign capital and to develop the newly emerging technology-intensive industries, such as electronics.

In 1985, three further areas were established to attract foreign investment and were designated as Open Economic Zones (Chu 1988). These are the Yangtze River Delta, the Pearl River Delta and the Zhangzhou–Quanzhou–Xiamen region in the southern part of Fujian Province.

Hainan Island became a separate province in 1988 (Cheng 1988: 96). The revised regulations for this particular area have made foreign investment so convenient that foreign investors need no visas; will be able to lease land for 70 years; will have the promise of managing their business without Communist Party interference; and will have the right to keep a large proportion of their profits.

In order to improve the investment environment further, a number of incentives were offered under revised regulations in 1986 (CFRTGP 1986). These included:

1 Access to the domestic market for products of joint ventures that China urgently needs, or imports.
2 Access to foreign exchange funds for firms selling mainly to the domestic market.
3 Stable land use fee for five years.
4 The right to pay for local utilities at local rates.
5 Purchase of raw materials to be exempt from customs duties.
6 Firms that agree to operate joint ventures for at least ten years may be free from taxes in their first profit-making year, and will pay reduced taxes in the second and third years.
7 Removal of all limitations on the remittance of after-tax incomes by foreign staff and workers.
8 Curbing of unauthorized charges and interference by local government officials.

FORMS OF INVESTMENT

China's pre-open door strategy of developing known technologies either by copying imported equipment or by means of completely independent research and development (rather than importing technological know-how) was in sharp contrast to the absorptive strategies adopted by the newly industrializing countries of East Asia. International experience (for example, Japan and Korea) had shown that an absorptive strategy has many advantages for a technological late-comer, since selective importation of technologies involves lower risks, a shorter time lag, and a lower cost of acquisition (World Bank 1985).

More recent emphasis in China has been upon the need to import know-how (software) in addition to, or instead of, equipment (hardware). This is a significant alteration in technology policy, because it recognizes that the individual elements of technology complement each other, and that equipment is not necessarily the most important element. In addition, it has been observed that the latest technology is not necessarily the most relevant. Given the Chinese situation, older but more relevant technology may make better sense than the 'latest thing' (Pomfret 1991: 135).

Technology can be in the form of:

1   Machinery.
2   Knowledge.
3   Instructions.
4   Training.
5   Specifications.

An important aspect of technological knowledge is that much of it is not explicit, and cannot be easily transferred except by transferring people or a whole organization. Very often, technology comes from within an organization; that is, the ability to produce something with greater efficiency or of a higher quality without using different hardware.

Whilst the importance of the soft elements of technology has recently been highlighted by Chinese policy makers, most of the technology transfer, particularly in foreign direct investment, is still hardware focused. Other channels of technology transfer, such as overseas education and training of personnel, and hiring of foreign specialists, can be very important and cost effective. However, tight control of foreign exchange has deterred many enterprises from using these channels.

Growth of foreign direct investment since the open door policy was implemented in 1979 has been remarkable, even though it has not reached Chinese targets. Most of the ventures established to date are engaged in the exploitation of natural fuels (Bangsberg 1991), in labour-intensive manufacturing or tourism, and in some infrastructure projects such as power (both thermal and nuclear), highways, railways and port development (Pomfret 1991: 103). So many hotels have been built that it has been suggested by Vogel (1989: 136) that this gave rise during the 1980s to low occupancy rates.

All of these investments have useful economic impact but do not bring in much advanced technology. Political unrest in China in the late 1980s and early 1990s did not help in attracting foreign investors, and the level of new commitments fell during this period.

Foreign direct investment in China would appear to be capable of some six different guises. They are described below, drawing on a classification by the World Bank (1988). Most of the six categories provide at least some technology transfer. However, only the first two forms really constitute foreign direct investment, although custom and usage often includes the next two forms as well. With the last two forms of activity, little or no actual investment is involved.

Wholly foreign-owned ventures

This category, not surprisingly, includes corporate entities which are completely owned by foreign investors, established and operating in China.

Equity joint ventures

Sometimes referred to simply as joint ventures, these businesses are owned partly by foreigners and partly by the Chinese. Both parties decide through negotiation on the ratio of their equity holdings, whether investment should be in the form of cash or equipment, and profit shares. Both parties share the risks, and the profit or loss.

Contractual joint ventures

In many ways, these are similar to equity joint ventures, although they are not subject to the same comprehensive set of rules, being governed instead by general business legislation. However, in both forms the foreign parties usually contribute some or all of the machinery and/or other technology and are responsible for exports, if any. The Chinese usually contribute land, buildings, labour, and most of the raw materials. Both sides usually co-operate in some way in managing the enterprise.

Joint development

The essence of this form is that the returns of the various parties are in the form of specified shares of the physical output of the enterprise. Typically, the Chinese parties use their share for domestic purposes, while the foreign partners are required to sell their shares abroad.

Compensation trade

In this case the purchase of machinery from abroad, by a local enterprise, is financed in whole or in part by goods produced after the purchase. With this arrangement, the Chinese partners are responsible for providing buildings and labour, while the foreign investors supply any agreed-upon combination of services, equipment, technology, materials, or technical and supervisory personnel.

Processing and assembling

In this arrangement, the foreign parties provide some or all inputs to a product. The Chinese contribution is to use the inputs to make the product, which is then returned to the foreigner investor, who pays a fee for the service.

REASONS FOR INVESTING IN CHINA

Whilst difficult to categorize, the rationale for investing in China can be examined under the four headings of strategic, market related, production related, or concerned with the special incentives provided by the Chinese (Kemp 1987).

Strategic

Most strategic factors centre on the issue of the business striving to secure its place among competitors, or on its attempting to gain a strategic advantage over them. The most commonly encountered strategic behaviours are 'follow the leader' (bandwagon effect) and 'pre-empt the competition'. Applying these in the context of investing in China would appear to imply the following motives.

Looking for new markets

Investors who produce or operate in China do so either to satisfy local demand or to sell in markets other than their home market.

Looking for new sources of raw materials

Businesses extract raw materials wherever they can be found, either for export or for further processing and sale in the host country.

Raising the efficiency of production

Businesses produce in China where some factors of production are under priced relative to their productivity.

Market related

Domestic market attraction

China imposes import quotas, and individual enterprises in China have very little freedom in importing and exporting. Therefore, an advantage is gained by foreign operations that have established production or trading operations in China.

Market and customer knowledge

Once foreign enterprises are established in China, benefits are gained because of access to first-hand information about the market and its requirements. It is not unusual for foreign companies to produce one product in China and market several other ancillary products as part of their sales strategy.

Service industries

Enterprises that are in the service sector, such as telephones and tourism, must locate in the host country. At present, the Chinese encourage manufacturing and export-oriented industries in order to earn foreign exchange to finance more technology transfer. Therefore, service sector activities are not invited. However, certain service industries that generate foreign exchange earnings, such as tourism, are allowed to develop.

Service of third country markets

China is an excellent base for export to the rest of the Eastern world, and foreign investors are able to enjoy preferential treatment if they are engaged in export-oriented industries.

Production related

Cheap land and low wages

For labour-intensive operations, the availability of cheap labour acts as a major incentive for foreign direct investment with regard to the savings in production costs (although a study by Wang [1992: 12] found that this feature was ranked only sixth by foreign partners as their reason for investing in China). The creation of the SEZs and the treatment of the coastal cities is intended to create incentives comparing favourably with other low-cost production centres in the Far East. However, the actual costs may be considerably higher than stated owing to hidden costs and unexpected production difficulties (Warner 1985).

Raw materials

If a steady long-term supply of raw materials is to be secured, investing in China may be worthwhile. This is especially true for textiles, chemicals and food processing industries. To be competitive in international markets and to achieve low-cost production, investors must be prepared to combine their technological advantage, such as improvement of existing obsolete production processes, with the plentiful supply of raw materials.

Special incentives

By 1988, investment incentives in China were considered to have compared favourably with those available elsewhere in Asia (see Chapter 3).

Tax incentives

Tax holidays and a reduced rate of corporation tax are offered to foreign enterprises according to various types of industry and location. The range of special incentives offered by the government has been a major contributing factor to the success of foreign investment in China, especially within the SEZs and coastal cities. These tax incentives are most important for investors with low-cost production strategies, or who want a fast return on investment.

There is little doubt that the Chinese government has used such incentives to guide the orientation of investment. Thus foreign businesses that invest in enterprises producing goods for export and with advanced technology have been charged less for services and use of land as well as enjoying tax reductions (Yu 1988: 182).

Preferential treatment

The preferential treatment of land and buildings does not in general act as a major incentive to foreign investors, since the hidden costs can be numerous and hefty. The true costs are not particularly cheap compared to other areas, such as Malaysia and South Korea. Electricity and power are not delivered at a reduced rate, being in short supply throughout China, especially in Guangdong, where the majority of foreign joint ventures are located.

Despite all of this, as has been pointed out with joint ventures undertaken in other countries:

> Investors should take into account not only the preferential tax treatment guidelines, dividend transfer opportunities or (simplification of) bureaucratic formalities required for registration, but also the economic stability . . ., the economic infrastructure, the finance and banking systems and the efficiency and supportive attitude on all levels of the country's business administration.
>
> (Bojar 1994: 29)

In other words, it is not all plain sailing, as will now be discussed.

POTENTIAL PROBLEMS

Most of the problems commonly encountered by foreign investors during planning, negotiating and administering ventures in China are explained in this section. Through understanding these problems, it should be possible to formulate strategies to mitigate their effects, as far as is feasible.

Bureaucracy and time delays

Bureaucracy is met by any investor wishing to do business in China. Much of the frustration generated results from long delays and misunderstandings. Because of the consequent stress put on foreign business people, adjustment is required to a generally slower pace of life. Investors must also be able to deal with a number of government bodies at the same time, and contradictions between the different officials are not uncommon (Hendryx 1986: 83). Vogel is well aware of the problems: 'Foreign business people had a reservoir of stories about Chinese bureaucrats who excelled in inefficiency, bureaucratism, personal profiteering, and a poor understanding of the needs of international business' (Vogel 1989: 135).

The extent of the bureaucratic problem has been considered to reduce the appeal of China's low land, labour and raw material costs that make the country a good manufacturing base (Anon. 1992b).

Incomplete regulatory and legal framework

The fact that China has such an incomplete regulatory and legal structure has led in the past to much confusion. Interpretation of some regulations or laws varies between bureaux, or (even worse) between officials in the same bureau (Lee *et al.* 1987). The legal environment in China is largely still being developed. Most 'laws' are drafted as statements of intent rather than as precise legal documents, which is more the Western model.

Lack of reliable statistics

The lack of reliable and comprehensive statistical and market information in China has created a host of problems (Lo and Yung 1988). This makes it difficult for investors to make predictions of return on investment, or payback period (a statistic of some interest, apparently, to the Chinese government). This problem will not disappear until better data collection methods are employed.

Evaluation of the respective contributions

Usually, the Chinese contribution to a joint venture will consist of land, labour, buildings and materials. Only when absolutely necessary will the Chinese, in addition, contribute a small proportion of the required capital in cash.

Arguments often ensue over the value of land and buildings assigned by the Chinese authorities, and the lack of an adequately developed real estate market in China means that values are easily inflated. The valuation of non-cash contributions from the foreign partner, such as technology, management techniques, services and training, is clearly error prone, and such items are frequently not valued by the Chinese as highly as their own contribution (Anon. 1987). Independent arbiters have had to be called in for an unbiased assessment.

Supply of raw materials

One feature of the investment regulations is that joint ventures are expected to give first priority to local suppliers. Problems then arise over pricing, quality, distribution and delivery. Raw materials are frequently in shortage, and a continuous supply is ensured only if the venture is featured in the State Plan. Very often, even when the venture is so included, supply is guaranteed only in respect of quantity, and not of quality (Lee *et al.* 1987).

Even when suppliers can produce the necessary materials on schedule, delays are common for the delivery and distribution of both imported and domestic goods (Lo and Yung 1988). The limited transportation system often holds up the manufacturing process and adds to production costs.

Quality of finished product

Export-oriented businesses face severe problems in achieving the sort of quality demanded by the international market place, stemming from the isolation of the Chinese economy over a period of so many years. 'Chinese workers and managers were usually unaware that quality was even a difficulty and even when they understood the problem, they were unaware what to aim for' (Pomfret 1991: 124).

Infrastructure deficiencies

Transport

All forms of transport are in need of improvement, expansion and modernization. This is recognized by the Chinese authorities as their top priority. All types of problems can be encountered, such as delays in supplies of raw materials and imported goods, whilst exports can be held up because of under-capacity at the ports.

Communications

Postal and cable communications between major cities are efficient. Telecommunication, however, is scarce and costly. Only 70 per cent of China's towns are equipped with telephone exchanges. In 1987, it was estimated that there was only one telephone for every 200 people, and the time from ordering to installation was over a year (Irvine et al., 1987: 74). More recent evidence suggests rapid improvement of the situation is planned by the year 2000 (Observer, 4 July 1993, p. 27).

Energy

Energy supply is a very serious problem. The worst situation is found in the southern part of China where power cuts are regular (Lee et al. 1987). In Guangdong, local factories are known to have worked a four day week. However, a guaranteed supply of energy can be obtained at a premium and if the venture has a high (i.e. State Plan) priority. Most foreign enterprises in Southern China have resorted to installing their own captive generating plants.

Labour availability and quality

Labour productivity in China's engineering industry is only one-twelfth that of Japan; in the steel industry one-twenty-fifth; and in electronics one-eighth. This low level of productivity can be explained as the result of low skill levels, insufficient motivation, poor management and antiquated technology.

The general lack of appropriate education in China is mainly responsible for the shortage of skilled labour. Training is thus expected to be provided by the foreign partner, and is seen as one of the main benefits flowing from foreign investment.

Low productivity alone does not, of course, lead to a problem if the labour cost is itself low enough to compensate. However, the seemingly low labour costs are inflated by additional expenses of housing, insurance, pensions and other benefits, imposed by the Chinese.

Management style differences

Pomfret (1991: 51) refers to cultural differences 'such as the Chinese desire to take decisions by consensus, even at the cost of delay, whereas the foreign investors tried to establish a managerial structure with clear job descriptions and responsibilities'.

Wang (1992: 13) reported that his study found that the overseas managers of joint ventures were more outcome oriented, emphasizing the quality of the outcomes no matter how the task was performed; whereas the Chinese managers tended to be more process oriented, and were more concerned with how a task was implemented, and in assuring themselves that all of the employees involved were satisfactory.

This incompatibility of Chinese and foreign management styles has led to conflicts in the board room. The lack of expertise and inefficiency displayed by the Chinese partners are thought to contribute to the generally low productivity. The following are some of the principal features of Chinese management and the background against which it operates:

1 Management responsibility is not clearly defined. Managers are reluctant to make independent decisions; even minor problems have to be reported to relatively senior levels.
2 Co-ordination and cohesion between sectors is almost non-existent. Several administrative sectors can be in the charge of one director instead of more specialist personnel.
3 The state-planned production quotas and guaranteed purchase of output have reduced the need for market research, so appropriate skills in this area have not been developed.
4 The Chinese approach to the export market is often to try to export what they have produced, rather than identify what the overseas markets require.
5 Quality control is poor by Western standards. Quantity is seen as more important than quality in order to meet production targets. The centralized distribution system and guaranteed purchase of output have done little to improve this situation.
6 Technical and professional skills are low. The percentage of qualified managers is very small.

Cultural differences

This aspect is clearly linked to that just discussed. Wang's (1992) field study revealed:

> some Chinese cultural traditions still had a strong influence on work behaviour in joint ventures ... Among the traditions, equality and egalitarianism were popular among many employees who, for example, were not comfortable about distinctive wage differences at different organizational levels ... Also, the traditional values of emphasizing interpersonal relationships and group responsibility were still quite dominating among Chinese employees
>
> (Wang 1992: 13).

There is nevertheless some suggestion that, whilst Chinese cultural traditions still have a strong influence on work behaviour in joint ventures, new management styles are being adopted (Chen 1991). Thus a major issue in managing joint ventures appears to be fit or comparability between different values, management approaches, and corporate cultures (Wang 1992: 13).

Remittance of profits

Under Chinese foreign exchange control regulations, foreign investors are responsible for maintaining a foreign exchange balance in their joint ventures. This means that enough export activity must be carried out so as to cover both import costs and remittable profits. The regulations allow joint ventures to be paid in foreign exchange for goods or services only if the ventures involve a high proportion of imported advanced technology, or are clear cases of import substitution.

However, owing to the unsuitability, or the price and quality, of the products supplied to foreign markets, many joint ventures have found it difficult to maintain this balance. The non-convertibility of the Chinese currency unit, the renminbi, and the tightening of foreign exchange control in 1985 have made the remittance of profits even more difficult.

Expatriate working and living conditions

There are three main problems for foreigners in China, namely, language, lifestyle and attitude of the locals towards foreigners. Some examples are:

1 The lack of accommodation means that foreign managers have to be housed in hotels.
2 Recreational activities are essentially geared towards Chinese requirements, except in the largest cities.
3 The lack of understanding of social norms and preferences may well turn an intended courteous action into a perceived insult or antagonism. As Pye (1986: 77) has commented, 'The Chinese approach calls for elaborate courtesy, gestured humility, and high sensitivity to perceived insult.'

Identifying the approval authority

One widespread characteristic of the environment for setting up a joint venture in China is the complex and ever-changing series of rules, procedures and incentives. Depending on their size and sector, joint ventures are subject to approval by a municipal, provincial or central authority. Each SEZ has its own set of procedures and incentives. Municipal and local authorities frequently issue new rules and grant new incentives, but these vary from area to area. The various rules and incentives are not collected together in one publication and even, in some cases, are not published at all!

It is also difficult to establish what level of approval in the hierarchy of Chinese government is required for different types of project. The only Chinese legislation that may give a hint in this situation is the Joint Venture Law, which requires that equity joint ventures be approved by the Ministry of Foreign Economic Relations and Trade (MOFERT). However, even this requirement has been altered since the creation of the Implementing Act of 1983, which gave to MOFERT the right to assign its approval powers to other authorities.

Difficulty of liquidating

For the sale of a share in a joint venture to occur, all of the partners must give their approval (see Chapter 3). Should the Chinese partner refuse, the only option open to the foreign investor is to abandon the investment and suffer the loss of the funds committed.

CONCLUSION

Chinese desire to 'catch up' with the West in technological terms is beyond doubt, and some success has been recorded, albeit not as much as the Chinese themselves would have liked. Joint ventures have introduced new technology, even if not of the very latest variety, and a significant modernization of parts of Chinese industry has occurred because of the level of imported hardware and software. Clearly, however, difficulty has been experienced in introducing radical change into an economy cut off for so long from commercial and technological developments occurring elsewhere.

The attitude of the Chinese government itself has been crucial in providing an impetus to overcome the problems imposed by an inconvertible currency, exchange control regulations and a general management ethos seriously out of line with twentieth century requirements. More investment incentives and policy changes of themselves would have been insufficient to achieve even the limited success that has occurred.

Many problems remain yet to be resolved. This chapter has attempted to identify those problems contributing to the lack of success, on the assumption that a recognition of these problems by foreign investors will serve to reduce their incidence. For example, prior knowledge of potential low quality supplies can be used as a negotiating weapon. If China cannot provide materials of the appropriate quality or price and at the right time, pressure can be exerted for permission to import.

Most companies will not encounter all of the difficulties outlined and experience suggests that, once the initial hurdles have been overcome, the majority of joint venture investments seem to have operated reasonably successfully (Stavis and Ye 1988).

REFERENCES

Anon. (1987) 'China officials keen to talk technology', *Financial Times*, 22 April, p. 4.
——(1992a) 'Amount of foreign investment', *Investing Licensing & Trading Conditions Abroad*, 1 February.

——(1992b) 'How foreign MNCs integrate operations in greater China triangle', *Global Financial Markets*, 3 June.

Bangsberg, P. T. (1991) 'Shell to study China refinery; report expected in 18 months', *Journal of Commerce*, 30 July.

Bojar, E. (1994) Joint Ventures in the Polish and Russian Economies, discussion paper released through Telford College, Edinburgh.

Chen, L. (1991) 'A perspective of new order in enterprise management in economic reform', *Chinese Journal of Applied Psychology*, vol. 6, no. 1.

Cheng, E. (1988) 'Development: no plan for an island', *Far Eastern Economic Review*, 26 May, p. 96.

Chu, B. T. (1988) *Foreign Investment in China: Questions and Answers*, Beijing: Foreign Languages Press.

Commission of Foreign Relations and Trade of Guandong Province (1986) *Legislation: Investment is Welcome*, CFRTGP: Guandong, PR China.

Hendryx, S. R. (1986) 'The China trade: making the deal work', *Harvard Business Review*, 64, 4: 75, 81–4.

Irvine, J., Croft, M. and Kelly, M. (with additional contributions by others) (1987) 'China: market is waiting', *Accountancy* 99 '1123': 67–75.

Kemp, L. (1987) *Investing in China: Where, How and Why?*, Economist Intelligence Unit, Dartford: Economist Publications.

Lee, P. K., Mun, K. S., Sit, F. S. and Wong, W. K. (1987) *Investment Climate in China: Problems and Prospects*, Feasibility Study Unit, Research Centre for Economic, Technological and Social Development, State Council, PR China.

Lo, T. W. C. and Yung, A. (1988), 'Multinational service firms in centrally-planned economies: foreign advertising agencies in PRC', *Management International Review* 28(1): 26–33.

Lockett, M. (1987) *The Regional Foundations of China's Foreign Trade*, Templeton College Research Paper 87/17, Oxford.

Pomfret, R. (1991) *Investing in China: Ten Years of the 'Open Door' Policy*, Hemel Hempstead: Harvester Wheatsheaf.

Pye, L. W. (1986) 'The China trade: making the deal', *Harvard Business Review* 64(4): 74, 76–80.

Stavis, B. and Ye, G. (1988) 'A survey of Shanghai joint ventures', *China Business Review*, March/April, pp. 46–8.

Vogel, E. F. (1989) *One Step Ahead in China: Guangdong Under Reform*, Cambridge, Mass: Harvard University Press.

Wang, Z. (1992), 'Managerial psychological strategies for Sino-foreign joint ventures', *Journal of Managerial Psychology* 7(3): 10–16.

Warner, M. (1985) 'Training China's managers', *Journal of General Management* 11(2): 12–26.

Woodward, D. G. and Liu, B. C. F. (1993) 'Investing in China: guidelines for success', *Long Range Planning* 26(2): 83–9.

World Bank (1985) *Country Economic Report — China: Long Term Development Issues and Options*, Baltimore, Md: Johns Hopkins University Press.

——(1988) *A World Bank Country Study — China: External Trade and*

Capital, Baltimore, Md: Johns Hopkins University Press.

Yu, Y. (1988) 'China's economic policy towards Asian-Pacific economies', in M. Shinohara and F. Lo (eds) *Global Adjustment and the Future of Asian-Pacific Economy*, Papers and Proceedings of the Conference on Global Adjustment and the Future of Asian-Pacific Economy, Tokyo, 11–13 May, Tokyo: PMC Publications.

Chapter 5

Chinese and Western stock markets

International influences and development

D. E. Ayling and Z. Jiang

INTRODUCTION

Stock exchanges are not new to China. They existed there prior to 1949 (when the People's Republic was founded). In the early 1980s, after many years without a stock market, China began once again to issue securities. It was not until late 1989, however, that securities received serious attention from the Chinese government. The consequent rebirth of the Chinese stock exchanges in Shanghai and Shenzhen, in 1990 and 1991 respectively, indicates that government attitudes are turning away from a highly centrally planned economy towards a market-oriented economy. The benefits of stock exchanges are becoming increasingly recognized by the Chinese government, which continues to offer them its support. In this Chapter the structure of the modern Chinese stock markets is compared with that of mature securities exchanges in the West. The focus is on administrative problems faced by Chinese markets and the measures available to alleviate them.

THE DEVELOPMENT OF CHINESE SECURITIES MARKETS

In 1979 China embarked on an ambitious reform of the economic system which led to great changes in Chinese politics and fundamentally influenced every corner of society. Attitudes towards the free market system changed dramatically. The same Chinese authorities who abolished securities soon after the founding of the People's Republic in 1949 re-approved the issue of treasury bonds in 1981. Treasury bonds (as allowed in 1981) were apportioned to public enterprises but were not allowed to be circulated or transferred between individuals. In 1986, in order to increase the liquidity and attractiveness of treasury bonds, bond transactions between individuals were made possible in Shenyang. This was, in effect, the rebirth of securities markets in China. These were now considered appropriate vehicles for economic reform. Following the Shenyang example, markets for bonds became established in other cities. Securities received further attention from the Chinese government in 1989. From this time onwards publications about securities trading became very popular and securities prices were frequently reported on radio and television and in newspapers. On 19 December 1990 and 3 July 1991, the Shanghai Stock Exchange and the Shenzhen Stock Exchange, respectively, were formally opened for trading equities. The establishment of these stock exchanges was an integral part of the Chinese government's strategy to move towards a market economy. Selling stocks to the public was viewed as a useful way to raise money to boost the economy and to lift the massive state industries out of the doldrums. Other sources of investment (such as government revenues and taxes) had dried up. In early 1992, Chinese senior leader Deng Xiaoping made an influential appearance in Shenzhen and bolstered support for continued economic reform. The influence of Deng's support on the Chinese securities market was dramatic. There followed a substantial rise in stock market prices around March/April 1992, as can be seen from Figure 5.1.

The number of securities listed on the Shenzhen Stock Exchange rose substantially from 6 (A shares) at the beginning of 1992 to 44 (24 A shares, 9 B shares, 10 corporate bonds and 1 warrant) at the end of 1992. Turnover in 1992 totalled RMB (China's currency) 43.8 billion ($US7.7 billion), 12 times larger than in 1991. The conversion to a market economy met with further endorsement by the Chinese Communist Party's Fourteenth Congress of late 1992. Formerly, the impetus for share issues came mainly from small enterprises. From 1993, however, more large and medium-sized state enterprises became stock firms. There are currently around 5,000 joint stock companies in China but only 124 of them are listed on stock exchanges.

HIGH = 312.2060   LOW = 107.0830

Figure 5.1 Shenzhen composite index daily movement, 1992
Source: Yu 1993

FOREIGN INVESTMENT IN CHINA

In December 1991 China opened up its securities markets to foreign investment. This was to be achieved via the issue of 'B shares' (available to foreigners only). Since then there have been two types of shares in China's stock markets: A shares (restricted to Chinese legal persons and individuals) and B shares (restricted to overseas institutions and individuals). On 9 October 1992, there occurred the first trading of Chinese shares on the New York Stock Exchange (NYSE). The letters 'CBA' (China Brilliance Automotive, a Shenyang producer of minivans) appeared above the trading floor of NYSE. It was necessary for CBA to meet strict US disclosure rules in order to provide foreign investors with adequate information about its activities. The offering was received well by US investors. It was also a coup for the Chinese government because it demonstrated a willingness to improve the international image of Chinese corporate names. The issue was viewed as a model for other Chinese firms wishing to meet the requirements of a mature stock exchange. Since the listing of CBA on the NYSE, nine more state-owned enterprises have been approved by the State Council to issue shares in Hong Kong. By

1 November 1993 four of these nine enterprises already had their shares listed in Hong Kong.

COMPARISON OF CHINESE AND WESTERN SECURITIES MARKETS

Mature stock markets such as those in New York and London are often described as being 'sophisticated, fair and accessible' in comparison with financial markets in developing countries. Some of the measures which are taken in practice by markets to secure these qualities are (from Ayling 1986):

1 High standards of information reporting and disclosure.
2 A substantial supply of stocks.
3 A professional, highly developed securities industry.
4 Well developed information and communication systems.
5 High standards of trading floor regulation.

Each of these desirable market attributes will now be considered in relation to Chinese stock markets.

Auditing, accounting, disclosure and reporting standards by listed companies

A high standard of information disclosure allows investors to make informed judgements about the intrinsic values of listed securities. Foreigners investing in markets where standards of disclosure are high have less to fear that the price paid for a stock is a poor reflection of its worth than if information reporting standards are low. Differences in national accounting standards reflect the influence of factors such as the structure and sophistication of capital markets, the role of government in the economy, business and tax laws, and the organization of the accounting profession.

Generally speaking, financial reporting in China is still in the early stages of development. The centrally planned economy influenced the Chinese information disclosure practices for about a quarter of a century. During this period, centralized material and product distribution policies were adopted. It is therefore not unsurprising that Chinese accounting standards lag behind international reporting standards. There has been a lack of statement standardization even when the information was available.

Traditionally, Chinese managers lack an understanding of the importance of disclosure. Consequently, information about the management performance of a joint stock enterprise is not always available to the Chinese public. Until recently, foreign investors, too, found it difficult to obtain solid financial data from companies listed on China's securities markets. The situation began to improve on 1 July 1993 when China adopted new rules relating to corporate financial affairs and new accounting standards. The new rules brought China more into line with international practice. Most Sino-foreign joint ventures in Shenzhen, a Special Economic Zone, have now adopted international accounting standards and procedures. In addition, several international accountancy firms have opened offices in China to audit certain categories of company and to improve their accounting systems. In the USA Chinese firms seeking stock market listing are required to provide financial information in accordance with US generally accepted accounting principles (GAAP). To prepare the required financial statements, CBA enlisted the help of the Hong Kong office of Arthur Andersen. The accounting firm dispatched a 30-person team to China from March to July 1992 and spent 11,000 hours reviewing and auditing the financial records. Finally, the team provided the statements required under GAAP, which allowed CBA's foreign listing. Following this listing it is reasonable to anticipate continued improved disclosure practices from Chinese enterprises.

It is now accepted that, in order to raise the interests of overseas investors, the financial situation of companies having their B shares listed must be audited by overseas — registered accountants. Lawyers' services are also bought in from overseas. This operation stimulates the improvement of China's domestic auditing systems. For example, to bring international accounting standards to A shares, China's central bank has appointed seven accounting firms in Hong Kong to audit the accounts of some companies whose shares are to be listed on the domestic stock market. There is plenty of evidence, therefore, that accounting practices in China are moving closer to international standards.

Supply of stocks

Stock markets grow in response to demand for services by capital users. Economies of scale may be reaped by stock markets if the supply of stocks is high. The overall supply of stocks is determined by factors such as the number and size of productive organizations, and political attitudes towards the free market, both domestically and worldwide. Governments are, of course, in a strong position to influence the supply of stocks coming on to the exchanges. Despite government support, however, the size of China's stock market is still small by international standards. On 25 October 1993, there were only 124 listed enterprises on the Shanghai and Shenzhen Stock Exchanges, with the total amount of 124 A shares and 33 B shares. The market's small size has, in the past, led to too much money chasing too few shares. Chinese investors, in general, anticipate far greater returns from buying stocks than from putting money in banks. In April 1992 anticipation of excessive returns pushed prices so high that the average share price on the Shanghai Exchange was 160 times the earning rate, and one company had a ratio of nearly 572 to 1. At the same time shares in Hong Kong were selling at 12.3 times earnings and on Wall Street the typical multiple was 13. On 10 August 1992, more than one million Chinese stood for days in Shenzhen's summer heat to buy applications for shares in newly listed companies. News spread that some officials had kept the application forms for themselves instead of selling them all to would-be investors. The ensuing riots (now referred to as the '8.10 riots') provide a graphic example of what can happen when too many Chinese chase too few shares.

The market's small size (especially the B share market) has also led to poor liquidity and erratic stock price movements. In mid-May 1992, B share prices in Shenzhen rose to nearly 240 per cent above the initial listings. Since then the market has edged downward. Traditional B share investment is consequently out of favour and foreign investors have found Chinese equities overseas listings more attractive in comparison. Overseas listings have better liquidity, more freedom of access, a broader investor base, more familiar trading practices and settlement procedures, and a consistently high quality of equity research from an experienced and well-qualified stockbroking fraternity.

Development and professionalism of the securities industry

Developed securities industries offer a wide variety of services from a large number of underwriters, dealers, brokers, analysts, money managers, mutual funds, unit trusts, investment trusts, and other providers of services for market users. In China there are two groups of brokers: local and foreign. In the B shares market, both types of brokers are involved in the trading of B shares. Approved foreign brokers can take orders of B shares from overseas investors and then commission local securities firms to execute the orders through a computerized trading system. Foreign brokers are not allowed to deal directly on exchange floors, leading to poor liquidity and share-trading inefficiency. For Chinese securities there has, consequently, been a wide divergence of professionalism and development between the domestic market (A shares) and the international market (B shares). The divergence is narrowing, however, as international pressures influence both markets.

Recently, for example, in order to make B shares transactions more appealing to foreign investors, China's securities exchanges have begun to set aside a few special seats for overseas securities dealers. The trend is therefore towards foreign investors having better access to B shares trading.

Information and communication systems

Information comes in many forms: in newspapers, on computer screens, in regular reports and accounts, through advertising in journals and trade publications, by radio and on television. The greater is public awareness of events as they happen, the more in touch investors are and the more informationally efficient the markets become. An important aspect of modern information systems is their range of facilities for collecting information at source. Unlike some other emerging markets, the authorities in China have always been aware of the need for information collection at the point of trading. Currently, in China's stock markets, all order placing, price matching and settlement of securities trading is achieved through scriplessness and computerization. China's securities industry, in this respect, stands amongst the leaders in securities market technology. Timely quotations are provided along wires, over the airwaves and by satellite. In the Shenzhen market an auto-matching system was introduced in February 1992. From May 1992 trading and information transfer was made possible between the exchange and the offices of local member-brokers on a real time basis via the intercity computer data line. Supported by the intercity computer trading network, the Shenzhen Exchange also provides a telephone auto-ordering system. From April 1993 the Shenzhen Exchange began transmitting the quotations to its non-local members. Trading information is now transmitted on a real time basis to 150 countries and regions in conjunction with Telerate. The Shenzhen Stock Exchange also recently managed to open another transmission system integrated with the IDN network of Reuters. Foreign investors are consequently provided with time-sensitive information on trades and shares prices. From the second half of 1992, the Shenzhen Stock Exchange has run an information centre to provide literature on developments at the exchange. The exchange has also begun a Shenzhen Stock historical database as an easy and accessible source of information and research.

Trading floor supervision

Market supervision may be exercised through legislation or internal regulations. Reliable and fair procedures for trading increase investors' confidence. The confidence of foreign investors, in particular, increases in the knowledge that trading floor procedures help to safeguard their interests. In China, trading floor supervision is governed by a two-tiered regulatory structure. The top tier, the State Council Securities Regulatory Commission, is in charge of policy decisions while the bottom tier, the China Securities Regulatory Commission, monitors the day-to-day regulation of the exchanges. Despite the existence of this two-tier regulatory structure, guidelines for trading floor supervision are not yet clear. To date there has been neither a national securities law nor a Companies Act in China to govern stock markets and listed companies. Instead, local rules and regulations have been relied on. In 1992 alone, thirty-plus provisions and detailed implemention rules in regard to share issue and trading were formulated in Shenzhen. There is a great deal of uncertainty surrounding the legality of these local rules. It is likely that a continued lack of legally codified investor protection for foreign investors would cause foreigners to remain wary of investment in China. The two-tier regulatory structure therefore has much ground to make up. A draft of a national securities law has been circulated within the Chinese government. The new legislation, which is intended to unify the markets and to clarify listed companies' responsibilities, is not yet finalized.

CONCLUSION

We have compared the development of Chinese stock exchanges with their Western counterparts with special emphasis on disclosure practice, supply of stocks, securities industry support services, and information and regulation systems. Our general conclusion is that, despite their small beginnings, Chinese stock markets have the potential to catch up quickly with those in the West. The impetus for this fast development comes from the interplay of China's need for development capital and the West's desire for overseas exchanges which operate along the same lines as their own. Consequently, higher accounting and disclosure standards are not only being imported from but also guided by Western market professionals. The supply of stocks to the exchanges at Shanghai and Shenzhen is increasing as many previously state-run companies seek new capital from private investors. Many of these firms also seek overseas capital and recognition. Information technology in the Chinese markets is highly developed even by Western standards. The main factors limiting the international accessibility of Chinese stock markets are the system of market regulation and the shortage of seats for foreigners to take an active part in trading. Market floor regulation and supervision is 'confused' rather than protectionist. There remain problems of reconciling local and national trading rules and guidelines against a background of uncertain but awaited government legislation. With regard to trading seats for foreigners, one such seat already exists (occupied by the Swiss Bank Corporation) on the Shanghai Exchange. Further seats for foreigners are being discussed but some reluctance in this direction is not entirely unreasonable. After all, it would not necessarily be a good thing for China to have a sudden, large influx of Western traders from exchanges which have not always been as consistently 'sophisticated, fair and accessible' as their regulatory authorities would have us believe. There is room for an Eastern influence on China's own stock markets, which would be lost if Western market philosophies, standards and practices were adopted totally.

Our expectation is that, in future, securities markets will become a major source of capital for today's state enterprises in China. The number of companies listed on the markets will increase substantially. More enterprises will also receive approval for stock listing outside China. The prospects are optimistic for

China's economy, with its abundant natural and intellectual resources, hardworking labour force, and an increased efficiency brought about by the economic reforms. If the trend continues, China's economic growth will be among the world's fastest in the next decade and, by the end of the century, China's securities market will have become one of the world's largest investment channels.

BIBLIOGRAPHY

Ayling, D. E. (1986) *The Internationalisation of Stockmarkets*, Studies in Finance and Investment, Aldershot, UK: Gower, pp. 29–31.

Chen, Y. S. (1991) 'New developments in mainland China's securities market', *Issues and Studies* 27 (8): 82–103.

Crossman, J. (1993) 'China-Shanghai', *1993 Guide to World Equity Markets* (*Euromoney* Supplement), May, pp. 66–7.

Sassoon, J. M. (1993) 'China-Shenzhen', *1993 Guide to World Equity Markets* (*Euromoney* Supplement), May, pp. 68–9.

Spencer, L. B. Jun., Randt, C. T. Jun., Bass, J. E. and Hsiaochiung, L. (1993) 'From Shenyang to Wall Street', *China Business Review*, May-June, pp. 44–6.

Swiss Bank Corporation (1992) 'China's stock markets: a guide for foreign investors', *Euromoney Supplement*, June, pp. 8–10.

Sze, J. W. (1993) 'The allure of B shares', *China Business Review*, January-February, pp. 42–8.

Yu, G. (1993) *Shenzhen Stock Exchange 1992 Annual Report*, Shenzhen: Stock Exchange.

Chapter 6

Re-emergence of the Chinese stock market

R. Brayshaw and Z. Teng

INTRODUCTION

This chapter aims to provide a preliminary analysis of the evolution and development of the Chinese stock market. It provides a basic analysis of the stock market with a view towards facilitating an understanding of the following issues:

1 Why did a stock market develop in China?
2 How does the stock market work in the context of China's 'socialist market economy'?
3 What have been the major problems in the development of the stock market and what are its prospects for the future?

Public ownership and a non-market economy are not commonly seen as providing the conditions necessary for the development of a truly functional stock market. It is thus essential to review the economic environment within which the Chinese stock market has developed in order to gain the necessary background information for an understanding of this unique phenomenon.

The economic and financial system in the pre-reform period

A highly centralized economic system was established in the early 1950s following the founding of the People's Republic of China. This system, a socialist economy was modelled on that of the former Soviet Union, and was intended to enable the government to exert direct control over aggregate demand and other economic activities. Under this system, privately owned enterprises were first controlled and later incorporated into state-owned enterprises;[1] investment was incorporated into the planning process, with the state determining the quantity and direction of investment; prices were regulated by wage and price controls with a system of commodity allocation etc. Thus most production decisions, including those relating to raw materials and production inputs, were made by the government. Profits were, in turn, remitted to the state. There was no sustaining linkage between an enterprise's efficiency and benefits accruing to those responsible for management. Supply and distribution channels were rigid and unresponsive to shifts in demand. One consequence of the practice of this economic system was that economic growth was achieved largely through the application of increased physical inputs, capital, and manpower rather than through more efficient use of resources. Prior to 1977, total productivity growth was zero (Xia *et al.* 1992: 21).

The financial system was based on this centrally planned economy, with a limited number of financial intermediaries and limited functioning of financial institutions. Under this system banking functioned as a part of the state administration: the banks were subordinated to the Ministry of Finance (MOF). Banking operations were generally inefficient, and clearly reflected the notion of 'politics in command' (Grummit 1986). During the Cultural Revolution (1966–76), the People's Bank of China (PBOC) was wholly incorporated into the MOF.[2] It was little more than a cash desk for that Ministry and the State Planning Commission (Reynolds 1988). In theory, the bank was in a strong position to monitor and control the activities of enterprises and other organizations as regulations obliged most state-owned enterprises and other organizations to keep all of their funds in a single account at the PBOC. In practice, however, as the bank had no power to refuse loans, this function had a marginal impact on the economy.

As far as the financing of industry was concerned, enterprises simply received necessary operating and equipment funds directly from central and local government. Investment in industry was thus overwhelmingly channelled through direct 'grants' from the MOF. On the other hand, enterprises had to hand over all of their operating profits to the MOF. There were, however, limited additional bank loans for enterprises' production funds and investments. Loans were normally granted to enterprises through the local branch of the PBOC. There was thus no need for enterprises to issue securities or try to raise capital directly from general investors at that time. There was also little accumulation of financial assets by the general public, and what there was was almost all deposited in banks, since there was no other way to invest. In short, the banking and financing system during this period featured a narrow role for the bank, a rigid industrial financing system, and no financial markets whatsoever. Given this situation, there was no possibility of, indeed no need for, the establishment of a stock or any other financial market.

Economic and financial reform

Economic reform was first introduced in rural areas in 1979. The basic thrust of the reform was to devolve production responsibility down to household level, thus encouraging the initiative of the peasants in their work by direct linkage between their performance and their rewards. The reform was then extended to the cities and focused on industrial sectors. The document of the Central Committee of the Chinese Communist Party on the 'Reform of the Economic Structure', issued in 1984, signalled the beginning of a major push to alter significantly the old rigid economic system. The long-standing pattern of industrial planning and operations began to change from that time. The major objectives of the economic reform were to reduce inefficiency and the distortions inherent in a purely centrally planned economy and to expedite economic development by improving allocative efficiency, relying on market forces and material incentives to motivate the desired economic behaviour. More specifically the reform aimed:

1 To increase industrial productivity by providing autonomy and incentives to enterprises.
2 To create a market which could produce correct signals.
3 To attract foreign capital.

As the economic reforms deepened, it was intended that the scope of mandatory planning should be increasingly restricted and a well functioning market mechanism became essential.

In the pre-reform period highly centralized planning was mandatory and carried out through two parallel procedures: the formulation of five year plans and annual aggregate plans; and individual project proposals. In this way both the state's overall economic direction and the production quota for each enterprise were determined by government administrators. This planning system did not of itself generate an efficient pattern of investment. The reform was therefore focused on reducing the scope of mandatory planning: on the one hand, planning was restricted to general overall direction of the economy; and on the other to the application of macro-economic policy instruments such as taxation, credit and interest rates. This was called the 'socialist market economy'. Under this economy only products essential to the economy of the state were kept within the State Plan. Other products were regulated through guidance plans, which provided collective enterprises and the private sector with greater flexibility and autonomy. Importantly, the private sector was allowed to re-emerge, grow, and compete. Eventually, the proportion of commodities falling under the mandatory plans decreased strikingly.

However, the use of macro-economic instruments within the reformed planning system was far from popular because of the lack of effective market mechanisms. Under the old economic system, price did not play an allocative role in the economy owing to the heavy reliance on administrative controls. The prices of most consumer goods and industrial raw materials were fixed by the state, and were largely determined by political and social considerations, with no proper adjustment mechanism built in to reflect changes in income and demand. Late 1984 saw the introduction of price reforms. This was considered the most radical and difficult reform. Since then prices have been gradually freed and a 'two track price system' has existed: first track prices are determined by the state and local government; second track prices are determined by market forces. In order to make use of credit, interest rates and taxation as instruments of macro-economic control, several reform measures were introduced simultaneously. These included reform of the financial system.

The lack of banks, money and capital markets has been shown to have been a deficiency since economic reform was initiated in 1979. As the market mechanism has been introduced into the Chinese economy, the proportion of government finances in GNP has fallen sharply (see Table 6.1). This has made it impossible for the state to continue to make huge investments and to spend large amounts of funds on enterprises. On the one hand the government has had to look for new resources to fund state expenditure; on the other hand, enterprises have had to find alternative ways to finance their activities, since they could no longer rely solely on state fiscal expenditures or bank loans for their projects. Furthermore, as a result of economic reform, the amount of savings accumulated by the general public has increased sharply. This has led to the highest level of personal savings in the Third World (see Table 6.2). It thus became necessary to convert these personal savings into production capital by providing diversified financial assets. To provide alternative investments money markets and capital markets were needed. These markets, in the eyes of reformist and liberal academics, can provide enterprises with a source of direct financing in addition to fiscal allocations and bank loans, so as to promote sound growth of the financial system (Xie 1990).

Table 6.1 A comparison of the proportions of expenditure and taxation in GNP

Year	Per caput income	Expenditure GNP %	Revenue GNP %	Deficit GNP %
1978	230	34.0	34.0	+0.2
1988	320	22.0	19.8	−2.2

Source: World Bank 1990

Table 6.2 Gross domestic investment and gross domestic savings as a percentage of gross domestic product in semi-industrial countries, 1965 and 1986

	Investment (%) 1965	1986	Domestic savings (%) 1965	1986
China	25	39	25	36
India	18	23	16	21
Brazil	20	21	22	24
Mexico	22	21	21	27
South Korea	15	29	8	35
Developing countries	15	29	20	24
Middle-income developing countries	21	23	21	24
Low-income developing countries	17	19	16	17
Industrial countries	23	21	23	21

Source: World Bank 1988

Further steps in the reform were taken in 1986, aiming to stimulate the initiative of corporate management in the operation of the banking sector. Perhaps the most important task was to change the funding channels for government-financed corporations. The financial reforms now targeted five main areas (JETRO Shanghai Office 1989):

1 Reform of the planning system.
2 Reform of loan funds.
3 Promotion of co-operation between specialized banks.
4 Strengthening of financial macro-management.
5 Development of financial markets.

The final area, which is the most relevant to the core discussion of this chapter, was the development of financial markets.

Development of financial markets

The savings of individuals and enterprises have increased since the reform of the economy began. It has become necessary to develop a system to recycle this money into ventures and projects. Meanwhile, the sustained growth and stability of enterprises will increasingly depend on the availability of new sources of financing as the economic reform deepens. The development of China's financial sector is heavily dependent on the development of financial markets, including short-term money markets and long-term capital markets, to facilitate the free flow of funds and to help to overcome price distortions in the credit market. There had been gradual development of financial markets from 1983, but substantial further development has been evident since 1986.

At the beginning of 1986, the government decided to make the opening up of the money markets a major part of the reform of China's economic structure over the following five years. Five major cities, Chongqing, Guangzhou, Wuhan, Shenyang and Changzhou, which had already been 'pioneer' pilot cities of economic reform, were also chosen for this reform. For the first two years the focus was on establishing an exchange for short-term loans between regions in order to ensure a rational distribution of capital, and to enable capital to seek out the most beneficial investment prospects. That is, money could now be borrowed or lent for short-term purposes. Interest rates are subject to negotiation between borrowers and lenders under the supervision of the PBOC. Generally speaking, they are slightly lower than rates for working capital loans. This has largely eased market liquidity. The positive outcome of the experiment of the five cities encouraged the further spread of the money market in the country. By 1987, regional money markets were beginning to open up in commercial centres in ten major cities. However, the importance of these money markets, which had been steadily increasing, suffered a setback when a credit squeeze was applied by the PBOC to control inflation in late 1988 and early 1989. This situation continued until early 1992. Since then the money market has been recovering, but it is becoming less important than another financial market: the capital market.

The issuing of share capital and the creation of a capital market has been the first priority of reform of the financial system since 1986. These are also potentially the most politically sensitive of China's financial reforms, because they raise the question of ownership of enterprises, and hence the question, crucial to a Marxist, of the ownership of the means of production. This is why the experiment of issuing stock started first with collectively owned enterprises: these enterprises were a small proportion of the nation's enterprises overall and not representative of the 'socialist publicly owned system' (*gun you zi*). The risks were therefore considered to be small.

The experiment of a stock share system was extended to state-owned enterprises later. Based on a study of the experience of reform in Eastern Europe, China decided to experiment with a limited scale stock share system in the state-owned enterprises. Under this system, the relationship of the employees with the enterprise is no longer just that of a wage earner. They have, in addition, an equity interest by being offered stock shares in the enterprise. The stock that they buy may be negligible compared to the total assets of state-owned enterprises, but can prove significant to the employees, by relating the operation of the enterprise to their personal income and bonus. This, it is claimed, creates stronger incentive pressures on both the employees and the enterprise. Moreover, this does not originate from negotiations with the state over specific assessment targets but from the enterprise's own interest in its survival and development. The mechanism of the stock share system as designed does not, however, seem to be working as intended. Problems include the tendency of shareholders to seek the highest short-term dividends, and an incompatible tax system.[3] The most serious problem in issuing new shares relates to the valuation of enterprise assets. In the initial stage, there is a tendency for assets to be undervalued because of low accounting standards and lack of professional experience.

The major underlying reason, however, for the failure to value and apportion assets properly was the lack of a well-functioning stock market. Although a share issuing market was created and grew, a primary market in the real sense of the word was not formed. There was, moreover, no secondary market for the trading of shares and other stocks. Under these circumstances, no quoted price was available to provide a value reference point. This, combined with the lower accounting standards, made it very difficult to value an organization's assets accurately. It was at this stage that the establishment of a stock market was recognized as an important factor in the building up of an effective market mechanism, which was seen as essential for the further reform of the financial system.

The establishment of a capital market focused attention on the need for a stock market. The establishment of two stock exchanges a little later, in the early 1990s, marked the formal creation of a capital market.

THE EMERGENCE OF THE STOCK MARKET IN CHINA

The Chinese stock market began to develop along with progress in reforming the financial system and in accordance with the need to build up financial markets. However, although the establishment and growth of the current stock market result from basic changes in the national economy brought about by the reforms made over the past fourteen years, the emergence of a stock market in China dates from the beginning of this century, when its establishment stemmed from completely different causes.

History of China's stock market

The origins of China's stock market go back to 1919 when Shanghai was considered one of the international financial centres of the Far East (Grub and Sudweeks 1988). The city of Shanghai established its first functioning stock exchange in 1919, and this served as one of Asia's major money centres during the period 1919–49. It was the only stock exchange of the time, all share buying and selling activities being transacted there. At its peak the shares of 76 companies were admitted for trading, 22 of them banks. Most major international banks had branches located there at that time. However, most trading activities took place outside the official stock exchange, and local interests even initiated an informal trading system. The stock exchange ceased to function during the period 1938–45 when the Japanese invaded China and occupied Shanghai. During the Civil War, 1945–9, the stock exchange barely functioned. When the Chinese Communist Party took control of Shanghai in 1949 the stock exchange was closed.

The new Chinese Communist government which came to power in 1949 viewed the stock exchange and financial intermediaries as among the most prominent symbols of an oppressive capitalist regime. In fact, all but four foreign banks left China, and the four which remained were stripped of their earlier status and prestige (Grub and Sudweeks, 1988). After the revolution, banks became the sole representatives of the financial sector in China and their function was very limited, as has been mentioned above. The stock exchange disappeared at that time, and people who were born after 1949 hardly knew the words 'stock' or 'stock market'.

It was not until the liberalization of 1981, when the Chinese government initiated economic reforms aimed at decentralizing production and investment decisions and subjecting these increasingly to market influences, that shares, or more exactly, non-voting participatory certificates, were first issued by a private company.[4]

Treasury bonds had been issued before this, but were not allowed to be floated until 1981. State-owned enterprises started issuing shares to the general public in 1985; nevertheless, no formal trading system was in place at that time. Indeed, the transaction of securities in a formal market only began on 19 December 1990, when the Shanghai Securities Exchange was founded. Since then, officially organized stock trading has becoming increasingly widespread in China.

As with the banking and financial markets, China's stock market developed initially with a 'dual personality'. China's native banking and financial markets, comprising indigenous bankers and their guilds, were once an important facet of local banking and finance, but were quickly surpassed by the markets which developed around Western banks. Further competition came as the modern Chinese banks became more important, and by the late 1930s the 'modern' money market, together with that of the foreign banks, comprised the bulk of the market. This situation was repeated in the securities industry. The first stock exchange in the history of China was established by foreign interests. These introduced a trading system similar to that on the London Stock Exchange, and most members of the Chinese Stock Promotion Committee (CSPC) were foreigners, as indeed were most of the listed companies. However, the stock exchange was open to a small number of very wealthy Chinese who had connections with their foreign counterparts. This stage in the early infancy of China's stock market is notable for limitations: limited financial resources for industry; limited influence on China as a whole; and a limited role in the economy.

The stock market which re-emerged in China after a gap of forty years exhibited completely different characteristics.

Re-emergence of the stock market

Re-emergence of share and bond markets

Although the official stock market was founded in 1990, the issuing and trading of stocks occurred much earlier than that. In 1980 the Wuhan municipal government issued bonds to finance the establishment of a trade centre building.[5] The bonds were mostly sold to state and collective enterprises. In 1981 a thermal power station in Shandong Province (east China) was financed by shares sold to state and collective enterprises. The Jinbei Automobile Co. Ltd in Shengyang (north China) issued shares to foreigners in 1988, the first since 1949.[6] The purchase price and dividends were payable in foreign currency. The shares issued during this period are not strictly comparable to shares in Western countries. They are more like 'non-voting, participating' certificates. The dividend rates are arbitrarily fixed without regard to the actual operating conditions of the issuing companies; stocks are bought back by companies after a fixed period. This makes them less stocks in nature than 'corporate bonds'. Furthermore, there is no official secondary market for trading these shares at this stage.

The re-emergence of the issue of shares is the result of both the reform of the financial system and the economic development of China. In 1985, a growing economy, the rapid extension of domestic lending, and injudicious use of national foreign-exchange reserves together created a situation which prompted tough new restrictions on China's bankers. (The same situation recurred in 1993.) This tightening of credit was an important incentive to companies and enterprises to raise funds through the sale of shares. Together with the fact that the question of introducing financial markets came more squarely on to the policy agenda at that time, the rate of share issues accelerated. Nationally the Chinese government agreed to extend the experiment of issuing shares beyond the five cities in which companies were allowed to issue shares.[7] This was partly because of the success of the experiment of issuing shares in those five cities and partly because the importance of the stock market in the Chinese economy was being recognized by increasing numbers of government officials. The Municipal Financial Trust Company in Wuhan, for example, expanded its share base with a public issue of 12 million RMB in July 1984, with the permission of the central government (*Huei Daily*, 7 July 1984). Between 1985 and 1989, regional markets for share and bond trading were formed in the five cities. This may be categorized as the infancy stage proper of the secondary market. Since then trading in these markets has been increasingly active.

In 1989 an official organization called the Stock Exchange Executive Council (SEEC) was established (see Xie 1990). The SEEC is engaged in the work of establishing and developing a Chinese national stock market. Its work includes theoretical research and specific design work, as well as work to establish the environment and conditions necessary for the development of the stock market. The SEEC assembled a study group comprising officials from regulatory organizations and research staff of the SEEC to conduct a comprehensive survey of the regional stock markets in Shengyang, Wuhan, Shenzhen, Shanghai and other cities where stock transactions were already active. This was probably the first time that the stock market had ever been surveyed in such a comprehensive way in China. This survey and its recommendations played an important role in the subsequent establishment of two official stock exchanges.

Since the issuing of stock is in an initial stage of development, stock circulation is also very limited. The primary and secondary markets have distinctively Chinese features.

The primary market

Shares

A primary market is one in which government, companies, enterprises and other bodies sell new securities to raise cash. As we have seen, Chinese enterprises and companies had started to issue shares in the early 1980s. This, however, was part of the experimental stage of the 'stock share' system. As part of the economic reforms, China started to expand the experiment in specified regions with the introduction of a system of stock share enterprises from 1984. Several thousand enterprises across the country introduced this system in 1984–9. The system was further developed in two main ways. First, the decision could be taken to convert existing companies to joint stock share companies. Second, the decision could be taken to establish joint stock companies through merger or division of enterprises.

In tandem with the introduction of the stock share system, stocks were issued through conversion of assessed assets of existing enterprises. However, for the most part enterprises were permitted only to sell stocks to employees or to related companies. A very small proportion of the stocks was allowed to be sold to the general public individually. For example, by 1989 only eleven out of 1,250 stocks issued by companies in Shanghai had made public offers, and only one of twenty in Guanzou (Xie 1990). A breakdown of the stock raised to 1990 shows the greater part, about 70–80 per cent, is stocks issued by conversion of existing state-owned assets, showing little new capital had been raised by share issues.

Bonds

Compared with the primary market for shares, the bond issuing market is much larger in scope. Over the last decade the Chinese government has issued massive amounts of bonds, and these bonds, together with the financial bonds issued through banks, companies and other organizations had reached RMB 2,573.25 billion by 1990 (see Table 6.3). Of this amount, over 68 per cent of the total is in national bonds. This shows the leading position of national bonds in the bond issuing market of China. For enterprises, the issuing of bonds makes it possible to raise funds for

Table 6.3 Total amount of domestic bonds and stocks issued, 1981–90 (RMB billion)

Items	1981–5	1986	1987	1988	1989	1990	Total
Treasury bill	237.21	62.51	62.87	92.16	56.12	93.28	604.15
Treasury bond				66.07		71.09	137.16
State construction bond				30.65			30.65
Key state construction bond				55.00			55.00
Special state bond					43.7	32.39	76.09
Inflation-proof bond					87.43	37.4	124.83
Capital construction bond				80.0	14.59		
Key enterprise bond			30.0	10.0	7.94	6.15	54.09
Financial bond	5.0	30.0	60.0	65.0	60.66	64.4	285.06
Local enterprise bond		100.0*	30.0	30.0	14.83	49.33	224.16
Short-term enterprise financing bill				11.78	29.72	50.15	91.59
Inter-enterprise bond				33.69	30.71	26.89	91.29
CDs				59.26	141.8	503.53	704.59
Sub-total	242.21	192.51	182.87	513.55	487.50	934.65	2573.25
Stock			10.0	25.0	6.62	4.28	45.9
Total	242.21	192.51	192.87	538.55	494.12	938.89	2619.15

* Includes amount for the previous year

Source: Reconstructed from China State Statistics Bureau 1991

production and operations by their own 'creditworthiness'. (A credit rating system has not yet been built up.) That is, they have the option of using 'direct financing'.

By floating a vast amount of national bonds the Chinese government was able to make up for shortages in its fiscal revenues and to raise funds for state construction, thus balancing its fiscal accounts. Since a market had yet to be constructed, the government was unable to rely on a market for sales of its bonds. Instead it resorted to administrative means to dispose of them (as it had in the pre-reform period), allocating purchasing quotas, and ordering or even forcing enterprises and individuals to purchase the stipulated quotas. This 'administrative flotation' remained the main technique for floating bonds for several years, but it ignored the desires of purchasers of bonds, and thus was inherently alien to the basic nature of the stock market (Xie 1990). This shows a basic dilemma: an old-fashioned administrative approach and a modern primary market mechanism. From 1990 repayment of previously issued bonds became due, so the government is forced to float a large amount of bonds each year, many of them rollover bonds. With such a large amount floated, it cannot hope to dispose of the bonds through a 'semi-primary' market, but has to construct a comprehensive issuing market, and in particular to introduce the market flotation method.

Secondary market

Shares

As we have seen, very limited stocks are issued to individuals, with less than 10 per cent of the stocks issued held by individuals. The secondary market is, therefore, very tiny. On 19 December 1990 a formal trading market, Shanghai Stock Exchange, was established. Before that, all public trading was carried on through securities companies such as Shanghai Investment Co. and, later on, through 'Securities Transaction Points'. The banks in China also played an equivalent role to a stock exchange. Banks such as the People's Bank of China and the Industrial and Commercial Bank had the function of issuing shares and bonds on behalf of enterprises, paying them the proceeds, and passing on to shareholders the interest or dividends.

By 3 July 1991 another stock exchange, Shenzen Stock

Exchange, was officially established. The establishment of the two stock exchanges accelerated the pace of stock transactions, since all deals are electronic. The number of companies whose stocks are traded 'over the counter' has increased rapidly. In Shanghai, shares of 80 companies had been listed by the end of 1993, compared with 7 by early 1990. Shares of 46 companies had been listed in Shenzen Stock Exchange.[8]

Nevertheless, many individual investors do not go to the securities companies or stock exchanges to make their transactions, but instead undertake them spontaneously on the streets. Meanwhile, as the amount of listed shares is still small, the supply of shares cannot meet the demand of investors. This, together with a high inflation rate and other factors, has caused the price of shares to rise rapidly. This will be discussed fully in the following sections.

Bonds

Regional bond circulation markets opened in several cities in 1987 and were used for transactions in a handful of bonds. In April 1988 treasury bond circulation markets were established in seven cities in the first instance, and later in another 59 cities. This gave a definite boost to the bond secondary market. In 1989 bond transactions reached RMB 3.0 billion. Since regional bond markets have separately opened in 61 cities, there is no unified national network of bond circulation spanning regional boundaries. This means that the stock managing organizations of different regions operate on their own in the different cities with very weak lateral ties. As a result, gaps between bond circulation prices among regions exist and are growing.

As with shares, the problem of a bond circulation market mainly derives from the unsoundness of the bond issuing market mentioned above. The dissatisfaction of purchasers with the 'administrative flotation' approach has created a flood of selling of national bonds on the circulation market and has all but ruined the supply and demand relationship. The price at which bonds are traded has plummeted and often drops below their face value. In this situation, the floater of national bonds, the Ministry of Finance, has been forced to intervene in price formation in the circulation market, creating another 'administrative method'.

The role of the stock market

The re-emergence of China's stock market has attracted much attention inside and outside the country. A debate has developed among economists concerned as to whether to continue the development of a stock market and, if so, how to proceed. One of the central issues of the debate was the impact of the stock market on the 'socialist market economy'. Although there is not much evidence on which to assess the impact of the fledgling stock market, there are analytical reasons for believing that it performs a number of functions. Indeed, a stock market in the context of China's 'primary stage of socialism' is seen as being capable of playing a lively role in the following ways.

Role of a stock market in the economic reform

One of the objectives of the Chinese economic reform is to build up a comprehensive functional market mechanism. The purpose of introducing a capital market is to increase the efficiency of financial resources used. A capital market enables this to be achieved by providing a more flexible and efficient mechanism for mobilizing and allocating investable resources, providing the central authorities with indirect instruments to control the macro-economy without having to intervene directly in micro decision-making, giving enterprises more autonomy over investment plans. The introduction of a well-developed stock market, especially a secondary market for shares, can allow the enterprises entry, exit, merger and takeover ideally according to the market rather than administrative criteria. A well-developed market can be used by enterprises and companies to raise the capital that they cannot obtain through other channels. It is in this way that the stock market is an indispensable part of the reform programmes.

Another target of the economic reform is to create a dynamic competitive context for fair competition among enterprises. Smaller enterprises, many of them with private owners, have been encouraged to expand. According to the *Journal of Commerce* (16 August 1993), 45 per cent of the Chinese economy is now in private hands. This rate is still increasing. Generally speaking, smaller enterprises have relied more on unofficial markets for their borrowing requirements. Although there is now in fact hardly any listing of small companies on the two official stock exchanges, a fully fledged stock market should be able to mobilize the financial resources for these small enterprises, and this is clearly a direction in which they need to move in the future.

The role of the stock market in corporate finance

The role of the stock market in raising funds is crucial in providing liquidity for the equity raised and price discovery for investors. The market can be used by existing firms to raise additional capital, or by new firms to obtain quotations for their shares and to raise new capital, although there are scarcely any data available from which to estimate the capital raised by new issues in China's stock market and stock exchange financing. The development of the market as an efficient, transparent and well-regulated market is, in a sense, inseparable from the degree to which the market can be used by large and small firms to tap investment funds.

Very little is known about the dynamics of corporate investment expenditure in China, and even less, or nothing, about the influence of developments in the equity markets on these decisions. This is because there is no evidence that variation in stock prices affects corporate investment decisions. Moreover, hardly any company reports are published, and the movement of the stock market index has more to do with speculation about political changes and rumours than with companies' activities. Thus stock index movements are not a particularly reliable leading indicator, and cannot influence the timing of investment, let alone corporate investment decisions.

The stock market does, therefore, play a positive role in corporate finance, but only to a limited extent.

CURRENT PRACTICE OF THE STOCK MARKET

Characteristics of the market

Since the stock market is in the primary stage and its emergence comes in the context of the Chinese 'socialist market economy', it has a number of unique features in terms of its market operation and trading activities. The following examination of the market is based on the data of the trading centres and stock exchanges; data collected from magazines and newspapers published inside and outside of China. As very little empirical research has been undertaken, and in the absence of systematic data, quantitative analysis is based primarily on figures reconstructed from limited resources by the present authors. These reflect the situation up to August 1993.

Market operation

Over the counter stock market operation started before the two stock exchanges were set up. From 1986 to 1990 about twelve trading centres were established. Except for those in Shanghai, most were fairly small and not equipped with modern communications equipment and facilities for handling large-volume trading. The trading activities at each centre were not connected via a network. There were usually about ten members of staff, including traders, brokers, administrative and logistical staff in each trading centre. In most cases, trading centres were run by the local branch of the PBOC or by a trust and investment department of a bank. The same organizations also often sold new issues.

The pricing mechanism of these trading centres is quite different from those in the stock exchanges of other countries. The auction system was not used for continuous price setting for all of the bonds and stocks listed. Selling and buying prices were artificially set, based on the following factors:

1 Interest rates (setting of maximum permitted capital gains).
2 The potential loss and gain of the sellers and buyers.
3 The supply and demand for a particular share.

In the case of bonds, the interest rate and the maturity were taken into account. This kind of mechanism, it is claimed, was suited to the trading centre's lack of facilities and capacity for handling large volumes of trading at that time.

The setting up of the two stock exchanges in Shanghai and Shenzhen rapidly changed the situation. With more advanced trading facilities, space, and trained staff, the operation of the market made significant progress. The stock exchanges were established following the model of the Tokyo Stock Exchange. In Shanghai Stock Exchange there are now about 25 members, all institutions. There are a total of six departments within the SSE. There is a trading floor which currently has 46 seats, and capacity for a maximum of 80 seats. According to a recent report, the SSE is planning a 30-storey building equipped with three trading floors accommodating 3,000 traders. The main floor will accommodate 2,000 trading seats (*Financial Times*, 2 June 1993). The other stock exchange in the country, Shenzhen Stock Exchange, is also evolving as a formal trading centre with a similar operation. Initially, however, its trading regulations were different. The operational structure and business scope of the two stock exchanges is similar (see Figure 6.1). To take Shanghai as an example: there are three managing directors, a general manager, a president, and a vice-president. They comprise a board of directors which is a decision-making body. The general manager is in charge of the daily operation of the SSE in the following respects (Xia 1992):

1 To provide for organized trading of securities.
2 To manage spot trading of listed securities.
3 To provide securities transfer and organized safe-keeping services.
4 To provide securities clearing and delivery services.
5 To provide market information.

In summary, the operation of the two stock exchanges has been rapidly built up towards a Western style in respect of the organizational structure and business management. These operations have been supported by a certain number of facilities, which evidently are not yet wholly adequate. A report of the British Trade Commission in Hong Kong (1991) comments:

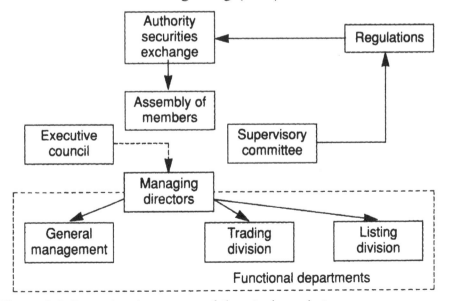

Figure 6.1 Operational structure of the stock market

Source: Reconstructed from various sources

There seemed to be little activity on the electronically computer-operated board when we surveyed events from the balcony above the trading floor ... Despite being fully automated, it seemed that all transactions were also recorded on paper and stamped in traditional Chinese fashion.

(BTC 1991: 11)

Trading activities

As of July 1993, 5,000 companies and enterprises were allowed to issue internal stocks, but only 1.9 per cent of these are presently listed on the two stock exchanges. The reasons for this are that the majority of bonds and stocks issued so far have mainly been sold by allocation to employees of the issuing enterprises.[9] Some of the enterprises did not even issue certificates, but made an entry in the books of the enterprise. According to the stock exchange regulations, no such enterprises are allowed to be listed by the stock exchange. Another reason is the limitation of the stock exchange's ability to handle large volumes, as described above. Third, as far as the listing requirement is concerned, although there are no specific rules about this, it is claimed that the selection of companies and enterprises permitted to issue bonds and stocks to the public is based on a thorough examination of their prospectus and past record. If the stock exchange believes that the companies are strong, well-managed, and fit for business, they will list them for trading. Table 6.4 provides an example of these requirements for being listed in the Shenzhen Stock Exchange. Nevertheless, the listing procedure is very slow and few companies succeed in being listed.

Since 1990, trading activities have increased sharply, both in the SSE and Shenzhen Stock Exchange. The comparatively more liberal regulations and the strong desire of companies to be listed led to a proliferation of listed companies. In Shanghai, for instance, ten new stock listings were approved in November 1991, increasing the total listings from 8 to 18. The total capitalization of the market doubled to approximately RMB 10 billion. By March 1993, this figure had increased to RMB 118.8 billion (see Table 6.5). Meanwhile, the number of participants also grew steadily. About 1 per cent of the population of Shanghai took part in securities trading activities in early 1991. In Shenzhen, more

Table 6.4   Conditions for companies wishing to be listed, 1992

Items	Requirements
Net asset value	> RMB 10 million
Total par value of shares which may be offered	SHK 28.4 million
Percentage of total capital	25
Net profit ratio	> 10% (preceeding year)
	> 8% (preceding 2 years)
Fees paid for listing	RMB 50,000

Others
Approved by Shenzhen and Beijing authorities.
Plans comply with requirements of Shenzhen government.
Have a good financial and operating record.
Able to provide details of assets and liabilities.

Note: The conditions were set up by the PBOC and the Shenzhen government

Source: Reconstructed from various sources

than 1 million people were involved in trading activities by the end of 1992. The individual participants ranged from students to professors, from the unemployed to managers of factories. At the same time, institutional investors, including insurance corporations, pension funds, and social welfare institutions also increasingly participated in securities trading activities. The growth trend continued until early 1993.

As far as total trading volume is concerned, the trading volume prior to 1990 was small. Because of limitations of the physical set-up and expertise, trading in the market at this stage was limited. Table 6.6 provides an example of the trading value in all of the Shanghai trading centres from 1984 to 1990.

Table 6.5   Statistical summary of Shenzhen and Shanghai Stock Markets, March 1993

| | Shenzhen | | Shanghai | |
	A	B	A	B
Number of shares	24	9	43	10
Market capitalization (RMB bn)	61.0	3.9	113.5	5.3

Source: Standard Chartered Research 1993

Table 6.6 Trading volumes in Shanghai as a whole, 1984–90 (RMB million)

1984–7	1988	1989	1990
40[a]	300	1,000	1,600[b]

Sources: Reconstructed from Xia *et al.*

Notes: [a] — annual average

[b] — the first half of 1990

Meanwhile, the kinds of securities handled by these trading centres were also limited. There were four securities traded: financial bonds, special bonds, corporation bonds, and shares. There were also restrictions on trading. For example, maximum daily fluctuation was limited in Shanghai to 0.5 per cent by regulation. However, trading volume in the two stock exchanges has grown sharply since 1990. By the end of 1990, turnover reached RMB 4 billion, compared with only 1 billion in 1989. The figure doubled in 1991, reaching RMB 8 billion. This simply reflects the fact that the trading volume moved from a low to a high level in a very short time.

During this period the most actively traded security among the four main types of securities mentioned above has also changed along with the growth of the market. Before the two stock exchanges were set up, the most actively traded security was corporate bonds. At that time, the total volume of shares issued was small. Holders of stocks, particularly those being paid good dividends, were unwilling to sell them. For example, the buying and selling ratio for the Yanzhong Industrial Company and Feile Acoustics Company was 11:1 in a survey of the period undertaken by Xia *et al.* (1992: 110). On the other hand, financial bonds issued carried more attractive terms, with interest rates far exceeding those on deposits for the same maturity. However, this has changed in the last two years with the main type of security traded in the stock exchange now being shares. The reasons are that more shares are becoming available and can produce instant profits from frequent trading activities. In addition, the popular awareness of the stock exchange has led to a sharp increase in the number of investors in shares, with stock exchanges making the fast transaction of share deals possible.

Depth of the market

One of the crucial characteristics of any financial assets market, according to A. F. Freris (1991: 99), is its depth. Depth of a market refers to the existence of orders to sell and buy above and below the current market prices. The result of depth is that excess demand or supply will have a smaller effect on the changes in prices. A shallow market will, however, tend to result in large price fluctuations. The excess demand or supply for the shares will generate large price changes precisely because there are no orders above or below the current market price to cushion it.

The trading activity in the SSE and Shenzhen Stock Exchange are concentrated in a relatively narrow range of shares in terms of the number of shares and sector distribution. Shanghai's board is dominated by big state-owned enterprises, while many of Shenzhen's existing companies are joint ventures with Hong Kong based companies, as these companies are easily listed in the stock exchange and attract investors. The listed companies are mostly in the fields of electronics, manufacturing, and property. Table 6.7 is a sample of listed companies in the Shenzhen and Shanghai Stock Exchanges. Trading activities in the market are thus dominated by a relatively small number of shares.

From this it follows that the market is shallow in terms of the number of shares and industrial sectors. This can partly explain the volatility of stock market prices. Other factors which contribute to the volatility of the market will be thoroughly examined later, when looking at problems and future prospects.

As large amounts of capital continue to flood into the stock market, the demand for stocks is much greater than the supply. When all of this capital comes into the market, the result will be sharply rising prices. When this is withdrawn, a sharp drop of price is unavoidable. A recent example can explain this point:

> More than 388.48 million shares were traded last week; 155 per cent more than in the previous week. Total transaction value registered a record RMB 6.1 million, 100 per cent more than in the previous week. Analysts said the rise was mainly triggered by more capital flooding into the market. They believed that real estate dealers would shift their investment focus to the security market ... They thought some industries, which are expected to receive more loans in the coming months, will probably pour some capital into the securities market.
>
> (*Business Weekly, China Daily*, 15–21 August 1993)

Table 6.7   Stock listing in the Shenzhen and Shanghai Stock
Exchanges,* August 1993

Shenzen

Stock	*Sectors*
China Bicycle	Bicycles
Chiwan Wharf	Port operator
Fiyta	Watch manufacturer
Huafa Electronics	Electronics
Jintian	Textiles
Konka Electronic	Electronics
Petrochemical	Petrochemicals
Properties and Resources	Properties
Shengbao	Soft drinks and property
Southern Glas	Glass products
Vanke	Property
Victor Onward Textiles	Textiles and property
Zhongchu	Property trading and finance

Shanghai

Stock	*Sectors*
China First Pencil	Pencil manufacturer
China Textile Machinery	Weaving machine manufacturer
Chlor-Alkali Chemical	Caustic soda products
Dazhong Taxi	Taxi operator
Erfanggi	Textile machinery manufacturer
Fridge compressor	Refrigerator manufacturer
Rubber Belt	Rubber belt manufacturer
Rubber & Tyre	Tyre manufacturer
Vacuum Electron Device	TV tube manufacturer
Wingsung	Pen manufacturer

Sources: Reconstruction from *Business Weekly*, 1 August 1993; *China Daily*;
and Standard Chartered Research 1993

Note: * The companies listed issue B stocks

Market performance

Indices

At present there are four stock indices in China: the Shanghai
All-Share Index and Shenzhen All-Share Index are used for
measuring price performance of A shares which are issued and
sold only to domestic investors, while the Shanghai B-Share Index
and Shenzhen B-Share Index are for B shares which are issued
and sold only to overseas investors. (A and B shares will be

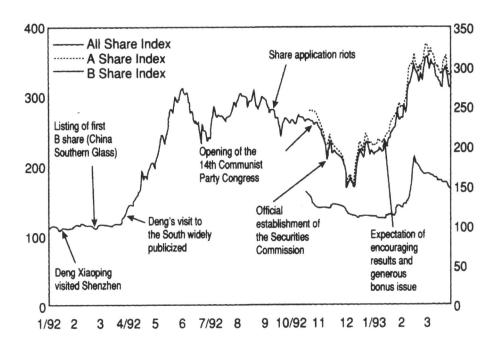

Figure 6.2 Performance of the Shenzhen Stock Market, January 1992–March 1993

Source: Standard Chartered Research 1993

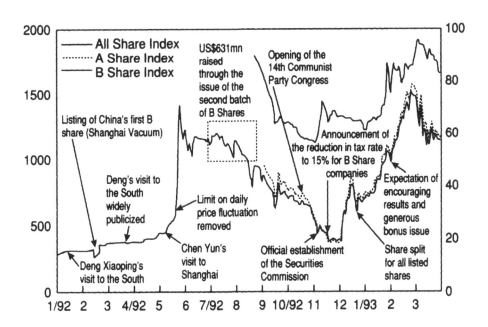

Figure 6.3 Performance of the Shanghai Stock Market, January 1992–March 1993

Source: Standard Chartered Research 1993

discussed later.) These four indices are compiled by the two stock exchanges and regularly published in *Business Weekly*, *China Daily* and other organs of the Chinese press. These indices are market-value weighted and cover all issued shares on the two markets. For example, the SSE Index is based on a weighted market capitalization of all stocks with the first day of trading in A shares (19 December 1990) as the basis with an index of 100. The B Shares Index is calculated from the first day of B share trading (21 February 1992). Besides the four indices, some overseas companies publish their own B share index. Among the best known is Standard Chartered B-Share Index.

The movement of the indices in the past few years reflects the volatility of China's stock market. Figures 6.2 and 6.3 chart the performances of the Shenzhen Stock Exchange and the SSE. From these Figures the following points may be observed. First, the trend of the two All Share Indices are similar in some crucial points. In April 1992, the All Share Indices in the two markets began to rise with the Shenzhen Stock Exchange moving upward more sharply. This reflects the high sensitivities of the market towards political events. Deng's visit to the south symbolized the political support of the market from the most powerful figure in China. After the event was publicized, the response of the two markets was quick, with about a 90 points increase in the SSE and 80 points in Shenzhen. A similar situation is observed subsequently.

After the Shenzhen stock market turmoil of August 1992 and the official establishment of the Securities Commission in October 1992, the market started to move downwards. This was partly because of a fear of the closing down of the market, and partly because of fears of strong anti-speculative sentiment from high-ranking Communist officials. In fact, there were official warnings against speculators at the Fourteenth Communist Party Congress of October 1992. The markets, however, have recovered since January 1993, when there was expectation of encouraging results and generous bonus issues. This also means that the development of the stock market has been seen as 'politically correct' for the time being. There followed a bull market which lasted for one month (February–March 1993), and the indices have been marking time since then.

Second, the movement of the B Share Indices are identical with those of the A Share Indices. This indicates that the B share markets are similarly sensitive towards the factors affecting the

market. Many foreign brokers and China funds have been authorized to operate in China's B share market. Indeed, overseas
investors, mainly institutional investors, have already built up their
expertise of China's politics, economics, and stock market.

Returns and risks

When analysing return and risk, three issues are generally considered: returns of shares in terms of their dividend yields and price-
to-earnings (P/E) ratios; sectoral returns in relation to risk and
the cross-relationships between returns of different shares and
different sectors (Freris 1991). Because there is very little data
available to enable an analysis of risk and returns to be taken,
this risk is examined in a discursive and qualitative manner while
the discussion on returns is based on estimates contained in
market analysis prepared by Standard Chartered Research. Table
6.8 shows estimated figures of the P/E ratio, earnings growth and
dividend yield of both exchanges for 1993 and 1994.

A cursory examination of the figures indicates that both
markets are driven by capital gains rather than dividends. The
relatively low dividend yield figures are much lower than the inflation rate, currently about 14 per cent nationwide, according to
official publicity. Another obvious deduction from Table 6.8 is that
the earnings growth rate in Shenzhen is much higher than that in
Shanghai. This may be because the Shenzhen Stock Exchange is
closer to Hong Kong and most companies listed are joint ventures.
In general the accounting and information standards are higher

Table 6.8   Returns of Shenzhen and Shanghai B Share markets,
1993 and 1994

	Shenzhen		Shanghai	
	1993	*1994*	*1993*	*1994*
P/E (times)	15.4	11.8	18.7	14.6
Earnings growth (%)	47.1	39.3	23.1	27.3
Dividend yield (%)	2.2	3.1	1.8	2.2

Source: Reconstructed from Standard Chartered Research 1993

Note: The P/E, earnings growth and dividend yield are calculated on the basis
of estimates on the listed B share companies only

in these companies than in state-owned companies, which comprise the majority of companies listed on Shanghai. This makes the shares, especially B shares, more in demand.

However, given the impossible task of a meaningful and consistent comparison of returns of the two markets, first impressions gained from simple numerical data may well be misleading, unless allowance is made for the risk factors involved. As a fledgling stock market, the information system is far from perfect and formal quantitative analysis not really possible. However, market risk (systematic risk) and company risk (unsystematic) can be examined in a rather general context. The inherent risk associated with the market and the company can be summarized as in Table 6.9.

The most risky factors listed in Table 6.9 are political, regulatory and legal. At present, the potential change in leaders is the most important factor affecting the fate of this emerging market. Most people now speculate about what will happen in the post-Deng Xiaoping period. The question is always there: can the stock market survive in the hands of new leaders who may or may not support the idea of building a 'market with socialist characteristics'? The outlook is still uncertain for China's equity market. The lack of a comprehensive legal system, especially poorly developed company law, leaves investors less protected. Last but not least, the regulatory risk is high because a long process is needed to set up a well-functioning commission. This issue will be addressed below. In short, although there are impressive current returns from investing in China's stock market, the potential risks in the long run are high.

Regulation and supervision

It was not until late 1992 that a set of formal regulations to govern the trading and issue of domestic equities nationwide was introduced. The new rules, which came into effect on 4 April 1993, unified practices on the two stock exchanges, which had until then operated under separate and very different regulations. This had caused problems for brokers and investors, especially foreigners. For example, Shanghai allowed buy and sell orders to be matched on the trading floor, while Shenzhen did not. Likewise, in Shanghai investors had to open an account with the Stock Exchange, while in Shenzhen investors could deal directly with

Table 6.9 Risks in China's stock market

Systematic risks	Factors
Political and regulatory	Changes of leaders Changes of politics Restriction on foreign investment Taxation
Economic	Overheating of the economy Inflation presure Administrative approach to manage the economy
General	Immature settlement procedures Immature operational framework No independent clearing agent
Marketability	Relatively illiquid: difficult to buy and sell shares

Unsystematic risks	Factors
Legal structure and information flow	Poorly developed company laws Low level of protection or rights to information Low transparency of listed companies
Accounting standards	Lack of qualified accountants Lack of property surveyors Accounting principles different from IAS No comparative historically adjusted financial figures Varying calculation of figures
Currency	RMB not convertible Exchange risks
Social	Low awareness of stocks and stock market Fraudulent market behaviour Easily guided by rumours

Sources: Compiled from various sources

brokers. Also in Shanghai, investors could cancel orders and change prices after an order was placed, but in Shenzhen neither was allowed. These different arrangements led to many conflicts. They also deterred foreign investors.

Eventually officials decided to set up unified regulations and in October 1992 a separate regulatory body was established: a two-part regulatory structure to oversee policy-making and day-to-day regulation. Figure 6.4 shows the framework of the new national regulatory system.

In the first part, the Securities Affairs Committee (SAC) will fall directly under the State Council and will consist of about twenty top officials from about seven relevant government departments. Its jurisdiction will include determining the number of listings and volume of issues allowed each year. The second part, the Securities and Exchanges Regulatory Commission (SERC), will be responsible for such tasks as designating firms for listing and licensing brokerage companies. As a 'quasi-governmental body' it will fall under the direction of SAC. It has about 200 employees, including lawyers, accountants, bankers and economists, but unlike members of SAC they are not employed in other government departments. Besides the two stock exchanges, the new regulators also oversee over-the-counter trading under the Securities Trading Automated Quotations System (STAQS — national trading network).

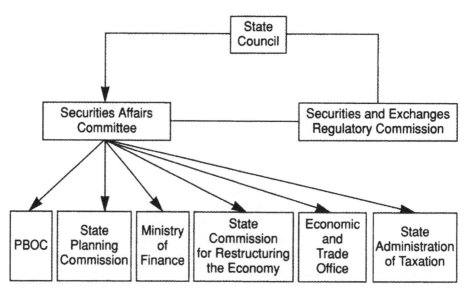

Figure 6.4 National regulatory structure

Source: 'China to overhaul regulation of markets', *Asian Wall Street*, 20 October 1992

Meanwhile, a national securities law was effected in April 1993 setting guidelines on a range of issues, including equity issuance and dealings, takeovers of listed firms, stock custodian and clearing procedures, disclosure practices investigation and penalty of unauthorized trading and arbitrage.

The object of establishing a nationwide regulatory system and law is to rationalize the stock market and protect investors. Under the new system, the authority to approve the establishment of brokerage companies, together with the listing and issue, has been transferred from PBOC to the regulatory commission.

Following the development of the regulatory framework and practice, three things have been observed. First, the regulatory situation of the stock market until 1992–3 was representative of China's reactive response to the market development. The national unified regulatory bodies and securities laws were established partly as the result of the 'August turmoil', following the realization of the conflicts of the old separated regulatory framework. Second, the weakness of the regulatory system of the stock market, like many other of China's regulatory systems, has been enforcement. The enforcement of regulations and laws is always difficult. There have been cases of a company seeking listing achieving success through political or personal links, despite its financial condition being below that required by the regulation. Another related problem is resistance from local authorities. If local authorities refuse to list a company from another province (this is always happening), it is unclear how the new regulatory commission could overrule the local regulators. Finally, the efficiency of the SAC is difficult to determine in a situation where so many different government bodies are involved and they are expected to meet only occasionally. As SAC exercises control over SERC, it could turn out to be ineffective.

Summary

The uniqueness of China's stock market shows in many ways. Public trading started from trading centres which had primitive facilities, limited expertise, and a small volume of transaction. The establishment of the two stock exchanges accelerated the trading activities by providing more advanced and sophisticated Western-style facilities. The number of companies listed for public trading has been increased significantly. The main type of securities in the market has been shifted from financial bonds to company stocks. All of this has happened in a period of only one and a half years. Prices are volatile owing to the market being shallow in terms of sectors' distribution and limited availability of stock. The market has been shown to perform well in terms of return, but the risk, particularly political risk, is high. A national regulatory framework has been built up to unify the formerly separate systems. However, problems such as enforcement of regulation and law, conflicts between the central regulatory body and local authorities, and efficiency are difficult to solve under the present system. These problems, together with other problems of the stock market, are addressed in the next section. They need to be clarified before the prospects for China's stock market can be predicted.

PROBLEMS AND FUTURE PROSPECTS

Primitive and premature is how China's fledgling stock market can be described from what we have seen. The issue and trading of securities undoubtedly opens an important avenue for China's financial development. However, a number of problems have already become evident and many more will no doubt appear with the further development of the market. Can these problems be solved? Will the Chinese government be able to continue this historic experiment? The problems will be discussed here in terms of accounting and disclosure standards, A shares v. B shares, and illegal trading and corruption. The future prospects of the stock market will then be considered.

Accounting and disclosure standards

As has been mentioned, the risk of investment in the Chinese stock market includes risk from lower standards of accounting and disclosure. This has largely affected the attractiveness of the market to investors, especially foreign investors. One report states that foreign investors may buy the shares of some of the companies listed on China's two official stock markets, but very few are doing so. Instead foreign investors are going to foreign markets, such as the Hong Kong Stock Market and New York Stock Exchange, for new Chinese shares (*Economist*, 31 July 1993, p. 74). As the Chinese authorities are planning for the stock exchanges to become major international stock markets, the problem of accounting and disclosure standards has caused widespread consternation.

The current practice of accounting dates from the time when the Communist government took over the country. Like other economic and financial systems, the accounting system is modelled on that of the former Soviet Union. The principles are very different from those of Western countries. During the Cultural Revolution (1966–76), accounting and accountancy professionals were considered among the most wicked emanations of capitalism and the principles of accounting were simplified to a mere bookkeeping level. The accounting system has been improved since 1980, but the standard is quite different from international accounting standards. In Group Accounts (IAS 27), for instance, a holding company should prepare group acounts in the form of a single set of consolidated financial statements covering the holding company and its subsidiaries. However, consolidated financial statements are not prepared and results of subsidiaries are accounted for on the dividend received basis according to China's acounting rule.[10] Most seriously of all, the accounting system distorts the view of firms' profits and losses. In 1991, the losses of state-owned firms was about RMB 55 billion. The government paid state firms subsidies amounting to 14 per cent of government revenues. Incredibly enough, this understates the problem because losses are disguised by accounting methods which put too high a value on stocks (inventories) which are quite unsaleable (*Economist*, 28 November 1992).

The problem has been recognized by the Chinese government and several new national regulations have been issued. These include the 'Financial Guidelines for Business Enterprises' and the 'Accounting Standards for Business Enterprises', which became effective on 1 July 1993 and provide requirements for disclosure in a listed firm's financial reports. These efforts are supposed to meet international acounting standards. The requirement is mandatory for all firms which issue B shares. This is indicative of the Chinese government's keenness to have its stock market recognized internationally. Nevertheless, the main problem is the lack of experienced accountants trained to internationally accepted standards. A more profound problem is compatibility between the system of accounting and the existing economic system as a whole. While the old economic mechanisms still dominate most of its enterprises, the transition from the old accounting system to widely accepted IAS is very difficult. The solution to this problem will depend on the successful transformation of the whole of China's economy to a market oriented system.

Public disclosure has been shown to be poorly practised since the establishment of the stock market. Many foreign investors hesitate to trust prospectuses scrutinized only by Chinese market regulators, who have been at their jobs for less than one year. Setting aside for the moment the problem of inexperienced regulators, let us look at the new law, which includes rules of disclosure practice.

Under the new equity law, listed companies must report any decisions or 'material changes that might affect share prices to the regulatory authorities who will decide whether to disclose the news to the public'. This is intended to force listed firms to disclose required information. However, two problems have arisen. First, is this feasible? As has been seen, the new national regulatory framework gives the Securities Affairs Committee (SAC) the greatest power, but the SAC itself may be inefficient, as many government bodies are involved. The development of the stock market will inevitably bring about the listing of more firms. This will make disclosure practice more complicated and difficult. It will require quicker and more accurate decisions to match the needs of frequent disclosure of information to the public. A committee which meets only occasionally will not be able to meet this challenge. Second, as with the accounting standard, a reasonable disclosure standard must be able to match the need for information from outside investors, professional managers and bankers. While there is no detail laid down about the standard of disclosure of information to the public, the decision whether to disclose news will largely depend on the personal judgement or preferences of the members of the SAC.

Reasonable, well-developed accounting and disclosure standards have always been considered to be an essential part of the infrastructure of the securities industry. The enforcement and supervision of public disclosure requirements are also crucial to the prevention of fraudulent market behaviour, such as concealing the current situation and prospects of a borrowing entity. Investors can determine the underlying value of risk capital only if they are well informed about the present financial situation of the enterprise in which they are considering investment. Such an informed judgement is possible only on the basis of the availability of information provided by companies (Xia *et al.* 1992:121) At this stage, however, it is difficult to raise the accounting and disclosure standards immediately, since the whole of the economic and financial systems are in a semi-reformed 'primary socialist market economy' stage. The non-enforcement of law, lack of expertise, and deficient regulatory systems are all barriers to the introduction of international standards. Nevertheless, these are the things which the Chinese authorities need to put right now and also the direction which future development needs to take.

A shares v. B shares

The most noticeably original quality of China's stock market is the practice of issuing A shares and B shares. As previously stated, A shares are for domestic investors, while B shares are only for foreign investors. B shares are traded for foreign currency and originally paid dividends in US dollars or in Hong Kong dollars. Both A and B shares are denominated in RMB, but otherwise carry the same rights and are subject to the same obligations. At present, the players on the A share market are mainly local individuals through domestic securities brokers, while the players on B share market are mainly foreign institutional investors.

The reason for dividing shares into two types is to help China to meet its need for foreign exchange by issuing a special kind of stock to foreign investors. The object, however, has proved difficult to achieve, owing to the lack of international standards regarding financial data and legally codified investor protection already discussed. Furthermore, the present clearing system scares away many foreign investors. Currently, one bank acts as a clearing centre for the Shanghai Exchange, while three act in this capacity in Shenzhen (Sze 1993). This system has hindered efficient clearing and settlement because of the slow procedure. Finally, the foreign bankers and brokers are not allowed to offer stock or to deal directly on the exchange floor. This in fact makes it very difficult to boost liquidity and to increase share trading efficiency. Conservative investors, such as pension funds, are likely to remain wary of China. Despite huge domestic demand for the A shares of listed companies, the demand from foreign investors for B shares has so far proved disappointing.

In order to improve the B share market, the Chinese government has taken several measures, including increasing the number of companies listed on the markets; enforcing more stringent disclosure requirements; and establishing a national regulatory body, all of which have been considered above. The issue of securities on overseas markets, however, is considered an indirect way to improve the B share market situation. In October 1992, China Brilliance Automotive, a Shenyang producer of minivans, became the first Chinese company to be listed on the New York Stock Exchange. The issue was considered a model for other Chinese firms wishing to meet the requirements of a mature stock market, and an incentive to the fledgling stock exchanges to achieve full maturity.[11] Nevertheless, this may not be the case, since the companies listed in overseas stock exchanges are all China's best companies, carefully screened by the government. This in turn is causing the domestic B share market to stagnate.

Illegal trading

Earlier, we mentioned that many individual investors do not make their transactions at a stock exchange, but instead undertake them spontaneously on the street. By early 1993, thousands of Chinese firms, especially rural and private enterprises, were issuing and selling internal shares without government approval. Black markets in the certificates sprouted in most major cities. The new national stock regulation prohibited this trading. Violators can be fined up to RMB 300,000. Quite apart from the legal risks, investors in illegal shares are taking big financial risks. For example, they may not be able to sell their shares. However, traders and local officials alike ignore the warnings. There are two reasons for this unstoppable illegal trading: ignorance about shares and the stock market and the difficulty facing private enterprises in obtaining loans from banks.

A 'stock trading fever' broke out in major cities in summer 1992 after China's leading newspaper published propagandistic articles praising Deng's philosophy and the stock market. Ignorance about stocks and the stock market and dreams of becoming millionaires overnight drove millions of people to go to great extremes to become shareholders. During that time, on Chinese television a typical image of a rich man showed a middle-aged Shanghaiese driving a Mercedes-Benz while dealing in shares over his mobile telephone. Eventually a tragedy occurred when about one million people rushed into Shenzhen in early August trying to buy shares there. Only a very few of them were successful owing to the shortage of issued shares. Angry people took to the streets in protest. Two main factors contributed to this 'August turmoil'. First was the immaturity of investors completely ignorant of the workings of a stock market. The Chinese public have little financial knowledge and are easily guided by rumours since the government-controlled mass media disclose little information. Second, rising inflationary pressures caused the withdrawal of money from banks in the hope of exploiting the economically vibrant stock markets.

On the other hand, as these private and rural enterprises cannot easily obtain loans from the state banks, issuing shares provides a source of capital for them. This creates a dilemma for the Chinese government: how is it to control their illegal economic activities without discouraging their developing initiatives? While there is high demand for shares, the issuing of shares of this kind goes some way to satisfying the need.

The unstoppable trading activities of both investors and suppliers arise to some extent from the imperfections of the law and a traditional disrespect for it. The basic reason for the phenomenon is, however, the widespread nature of corruption in China.

Since the early 1980s, the Chinese leaders have established policies to prevent Communist and government officials from abusing their power to gain from the nation's rush to a market economy. These measures, however, were adopted in the midst of a surge of corruption following Deng's promotion of a new wave of economic reform early in 1992 and the approval by the Fourteenth Communist Party Congress of a 'socialist market economy' in October. It is Deng himself who relaxed restrictions on participation of officials in business in order to increase the momentum of the reforms, but many officials have subverted market forces by using power as a commodity. The possibilities for using power to generate money have increased and have gradually emerged in the abuse of influence in the trading of stocks (*Wen Wei Daily*, 4 May 1993). The most profitable business in China now is stock and property speculation. Many officers could not resist this temptation.

Future prospects

As already seen, the stock market in China is underdeveloped in terms of scale in both primary and secondary markets; range of securities available; volume of transactions; and the regulatory and legal framework. Clearly many of the problems are unavoidable in any rapidly emerging stock market. The experimental setting up of a stock market in the most populous Communist country is a huge project, and the direction of its future development has attracted much attention. Based on the findings of the present study, it seems clear that future prospects for that development depend on the following three areas.

The infrastructure of the stock market

Inadequate facilities, lack of competent staff, low accounting and disclosure standards, and lack of efficient regulatory and legal frameworks have proved barriers to the development of the Chinese stock market. Its future development should therefore concentrate on the building of this infrastructure. If the use of securities for raising long-term capital is expected to expand further, it will be necessary to permit and to expand the operations of securities brokers and brokerage firms specializing in underwriting and marketing new issues. Their operations should gradually be integrated into a simple electronic trading network with a series of trading floors, effectively bringing together total demand and supply. A substantial increase in the number and quality of securities professionals with technical skills and analytical ability is urgently required.

Another critical aspect is the regulatory and legal framework. There is a need for comprehensive regulations and laws pertaining to companies, banks, investment firms, securities exchanges, accounting, taxation, and information disclosure. However, the enforcement and supervision of these regulations and laws are supremely important, since a significant problem currently facing China is the establishment of the primacy of the rule of law. This, however, will largely depend on how the potential conflict between the interests of Communist Party officials and the sovereignty of the law is tackled. Only when there is an efficient regulatory and legal system will it be possible to maintain good order in the stock market. Meanwhile, the law must seek to prevent any expansion of corrupt behaviour in the market.

Further reform of the financial system

The emergence of the Chinese stock market resulted directly from the reform of the financial system. As part of the financial mechanisms, development of the stock market will largely depend on the reform of the whole financial system. With restrictions on market participants, interest rates, and transfer of securities, financial markets, including money markets and capital markets, cannot fully play their roles as the markets themselves lack self-adjusting features to meet real supply and demand, which are currently unrelated. Thus it is important for the Chinese government to conduct a comprehensive and coherent reform. This will include:

1) Improvement of the banking sector in respect of the quality of the service it provides. At the moment, independent banking needs further encouragement. The government involvement in credit allocation should continue to be reduced. Meanwhile, the self-control of banking credit should be built up on the responsibility related system, in which the credit officers take full responsibility for the loans.
2) Introduction of a more market-oriented and integrated structure of interest rates and their determination. The interest rate has not yet functioned as a tool of macro-control, since the structure of the interest rate is too simple.
3) Dissemination of the knowledge of the benefits of financial savings, the functions and characteristics of different financial instruments, and specific investment techniques. This will increase financial awareness among the general public in China.

Deepening of the economic reform

The progress of the economic reforms in China has had a direct impact on the emergence of the stock market, as we have seen. Further development of the stock market will depend upon the success of these economic reforms. As has been discussed, the current practices of the stock market, which are far from the standardized operations widely used in other countries, are designed to cope with the current environment and to accommodate the present 'socialist market economy'. Therefore, the future development and gradual formalization of the market must be supported by fundamental changes in the overall economic system.

Currently, several issues need to be immediately resolved. First, ownership of enterprises needs to be further clarified so that the enterprises can fully utilize the equity market for raising risk capital. Transforming the state-owned enterprises has become imperative. Establishing a wider-ranging stock share system can improve the performance of these enterprises. Only when state enterprises of good size and strength participate in the equity market will the market show great vitality. Capital market development will mean that excessive emphasis on public sector enterprises must be significantly reduced, and that the economic and financial role of an efficient and dynamic private sector can be expanded (*Wen Wei Daily*, 4 May 1993). Second, further reforms of the investment system and budgetary system are needed. Government involvement in the allocation of funds for investment and in financial decisions must be further reduced, to allow the market and financial intermediaries to play an adequate role in terms of the level and direction of investment.

CONCLUSION

We have examined the emergence of a stock market in China and analysed its operation, performance and problems in the context of the development of capital markets under a socialist market economy. It has been argued that the reappearance of the stock market after more than thirty years of Communist government is the direct result of economic and financial reforms which aimed to build up a functioning market mechanism. This prompts the conclusion that it is not possible to separate the effects of issuing and trading bonds and shares from a plethora of other economic and financial reforms. At a deeper level, all of these reforms are reactions to political changes. Although the discussion can proceed only in relatively general terms at this stage, owing to the lack of systematic data, a clear trend in the development of the stock market can be observed. That is, the political situation is not only the driving force behind the emergence of the stock market but also a barrier to its development.

On the other hand, the stock market will develop only after China has achieved a degree of economic growth and stability. Initially, public trading was limited because of underdeveloped and primitive facilities, limited expertise and an immature regulatory framwork. However, significant progress has been made in a very short time in terms of market scale and trading facilities. The returns have been high and so too the risks. As the market has grown, it has attracted a large number of investors and stocks are becoming a widely accepted alternative investment instrument to traditional bank deposits. Meanwhile, the stock market has attracted an increasing number of international investors who seek international diversification. Nevertheless, it has not achieved full credibility owing to problems, such as an inefficient regulatory framework and wide corruption in the system, which largely damage its reputation.

At present, the issue is not whether China needs a stock market but how a fully fledged stock market can be established. A decisive move towards this will necessarily entail the removal of a variety of obstructions. Most significant will be complete political acceptance. The removal or reduction of these obstructions must form an integral part of any credible policy programme. A fully-fledged stock market would then be in a position to play a major role in the transformation of China's massive economy into a dynamic entity which would be internally consistent as well as externally competitive.

NOTES

1 Three types of enterprises exist in China: state-owned, collectively owned and privately owned. Privately owned enterprises had been almost totally suppressed by the end of the 1970s.
2 The PBOC was set up prior to the establishment of the People's Republic of China in 1948 to establish a unified currency in the areas of north China under Communist control.
3 Little has been achieved in respect of tax efficiency, tax administration, and closing loopholes.
4 In 1980, the state-owned Shanghai No. 17 Textile Mill issued shares solely to its own workers.
5 Wuhan is the largest industrial city in central China.
6 For the Wuhan share issue see *Dao Kung Pao* (*Tao Kung Daily*), 30 November 1980. For the Shangdong share issue see New China News Agency, 19 November 1981, in SWB W1161.
7 The five cities are: Chongqing, Guangzhou, Wuhan, Shenyang and Changzhou.
8 These included 20 companies issuing B shares in the SSE and 13 in Shenzen (see 'Securities market: regulators battle to catch up', *Financial Times*, 18 November 1993, p. 12).
9 Funds to buy these securities are automatically deducted monthly from the employee's salary.
10 From a reprint from Sun Kung Research Ltd.

11 A number of other companies have now been listed in overseas markets. The shares for the Hong Kong Stock Exchange are called H shares, while New York shares are called N shares.

REFERENCES

British Trade Commission in Hong Kong (1991) *Shenzhen and Shanghai Stock Exchanges*, Hong Kong.
China State Statistics Bureau (1991) *China Statistical Yearbook*, Beijing.
Freris, A. (1991) *The Financial Markets of Hong Kong*, London: Routledge.
Grub, P. D. and Sudweeks, B. L. (1988) 'Securities Markets and the People's Republic of China', Special Report, *China Newsletter*, no. 74, China–Britain Trade Centre, London.
Grummitt, K. P. (1986) *China Economic Handbook*, London: Euromonitor Publications, Chapter 8.
Japanese External Trade Organization Shanghai Office (1989) 'Reforms in the Shanghai financial system', *China Newsletter*, no. 71, China–Britain Trade Centre, London, pp. 19–21.
Reynolds, B. L. (ed.) (1988) *Chinese Economic Reform: How Far, How Fast?*, London: Academic Press and New York: Harcourt Brace.
Standard Chartered Research (1993) *Red Stars Over China: A compendium of China 'B' shares*, March.
Sze, J. W. (1993) 'The allure of B shares', *China Business Review*, January–February, pp. 42–8.
World Bank (1988) *World Development Report, 1988*, Washington, DC: World Bank.
—— (1990) *A World Bank Country Study — China: Revenue Mobilization and Tax Policy*, Washington, DC: World Bank.
Xia, M. Grub, P. D. and Lin, J. H. (1992): *Re-emerging Securities Market in China*, Westport, Virginia: Quorum Books.
Xie, S. (1990) 'China's stock market: problems and future development', Special Report, *China Newsletter*, no. 89, China–Britain Trade Centre, London, pp. 18–25.

BIBLIOGRAPHY

Books

Byrd, W. A. (1991) *The Market Mechanism and Economic Reform in China*, Armonk, NY: Sharpe.
Francis, J. C. (1990) *Investments: Analysis and Management*, NY: McGraw–Hill.
Knott, G. (1991) *Financial Management*, London: Macmillan.
Kornai, J. (1980) *The Economics of Shortage*, Amsterdam: North-Holland.
Nolan, P. and Dong, F. (eds) (1990) *The Chinese Economy and Its Future,*

Cambridge: Polity, in association with Basil Blackwell.

Rabushka, A. (1987) *The New China: Comparative Economic Development in Mainland China, Taiwan and Hong Kong*, London and Boulder, Colo: Westview Press.

Reynolds, B. L. (ed.) (1987) *Reform in China: Challenges and Choices*, London: Sharpe.

Senkow, B. W. (1993) *Taiwan's Financial Markets and Institutions: Legal and Financial Issues of Deregulation and Internationalisation*, Westport, Virginia: Quorum Books.

Shiller, R. J. (1984) 'Stock prices and social dynamics', in W. C. Brainard and G. L. Perry (eds) *Brookings Papers on Economic Activity*, Washington, DC: Brookings Institution.

Skully, M. T. (ed.) (1982) *Financial Institutions and Markets in the Far East: A Study of China, Hong Kong, Japan, South Korea and Taiwan*, London: Macmillan.

Sudweeks, B. L. (1989) *Equity Market Development in Developing Countries*, New York: Praeger.

Totten, G. and Zhou, S. (1992) *China's Economic Reforms: Administering the Introduction of the Market Mechanism*, London and Boulder, Colo: Westview Press.

Van Ness, P. (ed.) (1989) *Market Reforms in Socialist Societies: Comparing China and Hungary*, Boulder, Colo: Lynne Riener.

Articles

Authens, J. (1992) 'Stock needs time to settle', *Financial Times*, 25 July 1992, p. v.

Bowles, P. (1990) 'Inflation and economic reform in China', *International Journal of Development Banking* 8(3): 1–16.

Bowles, P. and White G. (1989) 'Contradictions in China's financial reforms: the relationship between banks and enterprises', *Cambridge Journal of Economics*, 13(4): 481–95.

——(1992a) 'The dilemmas of market socialism: capital market reform in China, Part I: Bonds', *Journal of Development Studies*, 28(3): 363–85.

——(1992b) 'The dilemmas of market socialism: capital market reform in China, Part II: Shares', *Journal of Development Studies* 28(4): 575–94.

Cheng, E. (1990) 'Chinese capital markets back on track: counters revolution', *Far Eastern Economic Review*, 26 July, pp. 54–5.

Cottrell, R. (1992) 'A death on the stock exchange', *Spectator*, 15 August, pp. 11–12.

Economist, China Correspondent of (1992) 'China's stockmarkets: open outcry', *Economist*, August, p. 50.

Hosoi, Y. (1987) 'China's Present Financial System', *China Newsletter*, no. 58, China–Britain Trade Centre, London, pp. 7–8.

Jarai, Z. (1989) 'Goals and conditions in setting up a stock market in Hungary', *European Economic Review* 33(2/3): 448–55.

Kornai, J. (1986) 'The soft budget constraint', *Kyklos*, 39(1): 3–30.

Masood, A. and Goopta, S. (1993) 'Portfolio investment flows to developing countries', *Finance and Development*, March, pp. 9–12.

Nuti, D. M. (1989) 'Remonetisation and capital markets in the reform of centrally planned economies', *European Economic Review*, vol. 33, pp. 427–38.

Schell, Q. and Lappin, T. (1991/2) 'China: going for brokers', *New Statesman and Society*, 18 December/1 January, pp. 46–50.

Summers, L. H. (1985) 'Does the stock market rationally reflect fundamental values?', *Journal of Finance*, no. 41 (July), pp. 591–601.

White, G. and Bowles, P. (1988) 'China's Banking Reforms: Aims, Methods and Problems', *National Westminster Bank Quarterly Review*, November, pp. 28–37.

Xu, J. A. (1987) 'The stock-share system: A new avenue for China's economic reform', *Journal of Comparative Economics*, no. 11, pp. 509–14.

Zhou, X. C. and Zhu, L. (1987) 'China's Banking System: Current Status, Perspective on Reform', *Journal of Comparative Economics*.

Articles published in China

Chen, X. (1992) 'Stockmarket chaos won't hold back reform — experts', *China Daily*, 22 August, p. 4.

Gou, B. S. (1992) 'On the internationalization of China's stock market', *Jingji Keixei (Economic Science)*, March, pp. 64–7.

Gou, L. and Zhang, G. B. (1992) 'Perfect the stock market by introducing self-regulating management', *Fujian Xeikan (Fujian Monthly)*, March, pp. 38–40.

Hu, M. L. (1991) 'On investment, speculation, and countermeasures', *Jinrun Yanjou (Financial Research)*, December, pp. 46–50.

Liang, Y. M. and Lin, P. (1992) 'Inside trading of shares and legislation', *Gangou Jingji (Gangou Economics)*, September, pp. 42–4.

Liu, G. D. (1993) 'Several issues of stockmarket development', *Jingji Yanjou (Economic Research)*, March, no. 3, pp. 12–19.

Liu, W. L. (1993) 'Top body banking on reforms', *China Daily (Business Weekly)*, 14–20 March, p. 3.

Ren, K. (1993) 'New regulations clarify procedures for the issue and trading of B shares', *China Daily (Business Weekly)*, 30 May — 5 June, p. 3.

Research Centre of China's Security Market (Beijing) (1992) 'The past and future of China's securities market', *Guanli Shijei (Management World)*, March, pp. 163–8.

Tan, L. (1993) 'A study on the financing mechanism of enterprises in innovation', *Jingji Yanjou (Economic Research)*, no. 2, pp. 7–13.

Wang, Q. H. (1993) 'The Shanghai Stock Market: a history of eight years', *Zhonggua Jingji Tizi Gaige (Economic Reform in China)*, pp. 37–9.

Wang, W. A. (1992) 'A strategic analysis of the conditions for a successful stock market in China', *Jinrun Yanjou (Financial Research)*, July, pp. 50–1.

Zhang, Z. (1992) 'B shares in mainland China', *Zhonggue Dalu (Mainland China)*, August, pp. 34–8.

Publications from government and other organizations

Demirgiic–Kunt, A. (1992) *Barriers to Portfolio Investments in Emerging Stock Markets*, Washington, DC: World Bank, Country Economic Department.

Guangdon Provincial Government (1986) *Provisional Rules of Guangdong Province on the Management of Shares and Bonds*, Guanchan.

Shanghai Securities Exchange (1990) *A Brief Introduction to the Shanghai Securities Exchange*, Shanghai.

Singh, A. (1992) *The Stockmarket and Economic Development*, Discussion Paper 49, United Nations Conference on Trade and Development, Geneva.

World Bank (1988) *China: Finance and Investment*, Washington, DC: World Bank.

——(1990) *China: Financial Sector Policies and Institutional Development*, Washington, DC: World Bank.

Chapter 7

Current financial problems and reforms in China

D. B. K. Hwang and Q. Tang

INTRODUCTION

Up until the end of 1992, there were more than 10,000 large and medium state-owned enterprises in China. This number accounts for only 2.5 per cent of the total enterprises, but their general product (GP) accounts for 46 per cent of the whole. Moreover, they contributed 60 per cent of the total profit and tax that the Chinese government received. Because large and medium state enterprises play such an important role in the Chinese economy, they usually are more heavily subject to regulatory control and economic planning. Financial regulation, such as a specific fund system, is implemented and strictly enforced in these enterprises. Unfortunately, at least one-third of them performed very poorly and inefficiently. According to the Chinese Industrial and Commercial Bank, more than 500 key state enterprises ran into increasingly serious deficits in 1990. Their total losses were 11.81 billion yuan ($US1 = 5.23 yuan in 1990).

Most rural and small enterprises are either collectively or individually owned in China. In 1990, they produced 700 billion yuan general product, accounting for 30 per cent of the whole nation's GP. Although their efficiency rate was better than that of the state enterprises, more than 400,000 of them became bankrupt in 1990, and the ratio of profit and tax over fund (the key indicator of fund efficiency) dropped from 13.8 per cent in 1990 to 10.7 per cent for the first quarter of 1991.

These statistics indicate that all Chinese enterprises, whether large or small, state-owned or private, have encountered serious financial crises. The Chinese government has implemented several reforms in order to rescue businesses from such extremities. The purpose of this chapter is to discuss the financial problems in China, the factors which contributed to them, and the proposed solutions to the problems, namely the recent reforms.

LITERATURE REVIEW

Carol L. Hamrin (1991) reviews political changes and economic reforms in China from 1979 to 1988. She divides the changes and reforms during this period into three waves. The first was an ebb tide and a search for a new model (1979–82). The second comprised an ideological struggle, policy breakthrough, and institutional changes (1983–85), and the final wave contained cross-currents: problems of systemic transition and political succession (1985–88). She also discusses the limits to reform, the crackdown on the Democracy Movement and the Tiananmen Square massacre.

Gordon White's (1991) edited volume, *The Chinese State in the Era of Economic Reform*, discusses the economic roles of different levels of governments in China, economic policies, rural and urban economies, and the population policy in China.

Tang *et al.* (1991) investigate the controversies over enterprise reform in China. They conclude that the business contract system allows management to adopt the strategy of maximizing short-term profit during the contract period. They also argue that, in the absence of a free market mechanism, the business contract system cannot be efficiently implemented.

Pitman Potter (1991) discusses the regulations on land development in China and concludes that land-user's right (LUR) provides an additional instrument for securing loans.

Lee Zinser (1992) reviews the economic performance of China for the period 1979–89. He also discusses the problems pertaining to the reform, such as the threat of higher inflation, increasing population and budget deficit, pollution, ideological conflicts, and political and policy stability.

FACTORS CONTRIBUTING TO THE CRISIS

Since the government of China utilizes centralized planning to direct almost every aspect of the nation's economy, and since centralized planning requires massive amounts of data and control to make the economy run as planned, the government has placed excessive controls and regulations on its accounting and economic systems. A restrictive fund accounting system is employed to monitor economic activities according to specific purposes. Prices and wages are placed under a certain degree of control. The management of enterprises lack autonomy in making decisions. The government tends to intervene in too many business affairs. In addition, the prevailing bureaucracy increases business costs and reduces efficiency. Generally, the economic and political systems should take most of the blame for creating financial problems in business in China.

Owing to the rigid control of the government and the lack of funds, most enterprises could not renovate their old plants and almost 70 per cent of production was processed manually. Modern facilities accounted for only 33 per cent of total capacity. High cost of production and poor marketing contributed to high inventory. It was estimated that about 130 billion yuan became idle funds because of the unsold inventory. When the enterprises began to experience financial difficulty, the rigid financial regulations aggravated the crisis. This finally developed into the so-called 'Triangular Debt Chain' problem: A was in debt to B, B was in debt to C, and C was in debt to A; A failed to pay B because C failed to pay A; C failed to pay A because C was short of funds owing to the delinquency of B. Since so many businesses owed money to each other, all debts became dead-locked and financial chaos ensued in 1990 and 1991. The central government formed a task force headed by the Vice-Premier, Zu Longqi, to solve this problem. Though tremendous efforts were made, very little was achieved. By the end of 1992, more than 200 billion yuan of due debt still remained unsettled.

THE RECENT REFORMS

In order to increase productivity and strengthen the financial position of business, the Chinese government initiated some important economic and financial reforms in the late 1980s. Although the positive impact of the reforms was not sufficient to cure the financial problems immediately, both the reforms of the late 1970s and the more recent reforms contributed to a general economic growth in China. An interesting phenomenon was seen in China in the late 1980s and early 1990s, when overall high economic growth co-existed with financial chaos in individual firms and general disorder in the financial market. Table 7.1 provides some key economic indicators which reflect economic performance in that period.

The following reforms are those that affected both the financial operation of enterprises and the national financial market.

Separation of ownership and management of state enterprises

In order to increase autonomy of management and to provide incentives for pursuing higher productivity and profit, the government enacted the 'Act of Contractual Operating Responsibility System'. Under this system, state enterprises are allowed to be leased to individuals and organizations who will assume full responsibility for fulfilling the economic target specified in the contract, though the government retains public ownership of the enterprises. A state enterprise run under contract must still comply with state economic plans, but the mandatory part of the plan has been reduced to the bare essentials.

Table 7.1 Key economic indicators in China, 1982–90

Year	1982	1983	1984	1985	1986	1987	1988	1989	1990
Real GNP growth (%)	8.0	10.5	14.0	12.5	7.8	11.0	10.8	3.9	4.4
Inflation (%)	2.4	2.0	2.6	7.8	6.0	7.5	17.5	16.0	2.5
Budget deficit ($US billion)	1.8	1.9	2.0	0.9	3.8	4.5	6.5	7.1	—
Per caput income (urban, $US)	—	—	—	—	—	272	320	270	—
Per caput income (rural, $US)	—	—	—	—	—	124	147	128	—
Exports ($US billion)	—	—	—	—	—	39.4	47.5	52.5	62.1
Imports ($US billion)	—	—	—	—	—	43.2	55.3	59.1	53.4
Trade balance ($US billion)	—	—	—	—	—	−3.8	−7.8	−6.7	8.7
Exchange rate (yuan/$US)							3.72	3.72	4.72	5.23

Sources: Compiled from official Chinese statistics

Lessening price control

Despite the shock of high inflation in 1988 and 1989 (see Table 7.1), cautious reform of prices continues. The government now controls the prices of only some key products, such as coal, steel and grain. The number of products subject to compulsory planning and control has been dramatically reduced. In 1990, the amount of goods under price control was 29.7 per cent (97 per cent in 1978), under market mechanism 53.1 per cent, and under state guiding price (between both control and market) 17.2 per cent (*People's Daily*, 26 September 1991).

Legislation on land-user's right

Legislation on land-user's right (LUR) was passed in May 1990. Under this enactment, the government retains the ownership of land. The land can never be transferred to private individuals or firms, but the right of land-use allows the users to utilize, transfer, lease, and pledge the land. Users of land may apply for the right for up to 70 years for residential purposes, 50 years for industrial, and 40 years for business use. Though the LUR legislation was primarily intended to encourage foreign investment in land development, it is available to all foreign and native businesses, organizations, and individuals. The real estate market has developed quickly and many transactions in LUR have occurred since the legislation in 1990. It is likely that the LUR will have a far-reaching effect on business finance because LUR provides a new instrument for securing funds.

Improving the banking system

Before 1979, China had only one bank, the People's Bank of China (PBOC), which issued banknotes and also dealt with general deposit and credit. Since 1982, the role of the PBOC has changed considerably. Now the PBOC acts in the same way as the central banks of other countries: issuing banknotes, managing foreign exchange, formulating financial policies, and controlling the money supply. Meanwhile, other specialized banks have been created to make up a banking system in China. They are: the Industrial and Commercial (specializing in industrial and commercial loans and city development), the Bank of China (foreign exchange), the Agricultural Bank (farming loans and rural development), the Construction Bank (long-term investment and loans), and the Investment Bank (use of loans from the World Bank).

Establishing money and capital markets

The new functions of the People's Bank of China and the creation of several new banks have helped the development of money markets. In addition, the government has approved the issuance of bonds and stocks and opened the first national securities exchange centre, the Shanghai Stock Exchange in December 1990. A number of major cities, such as Shenzhen, Beijing, Wuhan, Tianjin, Chongqing, Guangzhou, and Harbin, also started to create securities exchange centres. Both the money and capital markets have been gradually developed to increase the availability of funds and the efficient use of funds. Because both markets are still limited in terms of the variety and the number of each instrument and issuer, and because China lacks management experience in operating the markets, it will take some time for each market to become efficient.

Allowance for merger, consolidation, and reorganization

The government now permits any enterprise to engage in mergers, consolidations and/or reorganizations, in order to increase operational efficiency or to avoid insolvency.

CONCLUSION

Since China started to open its doors to the world and to implement its plans for modernization in the late 1970s, the country has experienced steady economic growth. During this transition from a socialist economy to a market economy, the Chinese have enjoyed higher production and living standards, but have also paid the price. In the late 1980s, China encountered high inflation and serious social unrest, and, into the early 1990s, has suffered from financial chaos. This chapter has discussed the financial problems, the factors contributing to them and the reforms aimed at solving them.

China has plans to transform some small state enterprises into privately owned enterprises. It is also proposed that the government should retain only 25–30 per cent of large state enterprises, with the remainder being sold off through the issue of stocks. There is much to do before China becomes an efficient economy. The reform plans must be implemented and checked continuously. As China becomes more Westernized, there is an urgent need to adjust its ideology and systems. For example, its accounting system and methods should be further reformed. The fund system no longer applies when more businesses in China are now organized in the form of a corporation. The Chinese must learn the concepts of cost, profit, information systems, etc. and must know how to apply these to management. Obviously, more utilization of foreign experts, foreign investment, and modern management and know-how will contribute to the success of the reforms.

REFERENCES

Hamrin, C. L. (1990) *China and the Challenge of the Future*, London and Boulder, Colo: Westview Press.

Potter, P. (1991) 'China's new land development regulations', *China Business Review* 18 (2): 12–15.

Tang, Y.-W., Cooper, B. and Chow, L. (1991) 'Controversies over enterprise reform in China: an accounting perspective,' *Proceedings of the Third Asian–Pacific Conference on International Accounting Issues*, Hawaii, October, University of California at Fresno, pp. 265–8.

White, G. (ed.) (1991) *The Chinese State in the Era of Economic Reform*, Armonk, NY: Sharpe.

Zinser, L. (1992) 'The performance of China's economy', *China's Economic Dilemmas in the 1990s*, Joint Economic Committee, Congress of the United States, pp. 102–18.

Part III

Developments in accounting regulation

The Chinese economic reforms have given rise to a demand for major developments in accounting regulation. In Chapter 8, Liu and Eddie explain the developments of a Chinese accounting standards programme and they offer an analysis of the first Chinese accounting standard. Aiken, Lu and Ji, in Chapter 9, explore the economic background to this first accounting standard and examine the conceptual approach underlying it. In Chapter 10, Xiao and Pan compare the Chinese accounting standard with conceptual frameworks in other countries. Liu and Turley, in Chapter 11, place the new Chinese accounting standard firmly in its historical context.

Chapter 8

Developments in accounting regulation

W. Liu and I. A. Eddie

INTRODUCTION

This chapter reports on the introduction of the 'Accounting Standards for Business Enterprises' (hereafter referred to as the Standards) promulgated by the Ministry of Finance of the People's Republic of China (PRC) on the 30 November 1992. The Standards were approved by the State Council on 16 November 1992 and became effective on 1 July 1993. Three main issues associated with this significant change in the direction of accounting reform within China are addressed. First, the major forces leading to the reform of accounting standards setting within China are examined. Second, the process for setting accounting standards within China is discussed. Finally, the Standards are outlined and issues associated with their implementation are considered.

FORCES AFFECTING THE SETTING OF ACCOUNTING STANDARDS

The Fourteenth National Congress of the Chinese Communist Party which was held in 1992 confirmed that the object of Chinese economic reform was to develop a socialist market economy. This conclusion resulted in the beginning of the historic transformation from a socialist planned commodity economy to a socialist market economy. These changes followed remarks by Deng Xiaoping concerning the issue of whether a market economy was socialist or capitalist in nature and confirmed that the primary goal was to improve the standard of living for the people. Deng's remarks established the new policy direction of carrying out deep economic reform of state enterprises, expanding the private market economy and providing a 'wider open-door' for foreign investment in China.

This change in policy direction represents the second step in the reform of the accounting process in China. Overall accounting reform in China can be characterized as comprising two steps, the first of which was the move from a central planning function to an enterprise management function. The second step involves the change from an enterprise management function to an external market decision function. This process is represented in Figure 8.1.

THE FIRST STEP

A perspective on the current reforms is best gained by reviewing briefly the historical development of accounting since the establishment of the PRC in 1949. During the first stage of development from 1949 to 1978 five distinct periods can be identified for the purpose of interpreting accounting reform: the infancy period, the suspended period, the recovery period, the catastrophe period, and the transition period. Each is discussed below.

After the foundation of the PRC the economic structure began to follow the Soviet Union with the introduction of central

	First step	*Second step*	
	1949–78	*1978–92*	*1992–present*
Economic structure	Socialist centrally controlled planned economy	Socialist planned commodity economy	Socialist market economy
Accounting function	Government planning function	Enterprise management function	External market decision function

Figure 8.1 The reform process

planning. The capitalist sector of the economy was gradually replaced by the state sector and worker co-operatives. The state sector was considered the leading force for socialist transformation which involved 'the transition from private management to joint state — private ownership and operation of private enterprises in industry, commerce, handicrafts and transportation; the organization of producers' co-operatives in both farming and handicrafts; and the restriction and gradual elimination of rich peasants' (Kwang 1966: 63). The Ministry of Finance (MOF) was established as the department in charge of accounting affairs and commenced to unify the variety of accounting systems inherited from the old society. The MOF issued regulations to ensure uniform accounting in enterprises. This period of introducing the socialist transformation lasted from 1949 to 1956 and is referred to as the infancy period.

The 'Great Leap Forward' was a catastrophe for accounting and led to the virtual collapse of the infant accounting systems established in enterprises. This second period from 1957 to 1961 is referred to as the suspended period. Comments on the lack of accounting during this period are illustrated by the following statements:

> Not only were the functions of accounting neglected as a result of the deviation from the principles of scientific management, but many absurd accounting concepts and practices were also encouraged and applied. A notable example was the practice of 'accounting without books', a reference not to the use of a computer but to the elimination of accounting journals and ledgers. Such a system might work briefly; over time, however, original documents such as invoices, receipts, and other documents accumulated, resulting in great confusion and disarray in accounting departments.
>
> (Bai 1988: 28)

> Drastic simplifications of accounting systems and procedures were made in order to make it possible for workers in the factories and peasants in the People's communes to participate in such work.
>
> (Kwang 1966: 79)

The period from 1962 to 1965 is referred to as the recovery period and is very important in the overall development of accounting within PRC. Two events are significant: first, the desire of China to recover from the problems of the 'Great Leap Forward' and, second, the ideological confrontation in the Sino-Soviet relationship. A new accounting system was proposed with Chinese characteristics and a self-reliance policy. This involved the development of Chinese authored textbooks and the introduction of new courses (Lin and Deng 1992: 166). The concept of accounting within a socialist economy was defined thus:

> Socialist accounting is one of the means of dealing with economic management under a socialist system. It is an approach through recording and examining in terms of money the supervision and evaluation of units, (e.g. enterprises, non-business units, public organizations, etc.) economic activities and financial situation in the processing of socialist expanded reproduction.
>
> (Tan Hui 1963, cited in Zhou 1988: 215)

The most significant development in this period was the introduction of the increase/decrease method as compared to the debit/credit method of bookkeeping. This method was considered to be easily learned and mastered and overcame much of the confusion associated with the debit/credit method. The increase/decrease method was implemented first in state-owned commercial enterprises and by 1965 was being adopted by many industrial as well as commercial enterprises. A discussion of this method is provided in Tang *et al.* (1992: 16–47) and Hwang and Tang (1991). During this period other accounting methods were developed for industries or sectors of the national economy. For example, a cash receipts and disbursements method was used for banks; a type of property receipt and disbursement method for rural units; and a fund receipt and disbursement method for government units and other organizations.

The newly established accounting systems were attacked when the 'Great Proletarian Cultural Revolution' was begun in 1966. Among the criticisms levelled at accounting was that it represented vestiges of capitalism which should be eradicated. Accounting education and training also suffered greatly during this period and the following comment illustrates this problem:

> By the time of the Great Proletarian Cultural Revolution (1966–76), intellectuals had become one of the primary targets

for revolutionary charges of elitism. Most academicians were humiliated and branded as reactionary academic authorities because of their 'inappropriate thinking' and 'bourgeois attitudes'. Intellectuals came to be known as the 'stinking ninth category' of class enemies.

(Watne and Baldwin 1988: 141)

After the Cultural Revolution the Chinese accounting system went through a transition phase. This was associated with a re-examination of the direction of the Chinese economy and the first steps towards opening China to international influences. The period from 1976 to 1978 is referred to as the transition period. This transition leads up to the first step in accounting reform as represented in Figure 8.1 above. In summary, this overview of the development of accounting in China is important because it provides a framework for understanding why reform was needed. Enthoven (1991) stated:

It is hard to comprehend Chinese accounting without a clear understanding of both its historical and recent (since 1949 and 1979) eco-political developments. These historical trends are extremely significant in trying to grasp the current Chinese accounting system, while Chinese accounting has its own characteristics resulting from these developments

(Enthoven 1991: 277)

Following the transition period, China's accounting system made the first step towards reform. This was heralded by the decision of the Third Plenary Session of the Eleventh Central Committee of the Communist Party in China to shift the work of the entire party to economic reconstruction. This programme of reform involved the modernization of key sectors of the economy and the recognition and practice of the planned commodity economy which has been described as 'China's nearest equivalent to the Western term of the market economy, that is, the integration of the planned economy with market regulation' Tang *et al.* (1992: 9). The accounting function changed with this first step from a tool of government for economic planning and control to an enterprise management aid.

The economic reform launched in 1978 involved a number of significant changes to the management and operation of the Chinese economy, each of which had important implications for the practice of accounting. Some of these changes are briefly discussed below. First, enterprises were reformed. This process saw a separation of government from the management functions of state enterprises. Managers were given power to make decisions concerning production, supply, marketing, finance, personnel, wages and bonuses. Enterprises 'were also given the responsibility for their own financial position and their successful performance under the pressure from outside competition' (Bai 1988: 29).

Second, the state began to reform the banking system in 1978. Prior to this, state enterprises obtained approximately 60–80 per cent of all funds from the state and the balance from the People's Bank of China. The reform of the bank system involved a reduction of the role of the state as a source of enterprise finance and an expansion of the role of banks in providing funds to enterprises. Several new banks were created to meet the increased demand for finance.

Third, the re-establishment of the audit system was begun. This requirement arose partly because of the separation of ownership from management in enterprises. The state was able to influence management indirectly through the audit system. The constitution of the PRC adopted at the Fifth National People's Congress on 4 December 1982 established the position of Auditor-General. The Auditor-General is a member of the State Council under Article 86 of the Constitution and is appointed by the President in pursuance of a decision of the National People's Congress. An observer at the time noted:

> With China's current modernization and the associated move to revenue raising based on taxation rather than the profit going to the State, there has been a recognition of the need to strengthen the planning, control and supervision of public enterprises to prevent unnecessary losses and expenses. This has led to a move to re-establish an auditing agency to operate at all levels of government.
>
> (Dick 1983: 169)

Fourth, and perhaps the most significant of all the reforms, was the start of the 'open door' policy towards foreign investment. China recognized the need for foreign investment to enable economic reconstruction and this move signalled the beginning of accounting reform towards the requirements in international accounting standards. Most of the major international accounting firms had opened offices in China by the early 1980s. Accounting regulations and laws were passed permitting joint ventures and wholly foreign-owned enterprises to operate in China. Details of these accounting rules and regulations have been extensively reported in the literature; see, for example, Tang *et al.* (1992: 49–87).

The framework of accounting and financial affairs follows the legal hierarchy and in 1985 the National People's Congress, which is the highest legislative body, enacted the Accounting Law of the People's Republic of China. The next senior legislative body is the State Council which has authority for approving regulations, administrative rules and decrees promulgated by the various Ministries and Commissions under its authority. The third level of government is the Ministry of Finance (MOF) which is in charge of the issuance of more detailed regulations to be applied by all enterprises throughout China. During the period 1978–92 the uniform accounting system used by industrial and commercial enterprises was improved three times. These reforms are discussed by Zhou (1988: 212).

The promulgation by the State Council in July 1986 of the 'Regulations on Certified Public Accountants' was a significant landmark in the reform of the accounting system. The Regulations defined the qualifications needed to become a CPA, including education and practical experience. Under the guidance of the Accounting Law and the Regulations, CPA firms are approved by the MOF and are then registered with local administrative units to undertake their work independently. Chinese CPA firms render a wide scope of services, including annual audits of financial statements, financial management consultative services, tax services, feasibility studies for investment, accounting system design, patent applications, business establishment, dissolutions and liquidations, settlement of claims and debts, preparation of articles of association, deeds, contracts and agreements and other business documents (Bai 1988: 47).

The final part of the first step in the accounting reform was the transformation of the accounting education system. The problems caused by the Cultural Revolution were addressed during the 1980s.

Accounting education, which was subject to stagnation in the 1970s, has received wide attention in China. China has clearly recognized the importance of sound accounting education in its new socio-economic development plan and process. Radical changes have occurred in the teaching methodology and coverage of accounting.

(Enthoven 1991: 279)

During the 1980s a diversity of options in higher education in accounting appeared in China. Regular college and university levels can be classified into the undergraduate programme and the graduate programme, which includes both Masters and Doctoral programmes. The professional training programme can be divided into an evening college programme, a correspondence college programme, television college programme, vocational college programme, and other on-job training. Accounting curricula and textbooks were updated and many included reference to foreign texts or involved translation. In some postgraduate programmes textbooks in English are used. For example:

> Many educators in the United States might be somewhat surprised to find that accounting departments and majors are commonly found in many Chinese universities and that well-known American accounting textbooks often appear on professors' bookshelves. In fact, American accounting texts, journals and monographs are often used as reference materials in advanced undergraduate courses and as basic texts in masters and doctoral level classes.
>
> (Watne and Baldwin 1988: 139–40)

These reforms were designed to enable Chinese students to master quickly the newest specialized accounting knowledge in order to assist with China's modernization programme.

In summary, the first step to economic and accounting reform involved the transformation of the economy from a centrally controlled and planned economy to a planned commodity economy. In order to complete this process the accounting function shifted from an emphasis on government planning to enterprise management. This shift was associated with reform of the management of enterprises, the banking system, the audit system, the legal system relating to accounting, public accounting firms, accounting education, and with the open door policy to foreign investment.

THE SECOND STEP

The reform process from 1978 to 1992 saw the completion of the first step in the reform of the Chinese economic system. The decision of the Fourteenth National Congress of the Chinese Communist Party in 1992 to proceed with economic reform and to develop a socialist market economy signalled the beginning of the second step in the reform process. The economic structure was to be transformed from a socialist planned commodity economy to a socialist market economy. Allied with this change, the accounting function needed to shift from an enterprise management function to an external market decision function. Three significant events have so far been associated with this stage of the reform process: the policy of deep economic reform of state enterprises, the expansion of the private market economy within China, and the 'wider open-door' to foreign investment. Each of these events is discussed below.

The policy of deep economic reform primarily refers to the separation of government influence and control from the management of state-owned enterprises. Deep reform of enterprise management commenced with the implementation of the State Council directive 'Provision for the Transformation of the Management Mechanism of State Owned Industrial Enterprises' in July 1992. The key to this reform was to turn these enterprises into separate legal entities responsible for their own decisions about operations and expansion and to make each enterprise responsible for profits and losses. Based on the reforms of the law concerning enterprises, each was granted autonomous management concerning such things as the purchase of raw materials, production targets and product mix, pricing and profit distribution. These reforms affected nearly 11,000 large and medium sized state enterprises, which contribute approximately 60 per cent of China's total industrial taxes and profits. The consequence of these reforms for accounting is that enterprise accounting systems have to change their orientation from producing information used in state planning and control to producing information useful for managerial decision-making. This change in the orientation of accounting has significant consequences for the nature of external financial reports prepared by state enterprises. Financial reports changed from disclosing fund balances to reporting assets, liabilities and owner's equity on the balance sheet and profit or loss in the income statement.

Coupled with the deep reform of state enterprises the government has initiated moves to expand the private economy within China. The private economy as at the end of 1992 comprised 15.3 million individual industrial and commercial units with 24.6 million employees and a gross output valued at 113 billion yuan (*Beijing Review*, 15–21, February 1993, p. 4). The range of industries and sectors of the economy available to the private sector is being increased and all private enterprises are being encouraged to become involved in export oriented ventures with overseas partners. Further, private businesses are being encouraged to establish equity interests in other business ventures. The consequence of these reforms for accounting enhance the exposure of Chinese businesses to foreign accounting practices and also create the need for the introduction of accounting standards on consolidation and equity accounting. Other accounting issues associated with deep reform include accounting for paid-in capital, fixed assets and depreciation, intangible assets and goodwill, and for tax and profit appropriation.

The other significant change has been referred to as 'opening the door wider' to foreign investment in China. According to the State Statistical Bureau, the State Council has approved more than 300 open cities to the world (*Beijing Review*, 11–17 January 1993, p. 16). By the end of 1992 over 84,000 foreign funded enterprises with a total of $US 178.46 billion in investments were registered in China (*Beijing Review*, 12–18 April 1993, p. 23). A total of 174,056 joint ventures were operating in China by early 1994 and their foreign trade accounted for approximately one-third of the country's total imports and exports during 1993 (*Sydney Morning Herald*, 12 March 1994, p. 40). The other side to the open door policy is that over 2,000 Chinese enterprises have now established overseas branches and outlets (*Beijing Review*, 5–11 April 1993, p. 25). Also, China has begun to list state enterprises on foreign stock exchanges. For example, de Freitas (1993) reported the following:

> In particular, the announcement by the Chinese that they had selected nine state enterprises as candidates for potential listing on the Hong Kong Stock Exchange promised tremendous opportunities for Hong Kong's accounting profession. The attractions of listing overseas as a source of foreign capital are high: the recent listing of a Chinese company on the New York

Stock Exchange saw its share value increase by 225 per cent within its first two days of trading.

(de Freitas 1993: 30)

The above forces promoting economic and accounting change in China have required the accounting system to adapt to the growing pressures of international business and the socialist market economy. Therefore, the next question that we address is, how have generally accepted accounting standards been set in China to guide the development of Chinese accounting and also to integrate the Chinese accounting system into the international economy?

SETTING ACCOUNTING STANDARDS

The structure and institutional arrangements for accounting standards in China are based around the legal and political system. At the first level is the accounting law issued by the National People's Congress in 1985. At the second level are the general rules and accounting standards approved by the State Council and managed by the Ministry of Finance. The third level involves detailed accounting regulations for different industries which are issued by the MOF. The overall structure of accounting regulations in China is illustrated in Figure 8.2.

Accounting standards are currently established in China in a co-operative way between the MOF and the Accounting Society of China (ASC). The motivation for setting accounting standards originated from the ASC which was founded in 1980. In 1987 the Research Group on Accounting Theory and Standards was established within the ASC. The objective of the Research Group was to explore accounting theory and the conceptual framework that would assist in setting accounting standards for China. The Research Group comprises fifteen members, the majority of whom are eminent accounting scholars from universities. Other members of the group include representatives from accounting practitioners, enterprise accountants, finance, tax and other administrative agency representatives (Tang *et al.* 1992: 132).

Shortly after the ASC launched its research project in 1988 the MOF announced that a working group on accounting standards had been founded within the Ministry. The working group formulated a plan for the establishment of accounting standards which

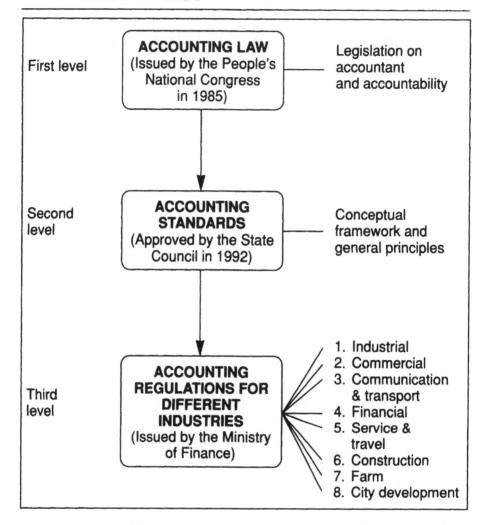

Figure 8.2 The structure of the Chinese accounting model

covered such issues as procedures for setting standards, methodology, structure and content of accounting standards. In 1988 a paper was published, entitled 'Discussion Paper on Major Issues Related to the Establishment of Accounting Standards', which represented an official guideline for setting accounting standards in China (Tang *et al.* 1992: 134).

Representatives of the MOF attended the first conference of the ASC Research Group and provided both political and financial support to the project. It was considered that a combination of the financial resources of the MOF and the human resources of the ASC would provide the best way to establish Chinese accounting standards. The ASC may initiate research concerning accounting standards, but only the MOF has the authority to promulgate accounting standards.

In January 1989 the first symposium on accounting standards was organized in Shanghai and the following themes were addressed:

1 The significance of accounting standards in the context of China's socio-economic development.
2 The content and level of accounting standards.
3 The relationship between accounting standards and existing accounting regulations.
4 The approach to the establishment of accounting standards.

The Research Group subsequently identified research issues and classified them into the following four areas (Tang *et al.* 1992: 132):

1 The fundamental theory of accounting, including objectives of accounting, accounting assumptions and definition of accounting elements.
2 Basic accounting principles, including relevance, reliability, comparability, historical cost, materiality and realization.
3 Accounting measurement and reporting, including recognition and measurement of accounting elements, and the function and purpose of various financial statements.
4 Operational accounting standards, including accounting standards for various business transactions such as hire purchase and lease transactions, intangible assets, fixed assets, right to use land, and long-term investments.

The Research Group then published two monographs in 1989 which not only served as a reference for but also have played a positive role in the development of draft accounting standards issued by the MOF. These monographs were respectively titled 'Research Monograph on Accounting Theory and Accounting Standards' and 'Recommendations on Accounting Standards'. Following this, the Department of Administration of Accounting Affairs (DAAA) of the MOF released an Exposure Draft on the 'Outline of Accounting Standards in the People's Republic of China' in November 1990. Using this exposure draft as a discussion paper the Research Group went to several cities and provinces to discuss and debate issues with accountants, academics and practitioners. This exposure draft was remodelled and reissued by the MOF as the 'Draft on Enterprise Accounting Standards No. 1' on 26 November 1991.

The pace of reform continued during 1992 and a speech delivered by the Vice-Minister of Finance, Zhang Youcai, at a seminar on International Accounting Standards on 26 February 1992 in Shenzhen, Guangdong Province demonstrated the focus of China's accounting reform. In this speech it was stressed that China wanted to communicate and share accounting knowledge with experts from all over the world and also to strengthen the relationship between China and the International Accounting Standards Committee. Extracts from the accounting standards currently published in the USA by the Financial Accounting Standards Board and in the UK by the Accounting Standards Board were translated into Chinese and published in Chinese accounting journals. After further deliberations the MOF officially issued the 'Accounting Standards for Business Enterprises' on 30 November 1992 after it was approved by the State Council on 16 November 1992. This accounting standard became effective for all enterprises on 1 July 1993. The process for developing accounting standards is represented diagrammatically in Figure 8.3.

This represents a major turning point in the history of accounting development in China. The following statement by the Minister of Finance, Liu Zhongli, highlights the importance of this event: 'The purpose of reform is to bring Chinese financial and accounting systems more in line with international practice' (*Beijing Review*, 7–13 December 1992, p. 14). These reforms have changed the orientation of accounting in China towards the provision of information for decision-making in markets and away from a central planning and managerial control orientation. In the next section the Standards issued by the MOF on 30 November 1992 are discussed.

ACCOUNTING STANDARDS FOR BUSINESS ENTERPRISES

The 'Accounting Standards for Business Enterprises' comprise ten chapters under the following headings: general provisions; general principles; assets; liabilities; owner's equity; revenues; expenses; profit; financial statements; and supplementary provisions. Overall, the contents of the Standards can be illustrated in the diagram in Figure 8.4.

In the chapter concerning general provisions, four key points are emphasized. First, the reason for issuing the Standards is

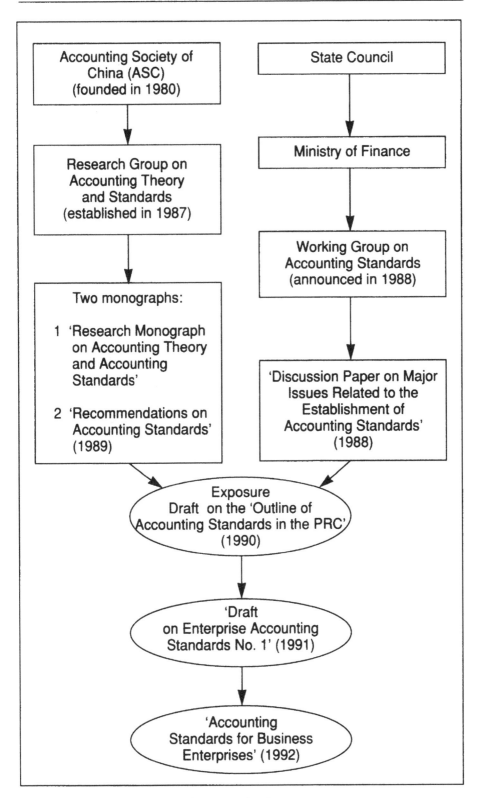

Figure 8.3 Setting accounting standards

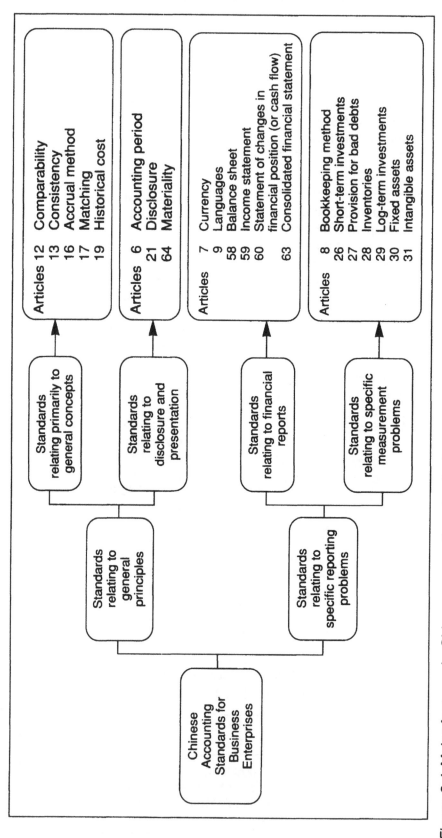

Figure 8.4 Major features in Chinese accounting standards

explained, namely that the Standards will improve the development of the socialist market economy (Article 1). Second, the scope of application of these standards is defined to cover all enterprises within China (Article 2). Third, the relationship between the existing accounting regulations and enterprise accounting systems adopted by enterprises is required to be consistent with these standards (Article 3). Finally, the chapter describes some general accounting requirements to be adopted by enterprises, such as the going concern concept (Article 5), the accounting year (Article 6), the currency unit (Article 7), the debit/credit system (Article 8), and language (Article 9).

In the second chapter general principles for the development of enterprise accounting practice in China are specified. Important general principles identified include: accounting information is useful for macro-economic management of the state and for decision-making by people concerned with enterprises (Article 11); accounting methods shall comply with the regulations to enable comparable reports to be produced (Article 12); accounting methods shall be applied consistently from one period to the next (Article 13); accrual accounting shall be used by all enterprises (Article 16); revenues should be matched with related expenses (Article 17); enterprises are required to adhere strictly to asset valuation on a historical cost basis (Article 19); expenditures of a capital nature need to be distinguished from those of a revenue nature (Article 20); financial statements should disclose fully the financial position and operating results of enterprises (Article 21). In addition, it is emphasized that accounting reports must be timely and understandable (Articles 14 and 15).

Assets are defined and guidelines for disclosure are provided in Chapter 3. The primary criterion for identification of assets is control of resources by enterprises (Article 22). In balance sheets assets should be classified in the following groups: current assets, long-term investments, fixed assets, intangible assets, deferred assets and other assets (Article 23). Special provisions are included for particular types of assets. For example, inventory valuation is required to be at historical cost, determined using any of the following valuation techniques: first-in-first-out (FIFO), weighted average, moving average or last-in-first-out (LIFO) (Article 28). In the case of investments in other enterprises, either the cost method or the equity method can be used (Article 29). Fixed assets are required to be reported at historical cost less accumulated depreciation calculated by using one of the following methods: straight line, production or service output or accelerated rate if approved (Article 30). Intangible assets can be recognized whether externally purchased or internally generated and should be amortized over the period of benefit attributable to the intangible asset (Article 31).

Equities in the balance sheet are covered in Chapters 4 and 5. Liabilities are defined and their classification and reporting in financial statements is outlined in Chapter 4. The primary division is between current and long-term liabilities (Article 35). Owner's equity is defined in Chapter 5 as the rights of investors to the enterprise's net assets and includes paid-in capital, capital reserve, reserve from profit and undistributed profits (Article 38).

Items involved in the income statement are discussed in Chapters 6 (Revenues), 7 (Expenses) and 8 (Profit). Revenue is defined to include all gains from operating activities (Article 44). Recognition is discretionary and may be at the point of delivery of the goods, provision of the services, receipt of the sale consideration or at the point of receiving an entitlement to the sale consideration (Article 45). Expenses are defined on a product basis to include direct materials, labour and overheads and other indirect expenses (Article 48). Period expenses are all of those attributable to the period including accruals (Articles 49 and 50). Profit is classified as operating profit, profit from investments and net non-operating results (Article 54).

The financial statements to be prepared by enterprises are the balance sheet, income statement, and either a statement of changes in financial position or a statement of cash flows (Article 57). Comparative amounts are allowed to be disclosed but such disclosure is not compulsory. If accounting practices have changed then there is a requirement that that adjustment needs to be disclosed (Article 61). Where an enterprise holds an investment in another enterprise equal to 50 per cent or more of the total share capital then the parent company is required to prepare consolidated financial statements (Article 63).

Finally, the supplementary provisions state that the MOF is responsible for interpretation of these provisions (Article 65). As these standards only became effective as from 1 July 1993 there will be many practical problems ahead in ensuring that they are uniformly implemented. The large number of accountants and managers that need to be trained will pose significant educational problems. It is expected that there will be a six-month transition period until 1 January 1994.

CONCLUSION

The current reforms of China's accounting system continue the long line of changes that have occurred since the establishment of the People's Republic of China in 1949. The 1992 reforms mark the beginning of a new era and of a greater consideration of the international forces that need to be harnessed to provide the people of China with the best opportunities to improve their standard of living and general economic well-being. Accounting reform has been recognized to be a vital ingredient in the overall process of economic reform.

The Standards herald a transition from a fund approach to an accrual approach for accounting practice and measurement (Maschmeyer and Yang 1993). The Standards developed so far have a conceptual orientation and cover many of the ideas in the conceptual framework projects of standard setting bodies in the USA, UK and Australia. For example, many of the elements of the conceptual framework project, such as a statement of objectives, the qualitative characteristics and the recognition and measurement of elements of the financial statements, are covered by the articles of the Standard. China now has the task of developing detailed standards for each of the items covered in the Standards and of producing a comprehensive set of accounting standards and regulations.

The second step of the reform process has only just been taken. A traditional Chinese saying is that a journey of a thousand miles begins with a single step. Reform and development of a socialist market economy will involve a broad range of economic, political, legal, social and accounting changes. There will be many more steps for China to take. The direction of the journey in which China is heading on its reform path is towards participation and co-operation on an international level. The changes in accounting are mirroring the journey of China and consequently the introduction of the accounting standards marks a move towards the internationalization of accounting in China.

REFERENCES

Bai, Z. L. (1988) 'Accounting in the People's Republic of China: contemporary situations and issues', in V. K. Zimmerman (ed.) *Recent Accounting and Economic Developments in the Far East*, Centre for International Education and Research in Accounting, University of Illinois, pp. 27–50.

de Freitas, G. (1993) 'Bringing China to the markets', *Certified Accountant*, February, pp. 30–3.

Dick, G. (1983) 'Auditing in China: the Australian involvement', *Australian Journal of Chinese Affairs*, January, pp. 169–74.

Enthoven, A. (1991) 'Accounting, auditing and education in the People's Republic of China', in C. Nobes and R. Parker (eds) *Comparative International Accounting* (3rd edn), Sydney: Prentice Hall International, pp. 277–80.

Hwang, D. B. K. and Tang, Q. (1991) 'Fund accounting and the increase decrease method in China', paper presented at the Third Asian–Pacific Conference on International Accounting Issues, Honolulu, Hawaii, October.

Kwang, C. W. (1966) 'The economic accounting system of state enterprises in mainland China', *International Journal of Accounting* 1(2): 61–99.

Lin, Z. and Deng, S. (1992) 'Educating accounting in China: current experiences and future prospects', *International Journal of Accounting* 27(2): 164–77.

Maschmeyer, R. A. and Yang, J. (1993) 'Financial accounting in China: new developments towards improved accountability', paper presented at the Fifth Asian–Pacific Conference on International Accounting Issues, Mexico City, Mexico, November.

Ministry of Finance (1992) *Accounting Standards for Business Enterprises*, Beijing: Publishing House of Law.

Tang, Y. W., Chow, L. and Cooper, B. J. (1992) *Accounting and Finance in China: A Review of Current Practice*, Hong Kong: Longman.

Watne, D. A. and Baldwin, B. A. (1988) 'University-level education of accountants in the People's Republic of China', *Issues in Accounting Education* 3(1): 139–55.

Zhou, Z. H. (1988) 'Chinese accounting systems and practices', *Accounting, Organizations, and Society* 13(2): 207–24.

Chapter 9

The new accounting standard in China

A critical analysis

M. Aiken, W. Lu and X.-D. Ji

INTRODUCTION

For many years, China employed uniform accounting systems.[1] The accounting reform that occurred in 1979 has focused attention on the relationship between uniform accounting and accounting standards. Questions have been raised as to whether uniform accounting includes accounting standards (Fang and Zhang 1988). In particular, is it necessary to establish Chinese accounting standards in addition to uniform accounting systems (Fang 1989)? At a special conference on accounting standards, held during the annual meeting of the Chinese Society of Accountants in January 1989, all Chinese accounting academics and practitioners agreed that it was indeed necessary to establish accounting standards.

In October 1988, a research group was formed within the Accounting Section of the Ministry of Finance to develop Chinese accounting standards. Three years later, the first draft of 'Accounting Standards for Business Enterprises No. 1: Basic Standards' (MOF 1991) was sent to accounting academics and professionals for comments (Gang 1992). An International Symposium on Chinese Accounting Standards was held in Shenzhen[2] in February 1992 (Yang 1992). International experts were invited to join the discussion.[3] In December 1992, 'Accounting Standards for Business Enterprises' was formally promulgated by the Ministry of Finance in China (MOF 1992) and was to be effective from 1 July 1993, along with accounting regulations for thirteen industries, which integrated the industrial characteristics and the requirement of accounting standards. It was a landmark for Chinese accounting reforms. Accounting practitioners and scholars in China had begun to use international accounting standards and Western experience as a basis for developing Chinese accounting reforms. This chapter will review the main contents of the Accounting Standards and will examine the main changes in accounting practices that resulted from the issue of the standards. The chapter also analyses the impact on the setting of accounting standards of economic developments, foreign investment, reforms of enterprise structure and the emergence of stock exchange markets.

MAIN CONTENTS AND CHARACTERISTICS OF THE ACCOUNTING STANDARD

The 10 chapters and 66 articles of the 'Accounting Standards for Business Enterprises' cover general rules, basic principles, assets, liabilities, owner's equity, revenue, expenses, profit, financial statements, and supplementary provisions.

The general rules include nine articles that explain the reasons for setting accounting standards, the nature and scope of accounting standards and the relationship between accounting standards and existing accounting regulations. The articles also cover accounting entity and tasks, the going concern concept, accounting periods, bookkeeping, recording currency and languages. It is stated clearly that the standard applies to all enterprises in China, including joint ventures and wholly foreign-owned enterprises. The standard also covers Chinese enterprises operating overseas.

The basic principles stated in the Accounting Standards include twelve fundamental accounting concepts: objectivity, relevance, comparability, timeliness, consistency, understandability, accrual basis, matching principle, conservatism, historical cost, separation of revenue expenditure and capital expenditure, and materiality. Chapters 3–8 each deal with one of six accounting elements: assets, liabilities, owner's equity, revenue, expenditure, and profit. The methods of identifying, measuring, recording, and reporting accounting elements are specified in each chapter. The major financial statements are described in Chapter 9 of the standard: balance sheet, the income statement, and the statement of changes in financial position. The Ministry of Finance is responsible for formulating, explaining and amending the Accounting Standards.

MAIN CHANGES IN ACCOUNTING PRACTICES THROUGH THIS STANDARD

China had not had its own accounting standards for over forty years. Accounting practice was governed by uniform accounting systems and regulations which differed from the accounting standard. Hence, promulgation of new accounting standards will bring many changes in accounting practices.

Basic accounting equation

The new accounting standards introduced the accounting equation

$$Assets = Liability + Owner's\ equity$$

which replaced the old accounting equation

$$Total\ fund\ application = Total\ fund\ source$$

in the uniform system. The old equation can be expanded into three sub-equations:

$$Fixed\ assets = Fixed\ funds;$$
$$Current\ assets = Current\ funds;$$
$$Specific\ assets = Specific\ funds.[4]$$

For a long time, the accounting authorities insisted on using the old equation, as this was considered to be the crucial distinction between socialism and capitalist accounting.[5] The major reason why Chinese accounting authorities made the crucial change was to make accounting practice in China more comparable with international accounting practice.

Financial management

Before economic reform, economic policy generally followed the classic Soviet model. The government directly provided most investment funds and directly or indirectly administered all economic enterprises (Myers 1980). The Chinese term for this policy is '*To Sou To Zhi*'. Although enterprises have had greater responsibility since the economic reforms developments in accounting regulations have not always kept pace with the reforms. Furthermore, enterprises had still not gained full rights and taken full responsibility for assets replacement. Investment decisions still remained with government authorities. For example, 50 per cent of the assets replacement reserve had to be handed over to the state and the government took care of assets replacement for enterprises. Thus, when assets were depreciated, journal entries were required to show how the total depreciation reserve was distributed between state and enterprise. Thus, if an item of plant costing $400,000 with nil residual value was depreciated at 20 per cent per annum straight-line method, then the required journal entries were as follows, according to uniform accounting legislation:

(1)   Dr.   Depreciation expense   80,000
      Cr.   Accumulated depreciation   80,000

      Depreciation of plant at 20 per cent

(2)   Dr.   Fixed fund – state   80,000
      Cr.   Special fund – replacement reserve 80,000

      Special fund of replacement reserve for fixed assets was created.

(3)   Dr.   Special deposit   40,000
            Special fund – replace reserve 40,000
      Cr.   Cash   80,000
      50 per cent of this reserve is handed over to the state and the remaining 50 per cent is left to the enterprise in the form of a special deposit.

These general entries show that when an enterprise depreciated assets it then set up the assets replacement reserve under a special fund, 50 per cent of which went to the state while the remaining 50 per cent was left in the enterprise to be used to replace the old plant. As a consequence the enterprise, when planning to replace old machinery, had to ask the bureaucracy for funding.

   In terms of the new accounting standard, only one journal entry is required when an enterprise depreciates assets. For example,

      'Dr. Depreciation expense
      Cr.   Accumulated depreciation'

No part of the replacement reserve based on accumulated depreciation will be out of operation. The enterprise will take full responsibility for assets replacement.

Manufacturing cost method

According to articles 48 and 49 of the accounting standard, the manufacturing cost includes direct materials, direct labour, and factory overheads. Administration expenses, financial expenses and sales expenses will be operating expenses to be deducted directly from revenue. This means that China has given up the full-absorption cost accounting method and adopted the manufacturing cost accounting method in practice. Before the promulgation of the standard the administration, financial and sales expenses had to be allocated to production costs. The reasons why China adopted the manufacturing cost method are that the community needs to simplify cost calculation, distinguish cost responsibility, and evaluate management performance under the reforms (Gang 1992).

Conservatism

'The general constraint of uncertainty has served as a basis for the traditional accounting concept of conservatism' (Hendriksen 1970). Conservatism is expressed in accounting as: 'to anticipate no profit, but to provide for all losses'. This idea has had great influence in the setting of accounting standards in many countries.

Conservatism was never previously adopted as an accounting concept by Chinese accounting practitioners and scholars. This can be seen in the old system. Under the old accounting regulation:

1 Short-term investment shall be presented at historical cost.
2 Inventory shall be calculated at historical cost, i.e. first-in-first-out (FIFO), specification identification, weighted average, moving average method and average cost. Cost or market, whichever is lower basis, is not allowed to be used.
3 No provision for doubtful debts is allowed.
4 Non-current assets shall appear at historical cost. Non-current assets revaluation is allowed only when enterprises are in combination, bankruptcy and liquidation.

In contrast, under the influence of leftist ideas, people talked only about good things; they liked to anticipate profit. Even when a loss was actually made, surprisingly one still can read profit in the profit and loss statement.

Even in the draft of the accounting standard, conservatism was not considered as an accounting concept (Lou and Zhang 1992). But when the standard was formally promulgated it was written in article 18: 'Accounting should calculate possible losses and expenses rationally according to the requirement of conservatism.' What had led to this change? There are three possible explanations:

High inflation

China's recent first-half economic statistics indicated that inflation was 17.4 per cent in the half, while GDP growth registered 13.9 per cent (*Far Eastern Economic Review* 1993). If the government does not allow enterprises to use the concept of conservatism in respect to accounting practices such as accelerated depreciation, provision for doubtful debts, and the last-in-first-out (LIFO) method of inventory calculation, the enterprises will not be able to maintain or increase their production capacity, take the necessary business risks or survive in the market competition.

Rationalization

As seen in the draft of the standard, Chinese scholars had tried to avoid recognizing the conservatism concept. However, some practice of conservatism was allowed. For example, 'The method of accelerated depreciation can be used under the approval of government agencies' and 'Provision for doubtful debts can be calculated in some circumstances according to the amounts of accounts receivable'. Obviously, this caused confusion and so, when the accounting standard was promulgated, the concept of conservatism was recognized.

International influence

Although in Western countries there is much criticism and argument about conservatism (Thomas 1966, Devine 1963), 'Unquestionably, conservatism holds an extremely important place in the ethos of the accountant. Indeed, it has even been called the dominant principle of accounting' (Wolk *et al.* 1992). If China persists in not recognizing conservatism as an accounting concept and does not allow some application of conservatism in practice, there is no doubt that assets can be overstated. It may disadvantage international trade and investment.

Financial reports

The financial reports are divided into two categories: external and internal. The external financial reports are: balance sheet, profit & loss statement, statement of changes of financial position, and supplementary statements, notes and statement of financial affairs. Internal reports, such as the statement of product cost can be designed according to various enterprises' own needs. Before the release of the accounting standard, enterprises had to submit many internal financial statements to the government, such as the statement of product cost and the statement of special funds application and source. This change obviously gives enterprises more flexibility to prepare internal financial statements to suit management needs.

The second change in financial reporting affects the content and structures of financial statements. As mentioned above, the basic accounting equation in China was

Total fund application = Total fund source
With its subordinate equations:
Fixed assets = Fixed funds;
Current assets = Current funds;
Specific assets = Specific funds.

The major contents of balance sheets were the fund application and fund source (see Table 9.1, format of the balance sheet used before the issue of accounting standards). But in the new accounting standards, it is required that enterprises prepare and submit their financial statements using internationally accepted structures and content, e.g. assets, liability and owner's equity.

Bookkeeping methods

The Chinese accounting authorities unified the bookkeeping method used in enterprises for the first time. Article 8 states that 'enterprises shall adopt the debit credit double entry method'.

The debit credit double entry method was used before only in large and medium manufacturing enterprises. Two other book-keeping methods were used elsewhere. The increase decrease

Table 9.1   Format of the balance sheet used before the issue of accounting standards

Application of funds	This month	Year to date	Source of funds	This month	Year to date
Fixed assets: Original cost of fixed assets Minus: Depreciation Carrying value of fixed assets			Fixed Funds: State fixed fund source Enterprise fixed fund source Capital construction loan		
Subtotal of fixed assets			Subtotal of fixed fund		

Current assets:
Sum of current assets with norm
Subtotal of current fund for
  procurement
(1) Raw materials
(2) Fuel
(3) Packaging materials
 	
(4) Low cost and short lived articles
(5) Work in process
(6) Material purchased
Subtotal of current fund for
  procurement
(1) Work-in process and self-manu-
  factured semi-finished products
Subtotal of current fund for
finished product
(1) Finished products
Sum of other current assets
  without norm
Merchandise shipped
Monetary funds
Trade accounts receivable and
  payment in advance
Other receivables
			Current Funds:
			State current fund source
			Enterprise current fund source
			
			Capital construction loan
			Current fund loans
			Trade accounts payable
			and advances on sales
			Other payable
			Accrued expenses
			Unpaid tax
			Depreciation payable
			
			Net income not
			turned over to the state
			Net income not retained		

Subtotal of current assets			Subtotal of current fund		
Specific assets: Bank deposits under specific fund Physical assets under specific fund Specific project expenditure Receivable and suspense debit			Specific funds Specific fund source Specific appropriations Specific purpose loan		
Subtotal of specific assets			Subtotal of specific fund		
Total fund application			Total fund source		

Source: Shanghai University of Finance and Economics and the University of Texas at Dallas 1987

double entry method was used in small manufacturing enterprises and merchandising enterprises and the receipt disbursement double entry method was used in government agencies (Wei 1984). These two methods emerged in the 'mid-1960s and were used widely during the period of the Cultural Revolution. They were the results of a leftist ideology that believed the debit credit method to be bourgeois and therefore not in the interests of the proletariat and so the proletariat should create new socialist or communist bookkeeping methods (W. Lu 1992). The different bookkeeping methods served to create obstacles in the communication of accounting information. Now it is certain that all manufacturing and merchandising enterprises will adopt the debit credit method. However, whether all government agencies will use the debit credit method is still doubtful. Historically, 'receipt' and 'disbursement' were used as recording symbols in non-governmental accounting as far back as the *Han* Dynasty (206 BC – AD 220) (Aiken and Lu 1993).

THE IMPACT OF PAROCHIAL FACTORS ON ACCOUNTING STANDARDS

Chinese accounting standards now reflect attempts to demolish the influences of Stalinist ideology that were seen in previous accounting practices. In the initial period of setting accounting standards, some scholars and practitioners in China advocated establishing Chinese accounting standards with Chinese planned market economy characteristics (Ge 1992). In the draft of the accounting standards, we can still find some Chinese characteristics such as the concepts of legality and uniformity. But when the accounting standards were formally issued, it seemed that some of these features were discarded. These standards are much more in harmony with the accounting standards in the West. One possible reason is that Chinese people have realized the need to move towards the internationalization of accounting. More importantly, economic and other developments in China itself are major factors inducing change. These factors are discussed below. They can be related to contemporary issues invoking strong public interest and might have significant implications for the future development of accounting standards in China.

Economic development

Economic development in China is now rapid. The growth rate of GDP in China was 12 per cent in 1992 compared with only 2–3 per cent in the main industrialized countries. With the development of this economy, new business activities emerged. For example, leases, business combinations, bankruptcies, land compensation, and intangible assets are now major areas of attention. Obviously, the old accounting regulations and central control of administration systems originating from previous ideologies are no longer seen to be appropriate.

Foreign investment

One of the most spectacular achievements since 1979, when China re-opened its doors to the outside, is the utilization of foreign funds. By the end of 1991, the contracted amount of foreign investment had reached $US 50 billion. The foreign investors participated in joint ventures, collaborations, wholly foreign-owned enterprises, and other areas (X. -L. Lu 1992). Several Special Economic Zones were established. Foreign accounting practices arrived with increasing foreign investment. The 'Accounting Regulations for Joint Ventures Using Chinese and Foreign Investment' was promulgated by the Ministry of Finance in 1985 in order to match the special needs of foreign investment. This regulation was different from others used by state-owned enterprises at that time. It was written by using internationally recognized accounting rules. The introduction of Western accounting thought and practice as well as accounting regulations for joint ventures were major challenges for the existing accounting system.

Reforms of the enterprise structure

Even after fourteen years of economic reform in China, large and medium state-owned enterprises are still often inefficient and uncompetitive. One reason is the lack of structural change in enterprises. Since 1979 the Chinese government has made many attempts to change the management of state-owned enterprises: from profit appropriation (*Li Run Liou Chun*) to tax levying (*Li Gai Sun*); from tax levying to operating responsibility (*Cheng Bao Jing Ying Zhe Ren Zhi*). However, the efforts have not essentially changed enterprise structures, and so the results of the reforms have often been unsatisfactory. In 1991, the Chinese government decided on a fundamental change to the structure of state-owned enterprises. Most of the state-owned enterprises have been or will be transformed to share-holding corporations. Individuals and legal entities will be allowed to buy shares in state-owned enterprises. Considering the great significance of corporations in the history and development of accounting in Western countries, it seems obvious that Chinese accounting will change widely and quickly.

The diversity of ownership and the stock exchange markets

In Chinese Society there are several types of enterprises: state-owned enterprises, collective enterprises, single proprietorship share-holding corporations, joint ventures, Sino-foreign collaborations, and wholly foreign-owned enterprises. Until 1993 the MOF issued individual accounting regulations for each kind of enterprise. With increasing private ownership and joint ventures, this administrative method is no longer suitable for the demands of equal opportunity under competition. That is why the government must urgently promulgate accounting standards governing all enterprises in China.

In 1990, the Chinese government officially opened stock exchanges in Shanghai and Shenzhen. The demands for disclosure of accounting information by corporations have accelerated the formulation of accounting standards.

Other factors

Aiken and Lu (1993) claim that accounting development in any country is strongly influenced by its culture and its political, social, and economic environment. We analysed the economic influence in the setting of Chinese accounting standards. According to Mathews and Perera (1993:105): 'Most accounting issues are politically sensitive because of (a) the need for standards which often arises where there is controversy, and (b) accounting distributions affecting wealth between different individuals and groups.'

Is there some political or ideological influence in standard-setting in China? The old accounting systems are based on those from the Soviet Union. With the collapse of the Soviet Union, all

Chinese accounting scholars and practitioners have had to adopt Western accounting principles, put them into practice and thus to set new standards.

COMPARISON WITH WESTERN EXPERIENCE

Compared with International Accounting Standards and the standards in Australia, the USA and the UK, the newly issued Chinese accounting standard is more like a conceptual framework. Strictly speaking, the Chinese accounting standard serves as a guideline of how to set accounting standards rather than as an accounting standard itself. This guideline can be traced to a conceptual model (see Figure 9.1).

Comparison of the Chinese conceptual framework with others used internationally reveals significant differences (see Figure 9.2 and Henderson and Peirson 1993:6).

The purpose of setting the Chinese standard is to provide a guideline for producing standards while the purpose of a conceptual framework in Australia is to provide an explicit set of concepts for users, preparers, and auditors of financial reports, as well as accounting standard-setters (Henderson and Peirson 1993). A conceptual framework in the USA has been defined as 'a coherent system of inter-related objectives and fundamentals that can lead to consistent standards and that prescribes the nature, function, and limits of financial accounting and financial statements' (FASB 1978: 1). Attention is now being given to using the conceptual framework as a structured theory of accounting in order to review, and even to rewrite, accounting standards in a more scientific and logical way.

Procedures to develop conceptual frameworks

The Chinese accounting standard was developed by first selecting the common accounting assumptions and principles in accounting practices and, second, using these assumptions and principles to recognize, measure, record, and report accounting elements. In Australia, the conceptual framework is set by defining the scope and objectives of financial reports and by identifying qualitative characteristics of financial reports. This means selecting the basic elements of accounting reports and developing the principles and rules for measurement of the basic elements. The type of

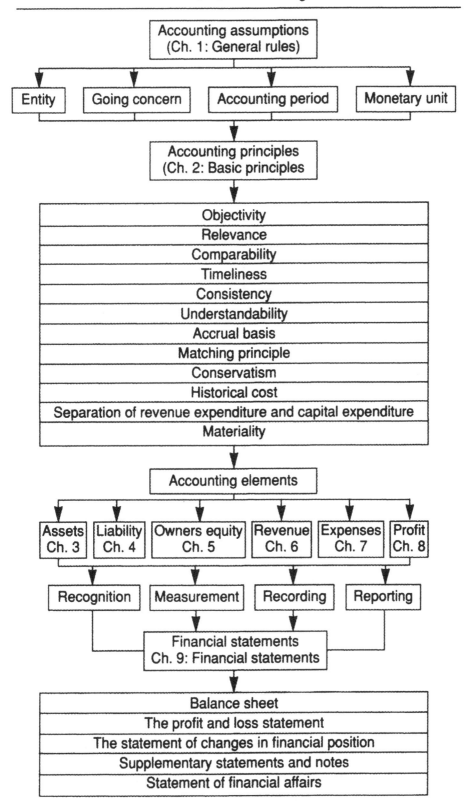

Figure 9.1 The structural model of the Chinese accounting standard

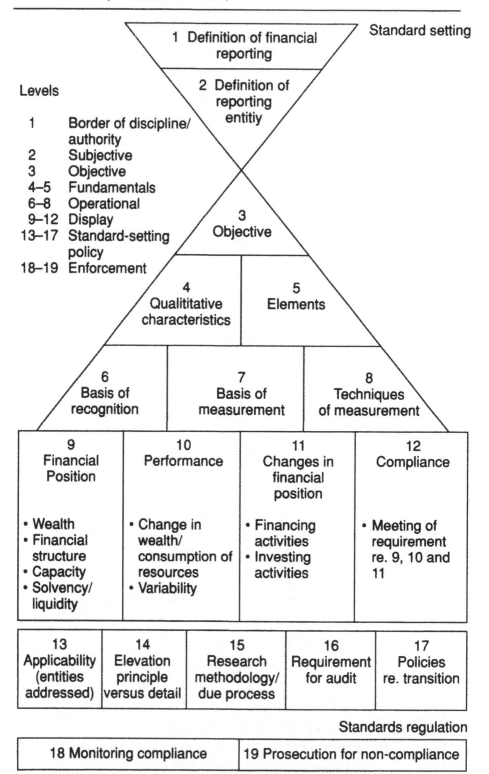

Figure 9.2 Tentative building blocks of a conceptual framework for general purpose financial reporting

Source: Australian Accounting Research Foundation

information to be displayed in financial reports is to be in accordance with these qualitative characteristics (Australian Society of CPAs and ICAA 1993).

Contents of conceptual framework

In the USA, there are six statements of financial accounting concepts (SFACs):

SFAC1 Objectives of financial reporting by business enterprises.
SFAC2 Qualitative characteristics of accounting information.
SFAC3 Elements of financial statements of business enterprise.
SFAC4 Objectives of financial reporting by non-business enterprises.
SFAC5 Recognition and measurement in financial statements of business enterprises.
SFAC6 Elements of financial statements: a replacement of FASB concept statement no. 3 (incorporating an amendment of FASB concept statement no. 2).

So far, the Australian Accounting Research Foundation has published four statements of conceptual framework and other documents. These are:

SAC1 Definition of the reporting entity.
SAC2 Objective of general purpose financial reporting.
SAC3 Qualitative characteristics of financial information.
SAC4 Definition and recognition of elements of financial statements.

These conceptual frameworks are more comprehensive than the Chinese accounting standard. Also, there are only five accounting elements — assets, liability, equity, revenue, expenses — included in the Australian conceptual framework. The Chinese has one more, profit.

PREDICTIONS OF FURTHER CHINESE ACCOUNTING REFORMS

Accounting developments depend on the developments in the economy and changes in social and political systems. With a stable, growing economy and improving legislative systems, Chinese accounting will be changed quickly.

The establishment of Chinese accounting standards is on schedule and includes:[6]

1 Accounting for state-owned property; depreciation; intangible assets; inventory; foreign currency translation; accounts receivable and provision of doubtful accounts; long-term investment; expenses on borrowing; recognition of revenue; division of revenue; share-holding corporations; securities; the effects of changing prices; liquidation.
2 Balance sheet: profit and loss statement.
3 The statement of changes of financial position.
4 Consolidation of financial statements.
5 Accounting for adjustment of previous events.

Now accounting in China faces two problems. The first is how to deal with the relationship between the new accounting standard, the Accounting Law, the Taxation Law and relevant company legislation. The second is how to deal with the relationship between the new accounting standards system and the old accounting regulation system.

The Accounting Law of the People's Republic of China (MOF 1985) was adopted on 21 January 1985 at the Ninth Session of the Standing Committee of the Sixth National People's Congress and was amended in 1993. The main contents of the Accounting Law, which reads like an accounting administration regulation or a code of professional conduct, can be summarized as follows:

1 The functions and sphere of responsibility of accounting officers of enterprise units
2 The legal rights and liabilities of accounting officers and related staff
3 The legal liability and obligation of the hierarchical administrative executives.

While accountants in Western countries face many alternative methods and procedures which can be chosen under accounting standards, their counterparts in China have almost no choice. Whether a tool valued at $100 is an asset or not is prescribed in accounting regulations. Also, the same tool may be treated differently in accounting regulations for other areas. It may be an asset in light-industry accounting and may be an expense item in construction accounting. This is one of the reasons why Chinese accountants want to change the accounting system. The problem is how to deal with the relationship between the accounting standard and existing industrial accounting regulations. Industrial accounting regulations can remain for a long time after accounting standards are set up. There are two reasons for this. First, there is an enormous number of state-owned enterprises in China, and the management of these varies greatly from industry to industry. Second, accounting standards, no matter how detailed they are, are to some extent abstract, and so pose difficulties in particular to some inexperienced Chinese accountants (Yang 1994). Practical demonstrations and guidelines are needed to promote the use of accounting standards.

CONCLUSION

With the development of the Chinese economy many accounting reforms will be accelerated. Accounting reforms could allow Chinese individuals and companies to do business more easily with other industrial countries such as Australia, the USA and the UK. This complies with the present trend towards the harmonization of accounting standards in the world, which the development of standards in China is intended to capture as market philosophies become more widely accepted in that country.

NOTES

1   From 1949 to 1979, the accounting system in China was mainly influenced by the former Soviet Union which had a uniform accounting system for every industrial sector. In a market economy, accounting information is used primarily by external users (e.g. investors, creditors) and by internal users (e.g. managers). In the former Soviet Union and in China before 1979, accounting information was mainly used by the central government for economic planning and control. Thus it was important for China to have uniform accounting systems. Under these systems, classification of accounting for reporting purposes is based on industrial sectors, such as uniform manufacturing, commercial, agricultural, banking and transportation accounting systems. There was also uniform budgetary accounting for government agencies and non-profit organizations. The ministry for each sector was responsible for the promulgation of uniform ministerial accounting systems subject to the approval of the Ministry of Finance.
2   Shenzhen was the first Chinese Special Economic Zone after China opened its doors in 1979. Its success has impressed the world and has

been the model for economic development in China.

3   Mr Arthur Wyatt and Mr David Cains, respectively Chairman and Secretary-General of the International Accounting Standards Committee, attended the Symposium and made speeches.

4   In most Chinese textbooks, 'fund' is defined as the monetary expression of property, goods and materials used in the production process. 'Fund source' is the channel for obtaining funds, while 'fund application' refers to the distribution, use and existing form of funds. Many accounting academics, both in China and overseas, recognize that the major differences between Chinese and Western accounting arise from the definition of financial source (see Lou 1984, Bromwich and Wang 1991). Thus, for Western accounting, capital structure includes both liabilities and owner's equity, whereas in China financial sources are simply called funds. The term 'capital' is not used because of political sensitivity.

5   In 1951, an article outlining the nature of accounting was published in a major accounting journal (Xing and Huan 1951). Subsequently, the debate on the nature of accounting ranged over such issues as the relevance of class, either socialist or capitalist. The contrary viewpoint was that accounting was a discipline with a specific methodology. Obviously, the first opinion dominated before 1979.

6   Deloitte Touche Tohmatsu International, after a process of tendering, was invited by the MOF to provide consultancy. Price Waterhouse was invited by the Bank of China to provide consultancy to develop accounting regulations for the banking industry. These accounting standards will be issued in three years (see Yang 1994).

REFERENCES

Aiken, M. and Lu, W. (1993) 'Chinese government accounting: historical perspective and current practice', *British Accounting Review* 25(2): 109–29.

Australian Society of CPAs and the Institute of Chartered Accountants in Australia (1993) *Accounting Handbook 1993*, Sydney: Prentice Hall.

Bromwich, M. and Wang, G. -Q. (1991) 'Management accounting in China: a current evaluation', *International Journal of Accounting* 26(1): 51–66.

Devine, C. T. (1963) 'The rule of conservatism reexamined', *Journal of Accounting Research*, vol. 1, pp. 127–38.

Far Eastern Economic Review (1993) 'Business briefing', 9 July, pp. 63.

Fang, Z. -L. (1989) 'Re-examining the accounting equation: how to report assets, liability and equity', *Accounting Research*, no. 3, pp. 21–9.

Fang, Z. -L. and Zhang, W. -G. (1988) 'New issues caused by economics structure reform in financial accounting and reporting', *Sichuan Finance and Accounting*, no. 2.

Financial Accounting Standards Board (1978) *Objectives of Financial Reporting by Business Enterprises*, Statement of Financial Accounting Concept no. 1, Stamford, Conn: FASB.

Gang, J. (1992) 'Initial practice in the development of the Chinese accounting standard', *Accounting Research*, no. 2, pp. 26–30.

Ge, J. -S. (1992) 'Learning from international experience to establish Chinese accounting standards', *Accounting Research*, no. 2, pp. 16–19.

Henderson, S. and Peirson, G. (1993) *Issues in Financial Accounting*, Melbourne: Longman Cheshire.

Hendriksen, E. (1970) *Accounting Theory*, Homewood, Ill: Irwin.

Lou, E. -Y. (1984) *Socialist Accounting Theory*, Shanghai: Shanghai Institute of Finance and Economics.

Lou, E. -Y, and Zhang, W. -G. (1992) 'A comparative study on Sino-foreign accounting standards', *Accounting Research*, no. 2, pp. 5–15.

Lu, W. (1992) 'Accounting development in China during the modern era', Masters thesis, La Trobe University, Bundoora, Vic.

Lu, X. -L. (1992) 'Prospect of foreign investment in China', International Conference on Trade, Investment and Economic Prospects in China's Three Economies: China's mainland, Taiwan and Hongkong, February, Monash University, Vic.

Mathews, M. R. and Perera, M. H. B. (1993) *Accounting Theory and Development*, Melbourne: Nelson.

Ministry of Finance (1985) *Accounting Law of the People's Republic of China*, Beijing: Chinese Financial and Economic Press.

——(1991) *Accounting Standards for Business Enterprises no. 1: Basic Standards* (draft), Beijing.

——(1992) 'Accounting standards for Business enterprises', *Accounting Research*, no. 6, pp. 7–11.

Myers, R. H. (1980) *The Chinese Economy, Past and Present*, Belmont, Calif: Wadsworth.

Shanghai University of Finance and Economics and the University of Texas at Dallas (E. -Y. Lou, S. N. Wang and A. J. H. Enthoven [eds]) (1987) *Accounting and Auditing in the People's Republic of China: A Review of its Practice, System, Education and Development*, Dallas: Centre for International Accounting Development, University of Texas.

Thomas, A. L. (1966) *Revenue Recognition*, Ann Arbor: University of Michigan Press.

Wei, Z. (1984) *Chinese Bookkeeping Methods*, Beijing: Chinese Financial and Economic Press.

Wolk, H. Francis, J. R. and Tearney, M. G. (1992) *Accounting Theory: A Conceptual and Institutional Approach*, Cincinnati, Ohio: South-Western Publishing.

Xing, Z. -J. and Huan, S. -G. (1951) 'How to establish new Chinese accounting', *New Accounting*, January.

Yang, J. -W. (1992) 'Address on the international symposium on Chinese accounting standards', *Accounting Research*, no. 2, pp. 3–4.

——(1994) 'Moving towards accounting internationalization', Sixth Conference of Accounting Academics, Hong Kong, 28–9 April.

Chapter 10

The Chinese approach to accounting standards and a conceptual framework

J. Z. Z. Xiao and A. Pan

INTRODUCTION

The last ten years have seen a proliferation of accounting regulations and standards.[1] Among these regulations and standards,
the 'Accounting Standards for Business Enterprises' (referred to
throughout this chapter as 'BAS' — Business Accounting
Standards) is said to have caused an 'accounting storm'. It has
made all of the existing accounting textbooks out of date. It has
created an urgent need for training almost every accountant.
Perhaps more importantly, it is expected to replace the old
uniform accounting systems (UASs) and to lead Chinese
accounting into line with internationally accepted practices.
Furthermore, BAS is also seen as a conceptual framework which
will guide the setting of the forthcoming accounting standards.
Can these expectations be realized? Can these claims be believed?

In an attempt to answer these questions, this chapter will
provide an analysis of the changes that BAS may bring about in
contrast with the UASs and the implications of these changes.
This is followed by a critical discussion on BAS as a conceptual
framework in comparison with other conceptual frameworks or
quasi-frameworks. But first it is necessary to give an introduction
to BAS.

AN INTRODUCTION TO BAS

In October 1988, an Accounting Standard Task Force (ASTF) was
established under the Department of Administration of
Accounting Affairs (DAAA) which has been the authoritative
body in dealing with accounting affairs and is itself subject to the

Ministry of Finance (MOF). ASTF was intended to develop accounting standards similar to those prevailing in the USA and in the UK. It spent a year in preparing a feasibility study and another year in drafting an outline of BAS. In November 1991 the BAS (Draft) was completed and formally published for public hearings in the name of the MOF. After wide consultation and discussion, including an International Symposium on Accounting Standards held in February 1992, the revised BAS was submitted to the State Council. Following the approval of the State Council, the MOF issued BAS on 30 November 1992 and it became effective on 1 July 1993.

BAS consists of ten chapters: general provisions, general principles, assets, liabilities, owner's equity, revenue, expenses, profit and loss, financial reports, and supplementary provisions. The main areas that it covers include the objectives of BAS, accounting postulates, general accounting principles, elements of financial statements, recognition, measurement and financial statements.

Objectives of the statement

Three objectives of BAS are stated:

1 To meet the needs of developing a socialist marketing economy.
2 To unify accounting standards.
3 To ensure the quality of accounting information.

In addition, it is also designed to guide the setting of further standards.

Postulates

Four internationally recognized accounting assumptions are adopted in BAS: accounting entity, going concern, accounting period and monetary measurement.

In addition, Chapter 1 requires the use of the debit/credit book-keeping method and prohibits other Chinese versions of double entry bookkeeping systems, such as the increase/decrease method and the receiving/giving method (Zhang 1981). It also contains rules about what language should be used in preparing financial reports.

Objectives of financial accounting and reporting

BAS does not discuss objectives in detail. A short paragraph in Chapter 2 states that financial accounting and reporting should:

1 Meet the information requirements for macro-economy management.
2 Allow relevant parties to assess the financial position and operating results of the business.
3 Meet the information needs of business management.

It is worth noting that the information needs for macro-economy management is placed at the top of the list. Equally notable is that BAS does not specify who are the relevant parties.

Accounting principles and qualitative characteristics

Chapter 2 is devoted to general accounting principles and qualitative characteristics. The principles proposed include accrual, matching, prudence, distinction between revenue expenses and capital expenses, full disclosure and historical cost. Objectivity or truthfulness, comparability, consistency, timeliness, understandability, completeness and materiality are stated as qualitative characteristics. It is rather surprising that relevance is not explicitly expressed in the list. It can only be inferred from a statement of the objectives of financial accounting and reporting as described above.

Elements of financial statements

As the headings of the chapters already show, assets, liabilities, owner's equity, revenue, expenses and profits are selected as the elements of financial statements. These elements are defined as follows.

1 Assets are economic resources, including property, rights to debts and other rights, which are owned or controlled by a business and are capable of monetary measurement.
2 Liabilities are obligations borne by the business which can be measured in monetary terms and can be discharged by assets or services.
3 Equities are the ownership rights of investors to the net assets of the business.

4 Revenues are realized operating revenues from selling goods or providing services.
5 Expenses are consumption (of assets) incurred in the process of manufacturing and operating.
6 Profits are the results of operations during a certain period, including operating profit, net investment income and net non-operating income.

Chapters 3–8 provide a detailed classification of the sub-elements of financial statements.

Recognition

BAS only provides criteria for revenue and expense recognition. Revenue is recognized when it is realized. Specifically, the business should recognize revenue when it has delivered an item of goods or service and in the meantime it has received cash or evidence for claiming the cash. On long-term construction contracts, revenue should be recognized using the percentage-completion method. Expenses are recognized applying the matching principle.

Measurement

Historical cost is the only measurement system considered appropriate in BAS. Alternative measurement systems are not discussed. As to the possible effect of price changes, BAS rules out any attempt to adjust the book values of assets unless other state regulations allow it.

Chapters 3–8 provide rules on some specific measurement issues. Variable costing must be used. For stock valuation, FIFO, LIFO, weighted average cost, moving average cost and specific identification methods are permitted. Accelerating depreciation can be used in addition to the straight-line method if other regulations allow. Other areas for which rules are available include: long-term investment, leasing, deferred assets, intangible assets, and so on.

Financial statements

The business must prepare a balance sheet, a profit and loss statement, a statement of changes in financial position or a cash flow statement and an explanatory statement on financial condition. If the business owns more than half of the capital of another company or actually controls the invested company, it must also prepare consolidated statements.

CHANGES PROPOSED AND THEIR IMPLICATIONS

China adopted the so-called uniform accounting systems (UASs) before BAS became effective. Those systems differed sharply from internationally recognized accounting practices. Ironically, the systems produced inconsistent practices among businesses in different sectors or industries although they were labelled as uniform systems. The systems were built to operate in an environment of centrally controlled economy called a planned economy and therefore incorporated no elements of a market economy.

It is not possible to perceive the value of BAS without investigating the changes that BAS has made or purports to make to the UASs. This section, therefore, discusses these changes and their implications.

Domestic harmonization

The old UASs were essentially a collection of a chart of accounts and detailed explanations as to how and where to use the accounts, plus detailed rules or regulations for costing, profit distribution, depreciation and other matters. These systems were either directly set by the DAAA under the Ministry of Finance or set by DAAAs in other ministries and then approved by the MOF which was and still is the major statutory accounting rule setter. Different systems were developed for accounting entities in different sectors or industries (commercial enterprises, manufacturing enterprises, energy enterprises, etc.), with different ownership (state-owned businesses versus collectively owned firms), and with different budgetary status (budgetary units versus non-budgetary units). These systems used different accounts and accounting methods for the same or similar transactions. They differed too not only in the types of financial statement but also in the structure of the same type of financial statement. These systems were also supplemented by local government departments (usually at provincial level) and this added to the complication and inconsistency among the systems. A typical example of this incomparability was the use of different bookkeeping methods. Three types of systems were used. Some commercial enterprises used the increase/decrease method, industrial enterprises and other commercial companies applied the debit/credit system, while financial institutions, budgetary units and agricultural firms adopted the receiving/giving method. Because of the differences among the UASs, it was difficult to obtain consistent and comparable information and this made it very hard to aggregate accounting information for the purpose of macro-economy management.

BAS intends to eliminate these variances. It is applicable to all domestic and overseas companies. As already described, BAS allows only the debit/credit bookkeeping method to be used. It prescribes the financial statements to be provided by all of the entities. It requires the use of the same treatments for the same or similar transactions across industries. By classifying each element of the financial statements in great detail, BAS provides references for a company to establish a specific financial accounting system.

Having recognized the difficulty in switching from the UASs to BAS based systems, the DAAA has also issued several industry specific accounting systems based on principles set in BAS.[2] These systems are temporary in nature and are not compulsory. They act only as a guide to help businesses to transfer from their old systems to BAS based systems and thus are a means of implementing BAS. They generally consist of a table of accounts and their explanations as well as forms of financial statements and how to prepare them. The accounts and financial statements are derived directly from BAS. Unlike the old UASs, these systems apply the same accounts and treatments to the same or similar transactions, and they all use the same financial statements specified in BAS. Furthermore, the number of these industry specific systems are far fewer than that of the old UASs.

Several implications arise from this change. First, it will result in more consistent and comparable information produced by different accounting entities, which in turn will lead to more meaningful aggregated information. This will benefit users greatly in comparing the performances and financial positions of different companies. Second, when any companies expand their business into a different industry or market, they need not worry about having to comply with different accounting systems. Thus, the corporate management will have less difficulty in evaluating the performances of businesses in different markets or industries. The investors will benefit from this as well. Third, in the long run, the above-mentioned industry specific accounting systems will vanish. This implies that resources and efforts can be saved in setting and implementing these accounting rules and in educating accountants. Finally, domestic harmonization will also make it easier for accountants to transfer from one industry to another.

International harmonization

The Chinese economy was a closed economy prior to the reforms started in the late 1970s. The country had hardly any overseas adventures and few foreign businesses had any investments in the country. The economy was also a tightly centrally planned economy modelled on the former Soviet Union's system. Correspondingly, the old Chinese accounting systems were also closed and centrally controlled. That is, they used principles, concepts and methods quite different from those widely used in market based economies. Because of the nature of the economy, the accounting systems were designed mainly to serve the information needs of government, in order to implement macroeconomic plans. One implication of these characteristics is that it is very difficult to communicate between Chinese and foreign accountants and users of accounting information. It could create barriers for foreign investors in making feasibility studies and other decisions should they intend to invest in the country.

BAS will make financial statements prepared by Chinese companies understandable and communicable, as it has incorporated many internationally accepted features. First, BAS has included accounting entity, accounting period, going concern and monetary measurement as basic assumptions about the environment of accounting systems, in terms of time, space, measurement unit and the future perspective of the entity. These postulates were not explicitly expressed in previous accounting regulations although they were actually the underlying assumptions in accounting practices. Second, BAS has drawn upon qualitative characteristics and accounting principles generally recognized world wide (although some of them were applied before). In the meantime BAS has abandoned some principles previously prevailing under the UASs, such as the mass participation principle. Third, BAS has required the use of the same bookkeeping method that is applied in any other country. Fourth, BAS defines elements and sub-elements of financial statements which are commonly applied in the world. On the other hand it has invalidated a great many concepts under the UASs, such as specific purpose fund source, fixed fund, current fund, and so on. Lastly, BAS has defined three major financial statements which are used globally.

The new system of financial statements distinguishes itself from the old one in two ways. First, the old equation

$$\text{Fund applications} = \text{Fund sources}$$

in the Funds Balance Statement (equivalent to a balance sheet) has been replaced by

$$\text{Assets} = \text{Liabilities} + \text{Owner's equity.}$$

Second, the statement of financial position, or cash flow statement, was not required before and so was not prepared.

Apart from overcoming the above mentioned problems with the old systems, BAS will bridge the gaps in accounting research and education between China and other countries. It is obvious that the formulation of BAS itself has benefited greatly from the conceptual frameworks of the FASB and IASC and from other studies elsewhere. BAS may also bring about more chances for international accounting firms to practise in China.

Market economy orientation

Before China launched its economic reform and implemented an open door policy in the late 1970s, there were almost no companies which were not state owned; a few were collectively owned. Under the planned economic system, there were virtually no markets. Adam Smith's 'invisible hand' had no role to play there at all. The activities of companies had all been fixed by the government in its economic plans. The companies had no choice of their own. The state was the only investor in all companies, except for those collectively owned. The government allocated funds to companies via the Ministry of Finance and/or banks (which were centrally controlled and exclusively state owned).

In this situation, accounting systems were no more than a means of providing information for various levels of government. A main feature of the accounting systems was the nationwide hierarchical network of financial reporting, through which financial statements prepared by individual companies were aggregated all the way up to central government level. Another characteristic was the maintenance of a fund system instead of a capital system, owing to the fact that the state was the sole owner of the companies. Under the fund system, funds from different levels of government were divided into three classes: the fixed fund for fixed assets, the current fund for current assets and the special fund for specific uses. The three classes were not usually permitted to be used interchangeably. This was reflected in the Funds Balance Statement where three sections were maintained for the three classes of funds and their corresponding assets, and each section was supposed to be self-balanced or nearly self-balanced.

However, the economic situation has been changing dramatically since the late 1970s, with a trend toward a market based economy. Several features have emerged. First, the economic role of the government has been changing from the manager of both macro and micro-economies to the manager of the macro-economy only. The government is now not supposed to intervene in business activities of individual companies. Rather it is expected to use indirect means such as monetary policies and fiscal policies to monitor the economy at the macro level. In the meantime, previously existing plans for controlling most of the commodities have vanished. Companies have much more freedom in decision-making and managing their businesses. Second, commodity markets, capital markets, labour markets and technology markets have been developed. The booming stock exchanges in Shanghai and Shenzhen now allow companies to finance their businesses from sources other than the government and the state-controlled banks. Third, there have emerged many types of non-state owned companies, such as Sino-foreign joint ventures, foreign ventures, and especially the rising township enterprises which are private or collectively owned. Even in state-owned companies, the ownership structure has been changing.

Many such companies have been transformed into share-based corporations. Apart from the state, there are other owners, such as employees, external individuals and institutions. The government has established a special bureau, the Bureau for State-owned Assets Management, which acts as the owner on behalf of the state in relation to the shares held in the companies by the state (Zhang 1992). Many domestic private companies have also adopted the share-holding system (Xu 1993).

Obviously, the old accounting systems could not cope with these changes. BAS has thus been developed to re-orient the role of accounting in economic activities. First of all, BAS has relegated accounting policy-making to the companies themselves, although accounting standards setting is still in the hands of the government. This not only represents the yielding of part of the control over accounting by the government to companies but also gives accountancy a role to play in managing the businesses. BAS has also given up the above mentioned fund system and proposed a capital system of accounting for the capital structure of the company. Furthermore, BAS recognizes the uncertainty of the various markets in which a company may be involved and thus permits limited use of prudence as an accounting principle (for example, accelerated depreciation and provision for bad debts).

It is worth noting that one feature of the old accounting system remains unchanged, that is, the national hierarchical reporting system. One reason for this may be that the state is still the major owner of most companies and the government must have control over these companies. Also, accounting information has always been regarded as a major information source for preparing national accounts. As the macro-economic manager, government at various levels needs accounting information for decision-making. Perhaps this is why BAS states that financial accounting and reporting must first satisfy the information needs of macro-economic management.

BAS AS A CONCEPTUAL FRAMEWORK

Framework versus standard

Strictly speaking, there is a difference between a conceptual framework and a standard. The former deals with matters which are general, universal, abstract and fundamental, such as aims, assumptions, principles and elements. It is supposed to provide a structure to layer such fundamental issues in a logical way. The framework should also be capable of being used as a theoretical basis for developing accounting standards. On the other hand, standards involve matters which are specific, such as stock valuation and foreign currency translation. Although they are derived from theories, they should be practical and operational.

This distinction is supported by some of the existing frameworks (see, for example, ASB 1991-2, FASB 1978-85 and IASC 1993). These frameworks are issued as a means of reference for resolving accounting issues in the absence of a specific promulgated standard and as a guide or basis for developing new standards or revising existing standards. They themselves are not issued as standards. They do not override any specific standard.

However, the above distinction is not always clear cut in practice. A statement can be a mixture of both a conceptual framework and standards. Examples of this can be found in the Statements of Accounting Concepts (AARF and ASRB 1990-92) and ED59-65 (NZSA 1991).

BAS is another example of the latter approach. It deals with both fundamental issues and rules on detailed matters. It is issued as a standard but is regarded as a conceptual framework as well.

There is no evidence as to whether one of these two approaches is superior to the other. However, a framework is expected to be more stable than a standard. Thus, it seems desirable to develop the conceptual framework and the standards separately. BAS may be expected to suffer from too frequent changes and amendments in the future because it involves too detailed rules which are liable to revision. Furthermore, there may be some practical problems in developing a mixture of a framework and a standard. For example, the efforts and resources for developing such a statement have to be divided and consequently the resulting document may lack completeness either as a framework or as a standard. We will show next that BAS is weak as a framework because it neglects many fundamental issues or lacks sufficient discussion on some issues. On the other hand, it is obvious that one document cannot cover all of the areas where standards are needed. So we do not expect that BAS is able to provide an all inclusive standard. The following discussion therefore focuses on BAS as a framework.

User information needs and objectives

User information needs and the objectives of financial accounting and reporting are the starting points for developing a conceptual framework, although this is not always agreed upon (see, for example, Most 1982). Because of this, the importance of the issues relating to them cannot be overrated. In most existing frameworks or quasi-frameworks, both user information needs and objectives are discussed in detail.

A fundamental issue is whether or not the information needs of different users are similar or the same. Different views on this lead to different approaches to financial accounting and reporting, that is, general purpose reporting versus special purpose reporting. The former assumes that the information needs of different users are similar, while the latter assumes that they are different. Existing frameworks usually adopt the first approach but acknowledge that differences exist in users' information needs and that a set of general purpose financial statements cannot meet all of the information requirements.

Another important issue is whether or not different users have the same rights to and interests in financial information provided by a company. This involves equity, commercial secrets and information asymmetry. A specific problem arising from this is the moral hazard described in Agency Theory. However, this problem has so far not attracted much attention in conceptual framework formation, except perhaps for the document *Making Corporate Reports Valuable* (ICAS 1988).

Developers of a framework must also choose between stewardship and decision usefulness when setting the objectives of financial accounting and reporting. Decision usefulness has acquired a dominant position in existing frameworks but sometimes stewardship is still retained alongside decision usefulness, for example in the Statements of Accounting Concepts (AARF and ASRB 1990–92) and in *Making Corporate Reports Valuable* (ICAS 1988).

Unlike other frameworks, BAS devotes little discussion to user information needs and objectives. Only a short paragraph in Chapter 2 deals with the topics. Three groups of users and their information needs are distinguished. From this the objectives are also implied, namely that financial accounting and reporting should:

1 Meet the information needs of governments for macro-economy management.
2 Meet the information needs of management for managing a business.
3 Allow relevant parties to know about the financial position and operating results of the business.

It may be inferred from Chapter 9, concerning financial statements, that a general purpose reporting approach is applied in BAS. That is, the same set of financial statements should be provided for all three groups. However, possible differences between the information needs of different groups are not acknowledged and, of course, it is not proposed how to meet these different requirements. In particular, BAS seems to suggest that management information needs are the same as those of external users. This echoes the view held by ICAS (1988) in its document *Making Corporate Reports Valuable*. But BAS and ICAS approach this issue in totally different ways. BAS suggests that general purpose reporting can meet the information needs of management as well as external users while ICAS proposes that external users should be provided with the same information as management. Interestingly it is seen as one of the characteristics of BAS (Ge 1992).

BAS does not discuss users. It generally calls users, other than the government and management, 'relevant parties'. By doing so, BAS provides no reference as to whether or not these relevant parties are equal in terms of their rights to the financial information of a company. On the other hand, BAS seems to suggest that the three groups have equal rights to financial information published for general purposes. Such treatment may be appropriate in the current economic climate where users, apart from the government and management, are of little consequence. However, as the move towards a market economy progresses, more and more private and institutional investors and creditors are emerging. There will certainly be a burgeoning demand for greater recognition of their rights to accounting information.

Although BAS does not elaborate on the objectives that it sets, it does emphasize macro-economy management. It keeps up the tradition. This should not be a problem if the objective is useful and achievable. To assess this, the cost incurred in establishing and running a nationwide reporting system for achieving the objective must be taken into account as a constraint. More significantly, there is no convincing evidence to suggest that such an objective has ever been met in the past. Weetman and Gorden (1988) point out that objectives set in conceptual frameworks are very much matters of opinion which require testing to establish their usefulness. The objectives set in BAS relating to macro-economy management may well be desirable, but equally so are the empirical tests on the objective. It would also be interesting and useful if research were done to compare the Chinese approach to meeting the information needs of macro-economy management with alternatives used elsewhere. These two areas, unfortunately, have not gained the attention of either standard setters or academia.

Qualitative characteristics

Most of the qualitative characteristics described in BAS are similar to those in other frameworks. However, there is room for comment upon the way in which BAS deals with these characteristics.

First, BAS gives a sequential list of the characteristics but does not layer them as do the frameworks of the FASB (1980: SFAC2) and ASB (1991). Layering the characteristics denotes their relative importance. It is possible that BAS may have attached importance weightings to the characteristics according to their position in the sequential list, in which case objectivity is the most important followed by relevance (as implied), comparability, consistency, timeliness, clarity and understandability, completeness and finally materiality. However, BAS provides no rationale for this attachment of weightings. One would therefore ask why relevance is less significant than objectivity, why consistency is less important than comparability and what is the relationship between them, and why understandability should stand after timeliness.

Second, BAS does not acknowledge the conflicts between the characteristics, although it is very likely that trade-offs must be made in order to achieve some of the characteristics, for example, reliability and relevance, and timeliness and completeness. Because of this weakness, BAS of course cannot provide any guidance as to how to make such trade-offs. It must be pointed out that this is also a problem in other frameworks.

Third, BAS fails to operationalize the characteristics. Both the preparers and users of financial reports need to know what constitutes relevant information and what makes information reliable, plus similar questions about other characteristics. In the FASB's framework, relevance consists of ingredients including timeliness, predictive value and feedback value, while reliability consists of ingredients such as verifiability, neutrality and representational faithfulness (FASB 1980: SFAC2). The ASB has made some plausible attempts in this respect (ASB 1991–2). In its draft framework, reliability is operationally defined as freedom from material error and bias and as representational faithfulness, and is further discussed under headings such as substance, valid description and measurement, neutrality, prudence and completeness. Relevance is operationalized as having predictive value and confirmatory value. Comparability is also defined in detailed terms such as consistency, disclosure of accounting policies and compliance with accounting standards. Because BAS does not give any operational definition, the list of the characteristics cannot be expected to have great value.

Noticeably, BAS does not show any interest in freedom from error as a qualitative characteristic. In so doing, reliability is reduced to objectivity, that is, freedom from bias (which is only one of the dimensions of liability).

Lastly, BAS fails to see cost as a constraint to obtaining useful information. Not only will this mislead accounting practices but it may also have led the preparer of this framework to give less consideration to the objective relating to macro-economy management.

Balance sheet centred approach v. income statement centred approach

In defining elements of financial statements, in setting recognition criteria and in choosing a measurement system, two different views are available: the asset and liability view and the revenue and expense view. The former is also referred to as the balance sheet centred approach (BSCA) and the latter as the income statement centred approach (ISCA). Solomons (1989) provides a detailed description of the two approaches.

BSCA has become rather popular recently and is followed in the frameworks or quasi-frameworks of the FASB, IASC,

Solomons, NZSA and ASB. However, there are some doubts about this view. One argument against it is that it tends to make income a more volatile figure than the other approach and so is not as good a representation of 'sustainable income'. Solomons attacks this argument by saying that 'sustainable income' is not an accounting concept and volatility is a fact of life (Solomons 1989: 18). Another doubt concerns practicability from the point of view of preparers of accounts, as this approach is a great departure from the implicit rules on recognition which are currently applied (Davies *et al.* 1992: 83). Finally, this approach is not workable at all under the historical cost accounting system, yet no alternative measurement has been developed and generally accepted (Davies *et al.* 1992: 85). Ernst & Young, in a recent discussion on the above mentioned ASB's draft framework, provides further arguments against this approach (Ernst & Young 1993). The firm holds that the balance sheet does not and cannot properly reflect the worth of a company and that the value of a company lies in its ability to generate future cash, not in the individual values of its present assets and liabilities. The firm also points out that financial reporting is not primarily a matter of valuation. It is the market which puts a value on a company, although accounting provides information for this purpose. Furthermore, the BSCA blocks good accounting practices by excluding all deferred costs and revenues from the balance sheet if they fail to meet the definition of assets and liabilities.

ISCA is favoured in Statement No. 4 of the Accounting Principles Board (AICPA 1970) and has prevailed in practice. However, it has also met several criticisms. One such is targeted at the abuse of the matching principle. Solomons argues that it opens the door to all kinds of income smoothing and that in general it leaves management free to decide what goes into the profit and loss account and what goes into the balance sheet (Solomons 1989: 18). This is said to be why preparers of financial statements mostly favour it. In Solomons' terms, this view also threatens the integrity of the balance sheet and its value as a useful financial statement. The use of LIFO is taken as an example.

BAS keeps to ISCA. It does not base its definition of profit on that of assets and liabilities. It does not think that there is a problem of recognition of assets and liabilities. It is not bothered to look for a new measurement attribute, rather it accepts the historical cost accounting convention. Matching and accrual are considered as two major principles among others and no constraints have been placed upon the application of the two principles. By following this approach, BAS complies with the current prevailing practice. However, although BAS favours ISCA, it defines revenues and expenses on the basis of its definition of assets and liabilities. This provides another example for Solomons who favours BSCA and who argues that, even under ISCA, revenues and expenses often have to be defined as the changes of assets and liabilities (Solomons 1989: 17). Furthermore, no matter what approach is taken by a framework, it should be able to develop useful and sensible measurement rules. However, the discussion under the next heading shows that this poses a serious problem with BAS.

Measurement system

Accounting measurement is perhaps one of the most difficult areas that standard setters encounter. The choice of a measurement attribute must answer some hard questions, such as whether relevant and reliable information can be obtained, whether the proposed measurement system is practical, and what capital maintenance concept should be used. However, these issues cause no problem if there are no continuous price changes.

Existing frameworks or quasi-frameworks either decline to prefer a particular measurement system and to suggest any improvements to existing systems or else run into trouble in trying to provide sufficient rationale for their preferences. Examples of the former are the frameworks of the FASB and the IASC. The latter is exemplified by the document *Making Corporate Reports Valuable* (ICAS 1988), which advocates the net realizable value, and by the Solomons Report which uses a concept of value to business (Solomons 1989). Perhaps because of this difficulty, the ASB has not been able to issue the chapter concerning measurement together with other chapters of its Statement of Principles (ASB 1991–2).

BAS does not avoid this problem. It openly adheres to the historical cost accounting system and does not even discuss any alternatives. However, this choice may be rather arbitrary because inflation has been a fact of life in the country.[3] By ignoring this fact, the choice made by BAS lacks a sense of capital maintenance, because in periods of price changes capital maintenance is problematic under the historical accounting system. Similarly, it lacks a sense of the importance of relevance as a qualitative characteristic because, given that inflation is a fact, information produced under the historical cost accounting system is hardly relevant although it may well be objective and reliable.

Capital maintenance

Capital maintenance is another major concern in developing a conceptual framework, especially when price change is a permanent phenomenon. However, it is a difficult area. First, this is because there are several variants of the concept of capital maintenance, such as physical capital, money financial capital and real financial capital. To choose a concept, to use it consistently and to make the concept practical is no easy task. Second, maintaining capital involves many aspects, such as the choice of a measurement system, the choice of a depreciation method and the choice of a stock valuation method.

No agreement has been reached as to which concept should be applied. The FASB's framework fails to prescribe a particular concept of capital maintenance that should be adopted by a company although the FASB bases its discussion on the concept of financial capital maintenance (FASB 1984: SFAC5). The IASC describes different concepts of capital maintenance but does not show its preference in its framework (IASC 1993). The concept of physical capital maintenance was used as the basis for discussion in the Sandilands Report (Inflation Accounting Committee 1975), while the Solomons Report insists on the concept of real financial capital maintenance (Solomons 1989).

Although BAS allows the use of LIFO and the accelerated depreciation method in a limited way, and this may have some effect on capital maintenance, BAS generally fails to incorporate the concept of capital maintenance. This can be seen from the fact that it does not discuss the concept at all and the fact that it exclusively chooses the historical cost accounting system. It may be at least partly because of this lack of a sense of capital maintenance that all alternative measurement systems are excluded from consideration.

There are other problems in BAS as a framework. For example, it defines the elements but does not discuss their attributes (Ge 1993). Moreover, the definitions of the elements also have room for doubts (for example, some of them may be too loose).

This section is quite critical of BAS, in the hope that such criticism may help to improve it in its future development. In summary, the following weak points existing within BAS may be worthy of consideration.

1 Neglect of user information needs and their differences.
2 Neglect of the importance of relevance as a qualitative characteristic and no attention paid to freedom from error which is a major dimension of reliable information.
3 Failure to see cost as a major constraint upon producing useful information and achieving the objectives of financial accounting and reporting.
4 Failure to provide a frame of reference about how to use the qualitative characteristics in preparing and using financial reports.
5 Failure to discuss the attributes of the elements of financial statements.
6 Lack of a sense of capital maintenance.
7 Neglect of the fact of price changes.
8 Lack of sufficient rationale for adopting the historical cost accounting system while ignoring all of the alternatives.

CONCLUSION

Admittedly, BAS has made a breakthrough in contrast with the old UASs. Its impact as both a standard and a conceptual framework on accounting practice, research and education will be far reaching. It may be expected to improve, to some extent, both domestic and international harmonization of accounting practices and to push Chinese accounting practice, research and education towards the requirements of a market oriented economy.

However, there is much room for improvement in BAS as a conceptual framework. A conceptual framework should be prescriptive rather than descriptive, but BAS fails in this. Because what is described in BAS is new to China, it is inappropriate to label BAS as a descriptive framework. Undoubtedly, BAS has proposed changes to the old UASs and does represent a real reform, but BAS is actually rather conservative in terms of looking to the future. For example, it does not discuss shareholders and creditors as separate user groups and therefore neglects their information needs. This problem may have arisen because BAS restricts itself too much to the current economic situation where shareholders and creditors are still very few in number. However, the trend towards a market oriented economy will lead to an enormous growth in their numbers. Apart from this, BAS has taken a far too simplistic approach. That is, it avoids or neglects too many fundamental issues or fails to elaborate on many equally important topics. As a result, BAS fails to provide prescriptive references for the preparers and users of financial reports in many areas.

NOTES

1   For example, Audit Regulations (1988), Accounting Act (1985), Certified Accountants Regulations (1986), Chief Accountants Regulations (1990), Financial Guidelines for Business Enterprises (1992) and Provisional Regulations on Managing Security Issues and Exchanges (1993).
2   The industry specific accounting systems that have been issued include those for industrial enterprises; commercial enterprises; post and communications enterprises; transportation and communications enterprises; banking and financial services; tourism services; construction enterprises; foreign economic co-operation enterprises; and agricultural enterprises.
3   The inflation rates of the retail price of goods from 1980 to 1989 are shown in Table 10.1.

Table 10.1 Inflation rates of retail prices of goods, 1980–9 (previous year as base year)

Year	1980	1981	1982	1983	1984	1985	1986	1987	1988	1989
Rate	6.0	2.4	1.9	1.5	2.8	8.8	6.0	7.3	18.5	17.8

Sources: For 1980–88, China State Statistics Bureau (1989); for 1989, China State Statistics Bureau (1990)

REFERENCES

Accounting Standards Board, (1991–2) *Statement of Principles; Ch. 1: The Objectives of Accounting Standards* (ED, July 1991); *Ch. 2: The Qualitative Characteristics of Financial Information* (ED, July 1991); *Ch. 3: The Elements of Financial Statements* (Discussion Draft, July 1991); *Ch. 4: The Recognition of Items in Financial Statements* (Discussion Draft, July 1992); *Ch. 6: Presentation of Financial Information* (ED, December 1991), London: ASB.

American Institute of Certified Public Accountants (1970) Statement of the Accounting Principles Board, no. 4: Basic Concepts and Accounting Principles Underlying Financial Statements of Business Enterprises, New York: AICPA.

Australian Accounting Research Foundation and Accounting Standards Review Board (1990–92) *Statement of Accounting Concepts (SAC) 1: Definition of the Reporting Entity* (1990); *SAC2: Objective of General Purpose Financial Reporting* (1990); *SAC3: Qualitative Characteristics of Financial Information* (1990); *SAC4: Definition and Recognition of Elements of Financial Statements* (1992), Melbourne: AARF and ASRB.

China State Statistics Bureau (1989) *China Statistical Yearbook*, Beijing.
—— (1990) 'Statistical Statements on national social and economic development in 1989', *People's Daily*, 21 February, p. 2.

Davies, M., Paterson, R. and Wilson, A. (1992) *Generally Accepted Accounting Practice in the United Kingdom* (UK GAAP; 3rd edn), London Ernst & Young.

Ernst & Young (1993) 'ASB has got it wrong, says E & Y', *Accountancy*, October, p. 11.

Financial Accounting Standards Board (1978–85) *Statement of Financial Accounting Concepts (SFAC) 1: Objectives of Financial Reporting by Business Enterprises* (1978); *SFAC 2: Qualitative Characteristics of Accounting Information* (1980); *SFAC 4: Objectives of Financial Reporting by Non-Business Enterprises* (1980); *SFAC 5: Recognition and Measurement in Financial Statements of Business Enterprises* (1984); *SFAC 6: Elements of Financial Statements*, Stamford, Conn: FASB.

Ge, J.-S. (1992) 'Learning from international experience to establish Chinese accounting standards', *Accounting Research*, no. 2, pp. 16–19.
—— (1993) 'The basic characteristics of China Business Accounting Standards', *Accounting Research*, no. 1.

Inflation Accounting Committee (1975) *Inflation Accounting: Report of the Inflation Accounting Committee* (chaired by F. E. P. Sandilands: Sandilands Report), London: Her Majesty's Stationery Office.

Institute of Chartered Accountants in Scotland (1988) *Making Corporate Reports Valuable*, London: Kogan Page.

International Accounting Standards Committee (1993) 'Framework for the preparation and presentation of financial statements', in *International Accounting Standards*, London: IASC.

Most, K. S. (1982) *Accounting Theory* (2nd edn), Columbus, Ohio: Grid Publishing.

New Zealand Society of Accountants (1991) *ED59: Explanatory Foreword to General Purpose External Financial Reporting*; *ED60: Concepts for General Purpose External Financial Reporting*; *ED61: Interpreting Concepts for General Purpose External Financial Reporting for Public Sector Entities*; *ED62: Framework for Differential Reporting*; *ED63: Application of Differential Reporting to Statements of Standard Accounting Practice 3 to 28*; *ED64 FRS1: Disclosure of Accounting Policies*; *ED65 FRS2: Presentation of Financial Reports* (all December), Wellington: NZSA.

Solomons, D. (1989) *Guidelines for Financial Reporting Standards* (Solomons Report), prepared for the Institute of Chartered Accountants in England and Wales and addressed to the Accounting Standards Committee, London: ICAEW.

Weetman, P. and Gorden, D. P. (1988) 'The philosophy and objectives of external corporate reporting, including users and their information needs', in ICAS, *Making Corporate Reports Valuable*, the Literature Review, London: Kogan Page, pp. 21–73.

Xu, X. (1993) 'Capital market development in China: the role of the private sector', *Chinese Economic Association Newsletter*, (CEA, UK) 5 (2).

Zhang, W. (1992) *Transforming Companies with Share Holding: The System in China*, Beijing: Beijing Publishing House.

Zhang, Y. (1981) *The Increase/Decrease Bookkeeping System*, Beijing: China Financial and Economic Publishing House.

Chapter 11

A comparison of international and Chinese accounting standards

Z. Liu and S. Turley

INTRODUCTION

The political and economic changes that have taken place in recent years in a number of countries, which were previously not well represented in the development of accounting at an international level, have given opportunities to observe the interaction between national traditions and international approaches in new and different environments. As countries have sought to promote international trade and economic growth, accounting has been seen as an important mechanism for facilitating such development. The People's Republic of China (PRC) is one such country where, over recent years, the economy has become more open to international interaction and where there has been major development in its accounting systems. This chapter reviews and evaluates the nature of accounting change that has taken place in China, particularly as judged against the benchmark of International Accounting Standards.

China provides an interesting case for observing accounting development for several reasons. The history of accounting in China reflects a number of influences, but the predominant traditions are very different to those exhibited in the mainly Western influenced international standards. The changes that have been introduced represent a fundamental redirection of accounting. These changes have been seen as necessary in order to promote certain national economic objectives, a different priority from that which has influenced the development of most international standards. Further, because of the fundamental nature of the changes introduced, the regulations have had to address many aspects of what would be involved in a conceptual framework for accounting in China.

The chapter is organized into five main sections. First there is a brief introduction to International Accounting Standards and their use subsequently for comparison with Chinese standards. This is followed by an outline of the history and traditions of Chinese accounting up to the point at which new standards were introduced in 1992. The third section describes the main structure and components of these standards before, in the fourth section, they are compared to the approach used in international standards. Finally, some concluding observations are made.

INTERNATIONAL ACCOUNTING STANDARDS

The standards of the International Accounting Standards Committee (IASC) are generally recognized as the most important source of recommendation on accounting at a global level (Nobes and Parker 1991, Radebaugh and Gray 1993). While in individual countries national or regional regulations will be more important, International Accounting Standards (IASs) provide international norms against which multinational reporting can be assessed.

Since it was established in 1973, the IASC, which comprises over 100 professional organizations from over 80 countries, has sought to harmonize financial reporting between various countries through issuing standards on different accounting topics. To date the IASC has published thirty-one standards (IASC 1993), covering basic accounting topics, more specialized topics which have become important over time, and disclosure requirements. In addition to the IASs, the IASC has issued a *Framework for the Preparation and Presentation of Financial Statements* (see IASC 1993). The IASC has also been pursuing a medium-term strategy of revising international standards to increase their comparability with national accounting requirements (IASC 1988), and has placed emphasis on the financial reporting needs of developing and newly industrialized countries.

Given the status and comprehensiveness of the publications of the IASC, they together provide a suitable basis for comparison with the ruling national standards in a country such as China. The espoused objective of the IASC to give priority to the needs of developing and industrializing countries also makes comparison between the new Chinese standards and IASs of interest from the perspective of IASC itself. For these reasons, the approach followed later in this Chapter to the evaluation of developments in Chinese accounting will rely on using IASC statements as the basis for assessment.

AN ABBREVIATED HISTORY OF CHINESE ACCOUNTING DEVELOPMENT

New accounting regulations were introduced in China on 30 December 1992, to be effective from 1 July 1993. The new rules, which are contained in two documents, 'Accounting Standards for Business Enterprises' and 'Financial Guidelines for Business Enterprises', involve a substantial amount of change in the system of accounting in China. In order to assess the signifi-cance of the changes introduced, it will be helpful first to review briefly the background of Chinese accounting and its historical development.

Chinese accounting before 1949

The history of accounting in China can be traced back 2,000 years. The earliest form of accounting appears in the record of the government offices of the Western Zhou Dynasty (11th century BC to 770 BC):

> Under King Zhou six official positions were created: Heaven official, Earth official, Spring official, Summer official, Autumn official and Winter official. The Heaven official, also called the major governor, was in charge of finance and accounting; the Earth official was in charge of education and taxation. Under the Heaven official two divisions were established, one respon-sible for storage and management of properties and wealth, while the other maintained the accounting system by recording receipts and disbursements.
>
> (Lu 1988: 122)

During the Tang Dynasty (AD 618–907), a budgeting system was established which could control the annual fiscal revenues from subordinate units and which applied the principle of 'budgeting fiscal receipts on the basis of fiscal disbursements'. Furthermore, annual financial accounting statements were produced (Lu 1988).

Further developments were apparent in the period of the Song Dynasty (AD 960–1279) when government accounting was rather more comprehensive and the 'Four Pillar Accounts' statement was used (Liu 1993). The four pillars were called 'original holding', 'newly received', 'newly disposed' and 'actually existing'. They are equivalent to the modern accounting concepts of 'opening balance', 'increase in current period', 'decrease in period' and 'closing balance'. This method established the fundamental basis of traditional Chinese accounting statements.

Accounting in business enterprises developed slowly in China because such organizations were few in what was a feudal society. During the Ming Dynasty (AD 1368–1644), the book-keeping method of *long men zhang* was created. This method was similar to double entry bookkeeping and was employed to provide records for traditional Chinese industry, especially in Zi Gong city of Sichuan province, which used to be a large salt producing area.

It was not until the twentieth century, however, when a large number of students went to Western countries as part of an effort to develop China's economy, that the debit credit double entry system was introduced. Xie Lin, one of the students who learned accounting in Japan, set up the first double entry book-keeping system for the bank of the Qing Dynasty in 1901 (see *Finance and Accounting* (Chinese journal), 1980). Although the introduction of Western methods was a significant point of development in Chinese accounting, it was not universally welcomed and:

> triggered a debate amongst accountants and academics in China. Those who favoured the traditional accounting system maintained that it was not necessary to follow a foreign accounting system, and that the traditional accounting system could survive in the new environment if necessary improvements were made. The resistance to adoption of the double-entry accounting system was, however, bound to fail. The new accounting system was soon installed in some of the large enterprises. In the universities, accounting and auditing textbooks published in the United States and the United Kingdom were used in teaching, and the influence of the western accounting system became established.
>
> (Tang *et al.* 1992: 2)

Chinese accounting 1949–78

1949–57: new accounting systems established

Since the creation of the PRC in 1949, China has been a centrally planned economy, under which all economic activities are carried out according to a State Plan. Individual enterprises have thus functioned as grass-root units of the national economy. The accounting system was stipulated by the government's Department of Administration of Accounting Affairs (DAAA; later to become the Department of Accounting Systems), under the Ministry of Finance (MOF), which is charged with full responsibility for directing and administering accounting affairs nationwide. In addition, industrial and local government bodies are empowered, subject to government approval, to issue detailed supplementary regulations and procedures whenever necessary.

When a new accounting system was established in 1950, Western accounting was considered unsuitable for the Chinese economic system and consequently the approach followed was based on the Soviet Union's methods. Between 1950 and 1955 many Russian experts visited China and helped the government to establish the new system. The Financial and Economic Committee of the State Council of China (FECSCC) published a Directive (on 9 March 1950) requiring unified accounting systems for enterprises within the area of responsibility of each government department. At about the same time the Department of Accounting Systems required every government department to submit to it their draft accounting system. From July 1950, different government branches developed and announced their unified accounting systems, which were then 'audited' by the FECSCC. The MOF published the 'Unified Chart of Accounts for State Industrial Enterprises' (December 1952) and announced certain special rules on accounting and financial management, for example the 'Temporary Regulations on Withdrawal of Profit for State Enterprises' (published in the *Journal of New Accounting*, 1951).

By 1952, complete accounting systems had been set up and the information they produced could provide the basis for national economic statistics. Generally each system comprised eight chapters dealing with: an overview, accounting statements, chart of accounts, books of account, accounting documents, accounting

procedures, organization of accounting and supplementary procedures. During the decades which followed some modifications
were made to accounting systems and additional rules and regulations were introduced.

The nature of this accounting system is one based on recognition of individual lines of business or economic sectors and
individual forms of ownership. It is a model which was suitable
for a product economy under centralized administration and it
played an important role in the Chinese centrally planned
economy over a considerable period of time.

1958–61: set-backs for accounting development

During this period, accounting became progressively less important. The national government wanted to reform management
methods and to devolve authority to the local government or
enterprise level. Under the influence of a strong Communist
philosophy, it was felt that the key to economic growth was the
enthusiasm of the workforce, and that this could be released by
devolving power to lower levels. Emphasis was placed on simplified working practices and, consistent with this, the MOF
introduced simplified rules for accounting systems and reporting. Attempts were made to reduce the number of government
officers and government expenditure, and as a result many
accounting officers were moved into other work. Clerical, office
or administrative activities were considered to be of less value
than practical work and it was thought that genuine knowledge
comes from practice. Taken to extremes, this approach resulted
in financial control being completely removed and in very limited accounting records, with reliance placed on people's con-
sciences. Over this period accounting became very weak and in
some areas there was little or no financial reporting. It became
difficult to determine exactly what was the state of national
enterprise and property.

1962–June 1966: a renewed emphasis on accounting

Between 1962 and 1966, the Chinese economy experienced serious
difficulties and the Soviet Union withdrew much of its support.
The government was forced to consider adjusting the national
economic plan. When re-evaluating government property, the

problems of incorrect and incomplete accounting records became apparent. Chinese leaders came to recognize the importance of accounting and re-established accounting rules and regulations. At the same time, many of the accounting positions which had been eliminated between 1957 and 1959 were reinstated. The re-established financial rules and regulations included 'Regulations on Duties and Rights of Accounting Personnel' (1963), accounting regulations for each department of government, and so on. During this period the first accountancy meeting to discuss accounting practice and theory was held in Beijing in 1962.

At the same time, some Chinese accounting experts continued to advocate the use of the traditional Chinese accounting system, and set up an increase/decrease double entry bookkeeping system. At the end of 1965, the Ministry of Commerce announced the use of this approach for commercial enterprises. This then spread to small and medium sized industrial enterprises. Thus, at that time, three kinds of double entry approach were concurrently being used in China: the increase/decrease, debit/credit and receipt/disbursement double entry bookkeeping systems.

During this period accounting was given considerable prominence. Many accountants were trained in special accounting schools and in colleges and universities. By 1965 18 colleges and universities offered accounting courses (compared with only 5 in 1954) together with 21 special accounting schools, and a total of 18,200 students were studying accounting, a considerable rise from the figure of 2,400 only three years earlier in 1962 (Yi 1986).

July 1966–1978: the effects of the Cultural Revolution

Another reversal in the position of accounting in Chinese economic life occurred as the Cultural Revolution began to influence working and living conditions. Although accounting continued, accounting records were very weak and there were less than 100 people working in the MOF. Accounting education at university was almost completely stopped for about ten years. For some five years no university offered accounting and by 1976 the figure had only risen to seven (Yi 1986). The model of accounting being applied continued to be that which had been adopted from the Soviet Union, although with some modifications introduced over the years.

Chinese accounting history 1978–93

1978–88: the role of accounting reasserted

After the Cultural Revolution, a new phase of reform in the Chinese economy began, with the object of modernizing and developing its productive capacity. For the purposes of monitoring the new situation the Chinese Accounting System was revised. A number of stages are evident in this process.

First, the State Council issued a directive which permitted every enterprise to value its assets and property. The statistical information which resulted, concerning the established property of the entire country, gave a measure of Chinese economic power at that time.

Second, different parts of the Chinese government issued a variety of accounting rules and regulations. There are five main government offices involved in regulating accounting:

1 The National People's Congress (NPC), which enacts the law of China.
2 The State Council (SC), which issues certain rules concerning enterprise management.
3 The Ministry of Finance (MOF), which issues the accounting rules and regulations.
4 The State Taxes Bureau (STB), which issues taxation law.
5 The State Auditing Bureau (SAB), which issues rules for enterprise auditing.

The relationships between these different sources of authority are shown in Figure 11.1.

The Accounting Law of the People's Republic of China, announced by the National People's Congress in 1985, represents the overriding regulatory authority for accounting. Examples of the regulations introduced or approved by the other structures referred to above are set out in Table 11.1, giving an indication of the diversity of accounting related rule-making in China.

The third stage in the development of the modern Chinese accounting system followed from China becoming more open to the rest of the world. Many joint venture companies, involving collaboration between Chinese and foreign investment, were set up and the government issued new rules to accommodate the fact

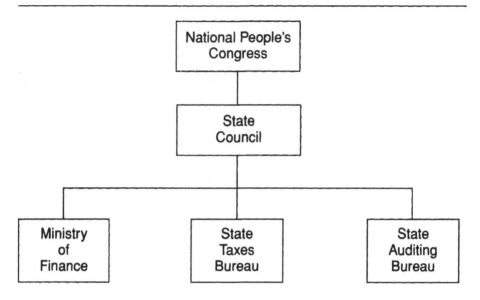

Figure 11.1 Sources of accounting regulation in China

that these enterprises differ from native Chinese companies. The rules included the Law on Joint Ventures Using Chinese and Foreign Investment (1985) enacted by the NPC; 'Accounting Regulations for Joint Ventures Using Chinese and Foreign Investment' (1985) and 'Chart of Accounts and Forms of Accounting Statements for Industrial Joint Ventures Using Chinese and Foreign Investment' (1985), both of which were issued by the MOF.

Most significantly, the accounting regulations for Sino-foreign joint ventures changed the traditional manner of accounting away from the Soviet Union model (Quan 1993). These regulations represented a first attempt at something which could provide a basis for unified accounting standards.

These accounting rules and regulations played an important role in the recent development of the Chinese national economy. However, the position remained that there was no unified system for every enterprise and companies in different areas of the economy followed different accounting systems. This not only made it difficult for potential foreign partners to evaluate Chinese business opportunities but also created problems for the Chinese themselves. The Chinese government therefore decided to introduce unified accounting standards, based on the joint venture regulations.

Table 11.1 Examples of regulations relevant to accounting from different governmental sources in China

Rules issued by the State Council

Rules of Cost Management for State-owned Enterprises (1984)
Tentative Regulations on Fixed Asset Depreciation for State-owned
  Enterprises (1985)
Provisional Rule on Cash Management (1989)
Regulations on Duties and Rights of Accounting Personnel (1978)
Regulations on Compilation and Submission of Financial Statements
  (1985)
Certified Public Accountants Regulations of the People's Republic of
  China (1986)

Rules approved by the Ministry of Finance

Accounting systems of various government departments (1980–88), e.g.
  Accounting Regulations for State Construction Enterprises — Chart
  of Accounts and Accounting Statements (1981)
Accounting systems of various collective departments (1980–88), e.g.
  Accounting Regulations on County and District Enterprises (1986)
  Accounting Personnel Working Rules (1984)
  Management of Accounting Records (1984)

Rules announced by the State Taxes Bureau

Income Tax Law for Industrial and Commercial Enterprises and the
  Detailed Regulations on Implementation (1985)
Production, Operation and Value Added Tax Law for Industrial and
  Commercial Enterprises and the Detailed Regulations on
  Implementation (1985)

Rules announced by the State Auditing Bureau

Internal Auditing Rules (1985)
Auditing Regulation of the People's Republic of China (1988)

1988–93: the development of modern Chinese accounting

In October 1988, the Department of Administration of Accounting Affairs under the MOF set up a Task Force on Accounting Standards and gave it responsibility for researching, designing and drafting accounting standards. The previous year, the annual convention of the Accounting Society of China had decided to change its approach to accounting research promotion, in order to help accounting to play a more active role in economic reform, and had appointed seven research groups, one of which was the Research Group on Accounting Theory and Accounting

Standards. Together the efforts of these initiatives resulted in the announcement of the 'Accounting Standards for Business Enterprises' on 30 November 1992 (MOF 1992a). To co-ordinate implementation, the Department of Industrial and Communications Administration of Financial Affairs, under the MOF, also introduced the 'Financial Guidelines for Business Enterprises' (MOF 1992b). This step in accounting standardization represents a major point of development in Chinese accounting history as it involves a general move away from the Soviet Union model, which had been followed for many years, and towards international accounting standards.

According to Liu Zhongli, China's Minister of Finance (reported in *China Daily*, 4 December 1992), the most significant areas of change resulting from the introduction of the standard are:

1 Accounting systems have been unified in a way which is applicable to all enterprises established within the PRC.
2 Domestic enterprises have been permitted to use accelerated depreciation methods in order to promote technological updating.
3 Manufacturing cost methods have been adopted for the measurement of production costs, instead of the previous full cost method, meaning that administration and selling expenses are now excluded.
4 Standards for capital maintenance are to be used to help to reduce financial losses.
5 The structure of accounts is to reflect an accounting equation of

$$\text{Assets} = \text{Liabilities} + \text{Owner's equity}$$

instead of the funds based formula used previously, where

$$\text{Fund applications} = \text{Fund sources.}$$

In addition to the two main regulations referred to above, there are still accounting standards and financial regulations for thirteen individual lines of business, which were re-established to play a supporting role to the new standards. There are also some provisional regulations in areas to be covered by later, more detailed accounting standards. At the same time, other accounting regulations, covering individual lines of business or individual economic sectors and individual forms of ownership, were cancelled, with the exception of those relating to enterprises involving foreign investment.

As a result of the changes introduced in the accounting standards, the Accounting Law of the PRC, which was designed to meet the needs of state enterprises alone, has been modified. The Eighth National People's Congress approved the new law on 31 December 1993. The NPC also announced a Certified Public Accountants Law (on 31 October 1993). The structure of the Chinese accounting system following these changes is shown in Figure 11.2.

Summary

The above brief outline indicates that, rather than following a steady path of development, Chinese accounting has undergone a number of radical redirections. At various times accounting has been emphasized and ignored, and has followed traditional

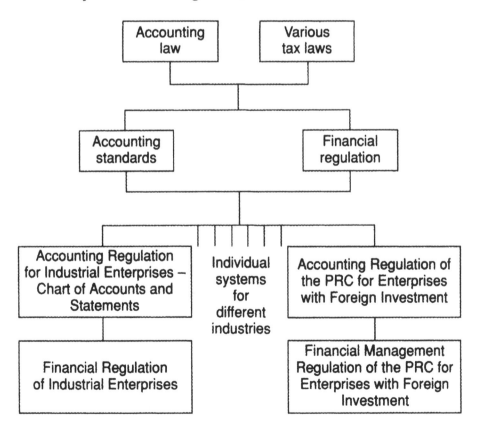

Figure 11.2 The structure of the Chinese accounting system

Chinese, Russian and Western approaches. The character of the Chinese system has been such that not only has it been subject to frequent change but also most of its recent experience has been based on non-western accounting approaches.

It is important to recognize this context as the background into which the recent standards and rules have been introduced. As will be shown later, these regulations effectively mark a move towards Western accounting practice, but the record of change in recent decades might suggest caution before concluding that the move is irreversible. The diversity in the history of Chinese accounting also raises questions about both the potential applicability of Western or international accounting approaches as a means of serving Chinese information needs and their likely success or ease of adoption. It is possible that, although the Standards will make Chinese enterprise more open to external participation, it will take some time before the entire domestic economy accommodates the new informational approach.

It is also interesting to note that the character of the system that is being introduced will impose a higher degree of uniformity in accounting than was previously the case. It is intended to eliminate much of the variation that has existed between accounting in different sectors and to move to a single common model, largely derived from the approach first introduced to accommodate the needs of joint ventures involving international investment.

The recent changes in regulation indicate a current desire to have forms of accounting that are appropriate for reporting on the individual enterprise. In the past, governmental control of state enterprises and resources dictated the objectives of accounting and there was little interest in the performance of the individual organization. Many enterprises are now more independent and the government itself is keen to promote forms of organization which can help to bring foreign capital into the Chinese economy. As a result, accounting for the enterprise has become much more important.

A final point worth noting is that, partly because of the recent history of Chinese accounting, the reforms have involved the laying down of the fundamentals of financial reporting. Although in no way equivalent to the scale or level of detail exhibited in the efforts of accounting regulators in some other countries, the new standards and rules have effectively had to address aspects of a 'conceptual framework' for accounting and to establish principles and concepts which have not previously been recognized or written down.

CHINESE ACCOUNTING STANDARDS AND FINANCIAL REGULATION

This section of the Chapter provides an outline description of the structure of Chinese accounting standards and financial regulations for business enterprises and the elements in these documents that have introduced major changes to the previous position.

Accounting standards

The new Chinese Accounting Standards comprise sixty-six articles organized into ten chapters, which provide statements concerning: a general overview of standardized accounting (Chapter 1), accounting principles (Chapter 2), accounting elements (Chapters 3–8), financial statements (Chapter 9), and some supplementary provisions (Chapter 10).

The first chapter on 'General provisions' provides an overview of points such as the aim of standardization (Article 1), the enterprises subject to the rules (Articles 2 and 3), the accounting period (Article 6), the unit of monetary measurement (Article 7) and the recording language (Article 9). The chapter also contains statements regarding the qualities of accounting, that it should 'accurately account' for transactions and 'provide reports of reliable quality' (Article 4), the assumption of a going concern (Article 5) and the standard use of debit/credit double entry bookkeeping (Article 8). Although issues concerning the purpose of accounting regulation were previously part of accounting theory in China and were also implicit in the old accounting systems, this is the first time that such matters have been explicitly written down in regulations.

A total of twelve principles are specified in Chapter 2. They refer to: representational faithfulness (Article 10), relevance for the users of accounts (Article 11), comparability (Article 12), consistency (Article 13), timeliness (Article 14), clarity and understandability (Article 15), accruals (Article 16), matching (Article 17), prudence (Article 18), historic cost valuation (Article 19), the distinction between revenue and capital expenditure (Article 20) and completeness (Article 21). Again, while many of these principles were implicit in the old accounting systems and Chinese accounting practices, this is the first time that they have been collected together and formally written down.

It is interesting to note the content of the article setting a standard of relevance to the needs of users (Article 11), as this refers to three rather distinct purposes: 'the requirements of national macro-economy control, the needs of all concerned external users to understand an enterprise's financial position and operating results, and the needs of management of enterprises to strengthen their financial management and administration'. It is ambitious, at the very least, to seek to meet all of these objectives through one set of measures, and there is no acknowledgement of the potential conflicts between them or of the limits on general purpose financial statements for meeting varied information needs.

The six chapters devoted to accounting elements deal in turn with: assets, liabilities, owner's equity, revenue, expenses and profit and loss. The concept of owner's equity and the focus on capital rather than funds are new developments in Chinese accounting. The accounting standards provide, for each of these elements, basic definitions and rules dealing with recognition, measurement, recording and reporting. A number of accounting methods and measurement issues are referred to in the regulations, including, for example, bad debt provisions, stock valuation, accelerated depreciation, and the equity method of accounting for long-term investments. The content of these rules in some ways makes aspects of accounting measurement more active and flexible than previously.

Three financial accounting statements are recognized in Chapter 9: balance sheet (Article 58), income statement (Article 59) and statement of changes in financial position (Article 60). Consolidated financial statements are required where there is ownership of 50 per cent or more of the capital of another enterprise (Article 63). There are also rules concerning disclosure of financial information in notes to the accounts (Article 64). The main changes resulting from this section of the Standards are the form and content of the financial statements, the introduction of a statement of changes in financial position and the new requirement for consolidated accounts.

Financial guidelines for business enterprises

In addition to the Standards, the 'Financial Guidelines for Business Enterprises' contain a number of matters of accounting significance. These rules are intended to 'meet the needs of developing the market economy in our country, normalize the financial behaviour of the enterprises so as to conduce to fair competition among enterprises, strengthen their financial management and economic calculation' (Article 1). The forty-six articles in the Guidelines are contained in twelve chapters, covering: general provisions (Chapter 1), raising funds (Chapter 2), the financial management of assets, expenditure and profit (Chapters 3–8), foreign currency (Chapter 9), liquidation of enterprises (Chapter 10), financial reports (Chapter 11) and supplementary provisions (Chapter 12).

The general provisions state that the fundamental principles of financial management include to 'reflect truthfully the enterprise's financial situation' (Article 4). This is the first time that aims, principles and methods of financial management have been established in official regulations.

The chapter dealing with the raising of funds includes certain points relating to the accounting for equity capital and long-term debt. Equity may be subscribed by the state, by corporate bodies, by individuals and by foreigners. The rules state that any surplus on capital subscribed, including stock premiums, must be taken into capital reserves, as must surplus arising from the revaluation of assets. Such reserves can be converted into other forms of capital, subject to certain regulations, but withdrawal of capital is not allowed except for certain legally permitted transfers. Although the content of these rules is very limited and superficial in comparison with the volume of detail contained in accounting regulations in many Western countries, they are of interest because they indicate the adoption of a system of accounting which is equity capital based and which applies notions of capital maintenance commonly found elsewhere in the world.

Six chapters deal with aspects of financial management, including certain accounting issues concerning valuation and profit measurement, for: current assets; fixed assets; intangible, deferred and other assets; external investment; cost and expenses; and operating revenues, profits and their distribution.

For example, the standard includes a number of changes in permissible methods for depreciation of fixed assets. Classifications of the life of fixed assets and of legitimate methods of their depreciation are determined by the MOF, but the enterprise selects the specific depreciation method and is also permitted to determine amounts of accelerated depreciation (Article 18). To simplify the approach to depreciation, the asset classifications have been reduced from a system involving some 433 items to a list of just 32. There have also been some changes in the range of cost items that can be regarded as expenses in calculating profit, rather than being treated as appropriations of post tax profit.

Foreign currency transactions have only recently been possible for most Chinese enterprises. The standard permits the use of a foreign currency as the measurement unit for accounting records where an enterprise's operations are mainly conducted in overseas currencies (Article 33), and they specify the rate of exchange to be used in translation. Gains and losses on foreign currency translation are required to be taken through the profit and loss account, although some alternative treatments are permitted for gains and losses associated with establishing the enterprise.

Rules on enterprise liquidation cover the appointment and remuneration of a liquidator (Articles 37 and 38), the order of priority of claims (Article 38) and distribution of any profit on liquidation (Article 40). In the past, bankruptcy and liquidation of enterprises were not a problem in China because all enterprises were supported by the central or local government and liquidations were rare. As a result of the economic reform, bankruptcy is now a real possibility and regulation for accounting on liquidation is necessary.

The references to financial reporting in the standard include not only the basic financial statements (balance sheet, income statement and statement of changes in financial position Article 41) but also the 'explanatory statements on financial condition' (Article 42). These are expected to provide information on the status of production, profitability, and matters affecting the current or future financial position of the enterprise, including post balance sheet events (Article 42).

In addition, a number of key ratios are mentioned in the Rules, although they are stated as an illustrative rather than a complete list (Article 43). They include: liquidity ratio, quick ratio, inventory turnover and certain profit based ratios. There is, perhaps, a change in this set of measurements away from the pre-existing emphasis on the funding of activities to concern with the enterprise's capacity to pay debts, its operating capacity and its profitability.

The relationship between accounting standards and the financial regulations

The accounting standards and the financial regulations are intended to complement each other, both pursuing the same objectives of unifying and standardizing financial and accounting behaviour. They differ in emphasis, the accounting standards being most concerned with accounting methods and reform of the accounting system while the financial regulations deal with financial management and the management system.

The presence of financial regulations which to some extent overlap with and supplement the accounting standards reflects the pre-existing structure of regulation in China. Under the old structure, different accounting systems applied for different lines of business, organizational forms and ownership structures. These systems were accompanied by financial regulations which were produced by the MOF and which governed aspects of financial management, such as distribution of profits. In future, it will be difficult to sustain a unified accounting system unless these financial regulations are similarly unified.

The existence of the financial rules also reflects the stage of development of the economic reforms. The Chinese government has for a long time relied on administrative control to supervise enterprise activity, and as a consequence has established regulations governing the raising of funds, making of payments, etc. As part of the process of economic reform, this management control by government is expected to be relaxed so much that government will establish guidelines on general management but individual enterprises will be more at liberty to adopt their own administrative and financing arrangements. Such change requires time, and so, until a suitable infrastructure for corporate control is in place, which involves, for example, the auditing system and the public practice accounting profession, the financial regulations will remain as an interim measure. Similarly, the financial rules have been used to protect the interests of government itself, for example with respect to taxation revenue, until such time as the tax laws are revised to accommodate the new economic climate.

The future of accounting standards in China

It is likely that future regulatory developments will result in the financial regulations being incorporated step by step into the accounting standards and tax laws. Accounting standards in future will come to comprise three main parts, as represented in Figure 11.3:

1 Basic accounting standards will include assumptions underlying accounting, general accounting principles, concepts applying to measurement, recognition and reporting of particular accounting elements, and financial statement concepts.
2 Detailed accounting standards will apply the general standards to more detailed aspects of financial statements, to particular types of transaction or accounting technique, (for example, depreciation, inventory, foreign exchange, leasing and liquidation of an enterprise), and to specific industries, (for example, natural gas, banking and agriculture).
3 Detailed accounting recording systems rules will refer to the structure of recording for charts of accounts, and to the forms of financial statement and their preparation.

The standards under parts 1 and 2 will collectively provide the framework of accounting policy for Chinese enterprises, while the rules under part 3 will explain the steps to be followed for recording and reporting the financial position, of an enterprise.

COMPARISON OF CHINESE AND INTERNATIONAL ACCOUNTING STANDARDS

Since the principal structure of the new Chinese accounting regulations has been described, the regulations can now be evaluated with reference to their compatibility with the International Accounting Standards published by the IASC. The general approach followed in the Chinese regulations, examples of the treatment of individual accounting subjects, and certain other matters are discussed below. However, before that, a number of background points should be acknowledged.

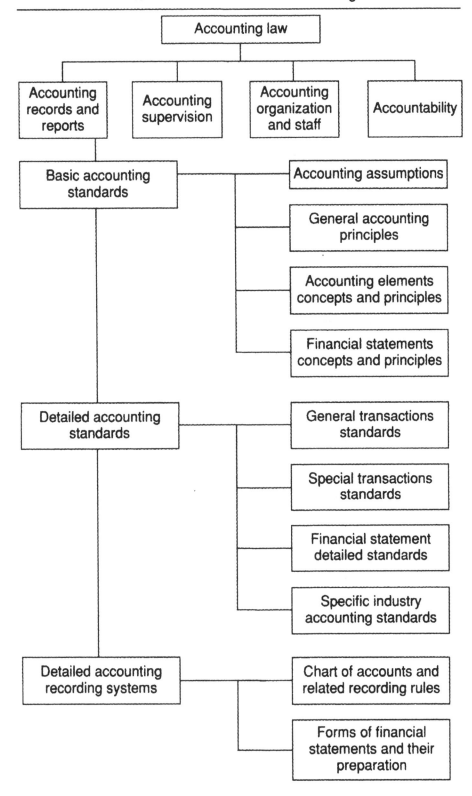

Figure 11.3 The future structure of accounting standards in China

First, it should be noted that some specific accounting methods which are recognized in IASs are not found or permitted in China, owing to both the economic background and the history of accounting development. For example, the need for a separate approach to accounting for the effects of inflation has not been an issue in China as this situation has not impacted on the financial environment.

Second, it must be recognized that the form of regulation introduced in China is in no way equivalent to the level of detail that is presently contained in the thirty-one IASs. There are no separate standards as such for specific areas of accounting, but rather one statement on Standards and one on General Rules, which possibly together in volume would be equivalent to the size of one IAS. To the extent that more detailed standards do exist they are contained in the old systems applying to different lines of business, but the situation continues to be that considerable development of accounting rules can be expected in future, along the lines noted above.

Third, IASs are intended to be suitable for application by all kinds of enterprises. Currently in China the position remains that, despite the move towards unitary regulation in the Standards statement, there are still some 14 systems (covering 13 industries and joint ventures) which can be followed by different types of enterprise. This situation should, however, be temporary and the Task Force on Accounting Standards is currently designing and drafting more detailed standards which will further help to unify the regulatory structure.

Finally, an important difference between the Chinese system and IASs is the existence of the associated financial regulations, which indicate an approach derived from concern with control of the organization and management of economic enterprises rather than simply the communication of information to external parties.

General approach

As discussed earlier, the introduction of new accounting regulations in China has involved the adoption of a new way of thinking conceptually about accounting. While not equivalent to what might be regarded as a conceptual framework in countries with longer traditions of Western accounting, it is none the less interesting to compare the main structural components in the regulations with the conceptual base that is represented in international standards and in the IASC Framework statement. This can be done by looking at the approach to the elements, assumptions and qualitative characteristics of accounting, and the types of financial statement and disclosure.

In the past, the approach to accounting in China has involved recognition of two basic elements: the application of funds and the source of funds. Under the new Standards, six elements are identified: assets, liabilities, owner's equity, revenue, expense, and profit or loss. Apart from some differences in terminology and the inclusion in the Standards of a separate chapter on profit and loss, this approach is very close to that of the IASC, and thus represents an effective step towards the dominant forms of accounting internationally..

IAS1 (IASC 1993) specifies three assumptions underlying financial statements (going concern, consistency and accruals) and ten qualitative characteristics (understandability, relevance, materiality, reliability, faithful representation, substance over form, neutrality, prudence, completeness and comparability). There is a considerable level of overlap between these items and the principles outlined in the Chinese Accounting Standards described earlier. Reliability, substance over form and neutrality are not mentioned, although the principle of representational faithfulness is taken to include reliability. The Standards stress consistency, matching, adherence to historical cost valuation, and the importance of the distinction between revenue and capital expenditures.

The new Standards also specify the same three types of financial statement as are recognized internationally: balance sheet, income statement and statement of changes in financial position. One possible area of variation in practice may be with respect to the last of these. In the Guidelines the statement of changes in financial position includes a reference to cash flow, but in the Standards it does not. It seems likely, therefore, that this form of statement will be used only in financial enterprises such as banks.

On the subject of disclosure, IASs require that all significant accounting policies which have been used to determine the profit or loss and the financial position of an accounting unit should be disclosed. Chinese regulations require that the notes to the financial statements should include the accounting methods adopted for the current and prior period, changes in accounting treatments, unusual items, detailed information on items in the financial statements, and other explanations. There are no requirements linked to specific common areas of accounting policy. The main difference between the Chinese situation and the international is thus not in the emphasis on disclosure but rather in the specification of individual items to be disclosed. The development of regulations in China has not reached the same level of detail as is common elsewhere.

Overall, despite certain differences in terminology, classification and level of detail, there is a strong degree of consistency between the basic conceptual aspects of the broad approach contained in the new Chinese Standards and that advocated by IASC, which is generally representative of common approaches internationally.

Examples of individual areas of accounting treatment

A number of examples are given below to illustrate areas of difference on specific accounting items between international accounting standards (IAS; see IASC 1993) and Chinese (CAS).

Depreciation

IAS4 applies no limiting conditions to the type of depreciation methods used but does require that the method chosen should be disclosed. In China the position is considerably more rigid as the state is involved in determining the life of assets and acceptable depreciation methods (Guidelines, Article 18). Depreciable assets are defined as those whose useful life is over one year, which have a value above the prescribed minimum (a standard not present in IAS4) and which retain their physical existence during the process of utilization. The Chinese standards generally permit the use of the straight line method for depreciation based on asset utilization ('the working capacity [or output] method'; Standards, Article 30). Accelerated depreciation is now possible but only if explicitly approved or permitted by specific relevant regulations. For example, the double declining balance method is permitted in joint ventures involving foreign investment. Under state rules enterprises can choose the method of depreciation and extent of accelerated depreciation.

Unusual items

The treatment of unusual items has been a source of controversy in Western countries for some time, reflecting concern over the measurement and manipulation of earnings figures in the financial statements. Thus, for example, IAS8 requires disclosure of the 'income from the ordinary activities of the enterprise during the period' and of the nature and amount of each unusual item. In contrast, this subject is not dealt with in detail in CASs. The definition of unusual items, one of the most critical points of debate, is left unspecified and there is simply a requirement for descriptions to be given in the financial statements.

Contingencies and events occurring after the balance sheet date

Under IAS10, enterprises are required to accrue the amount of a contingent loss through a charge in the income statement, but are not permitted to include contingent revenue. This standard also requires that assets and liabilities should be adjusted for any events occurring after the balance sheet date which provide additional evidence to assist with the estimation of amounts relating to conditions existing at the balance sheet date.

CASs approach these issues somewhat differently. While certain provisions for loss are possible, such as for bad debts, no general regulation exists to permit taking account of contingent losses. Even in the case of inventory, it is not possible to apply the lower of the cost or market value rule. Contingent income also cannot be recognized, in common with the IAS. The emphasis under CASs is placed on disclosure alone, as enterprises are required to explain the issues which may substantially affect the financial position of the enterprise after the balance sheet date and prior to the submission of financial reports.

Accounting for leases

There are strong similarities between the basic approach adopted in IAS17 for accounting for leases and that present in Chinese rules. Essentially, under both systems, there is a requirement for capitalization and depreciation of assets acquired under finance leases, and recognition of the associated liability for rental payments. The level of detail in the rules may result in some differences in valuation of assets acquired, but the principal approach is the same. For operating leases, the rental charges are to be charged to the income statement on a straight line basis under both IAS17 and CASs.

Accounting for group interests

Chinese standards provide for both consolidated accounts and accounting for long-term investments either at cost or by the equity method. Consolidation is required in situations of ownership of a minimum of 50 per cent of the capital of another company. The approach to long-term investments is less well defined, however, in that the CASs simply state that the cost or equity methods shall be used 'in accordance with different situations' (CAS, Article 29). International standards require the equity method for investments which constitute 20 per cent or more of the voting rights in another enterprise or where significant influence is exercised over the management.

Valuation of inventories

CASs do not permit the use of the lower of cost or realizable value in the valuation of inventories, in contrast to not only IAS2 but also the approach followed in most Western economies. Historic cost valuation must be used. There is greater flexibility, however, as regards the assumptions of the inventory flow underlying valuation, and methods based on FIFO, LIFO, weighted average, base stock and specific identification may be used.

CONCLUSION

This Chapter has described the historical background, the content and the degree of consistency with international standards of the new regime for accounting regulation in China, with a view to evaluating the changes in Chinese accounting following the 1992 'Accounting Standards for Business Enterprises'.

The Standards do represent a significant development in Chinese accounting. The extent of acceptance and formal recognition of conceptual factors is considerable. New concepts have been adopted and the purpose of accounting redirected towards a focus on the enterprise as the important unit of account, with a consequent need for financial information in order to make enterprise activity visible to outside groups, rather than to satisfy government information requirements. It would be wrong to imagine that all conceptual issues have been resolved, however, and there is still the possibility that the wide diversity of objectives for accounting, which are now recognized, will result in future problems. As noted earlier, the present Chinese approach may be over-optimistic about the potential contribution of general purpose financial statements.

It is important to note the interlinking between accounting development and economic objectives in China. The desire to promote economic activity through international trade has led to an obvious emphasis on 'modernizing' accounting practice and to a predictable policy of achieving compatibility with internationally accepted norms. In this process, the treatment of joint ventures involving Chinese and foreign capital has been an important intermediate step, through which accounting innovation was first introduced and then used to provide a basis for more general reform. The use of accounting in the promotion of economic objectives is evident not only in China but also in certain other newly industrializing nations.

Reviewing the history of Chinese accounting does raise some further questions regarding this latest stage of development. The reliance on different models of accounting in the past and also the periodic shifts in the importance attached to accounting may mean that some caution is warranted before concluding that the recent changes will be entirely sustained in the long term. Also, the diversity of traditions and systems of accounting may result in certain difficulties in the implementation, application and acceptance of the new regulations.

It must be recognized that the new standards are still only the first stage towards accounting regulation which is equivalent to that implied in IASs and found in most Western countries. The Standards and Guidelines are relatively brief statements with little explicit treatment of important individual areas of accounting policy and controversy. A process of considerable development of more detailed standards is still needed before the body of regulations will match that found in most developed economies internationally. In the short run some individual areas of valuation and income measurement may vary from international practice, and the approach to disclosure will be of interest. As more detailed standards are published it will also be interesting to observe the balance that is struck between uniformity and flexibility for accounting for particular items.

The approach to accounting that is contained in the Standards is, however, broadly consistent with international accounting norms. Using the IASs as a comparative standard, the above discussion has shown that, while there are certain differences in terminology, classification and the accounting treatment of certain items, as well as in the level of detail and comprehensiveness of the regulations, there is none the less a considerable measure of overlap between the approach embodied in the Chinese reforms and that found in IASC statements. From the perspective of the IASC, which is seeking to promote international accounting standardization, the changes that have been introduced in China must be seen as a positive development, although it is still the case that the national regulators are developing their own standards, rather than simply adopting those already produced by the IASC itself.

REFERENCES

International Accounting Standards Committee (1988) *Comparability of Financial Statements*, London: IASC.
—— (1993) *International Accounting Standards 1993*, London: IASC.
Liu, Z. (1993) *Fundamental Accounting Principles*, Beijing: Geological Press.
Lu, T. G. (1988) 'Governmental accounting and auditing in China', in J. L. Chan and R. H. Jones (eds) *Governmental Accounting and Auditing: International Comparisons*, London: Routledge, pp. 122–48.
Ministry of Finance, (1992a) *Accounting Standards For Business Enterprises*, Beijing: Publishing House of Law.
—— (1992b) *Financial Guidelines for Business Enterprises*, Beijing: Publishing House of Law.
Nobes, C. W. and Parker, R. H. (eds) (1991) *Comparative International Accounting* (3rd edn), London: Prentice Hall International.
Quan, M. Q. (1993) *The Finance and Accounting of Enterprises with Foreign Investment*, Beijing: Enterprises Management Press.
Radebaugh, L. H. and Gray, S. J. (1993) *International Accounting and Multinational Enterprises*, Hamilton, Canada: Wiley.
Tang, Y. W., Chow, L. and Cooper, B. J. (1992) *Accounting and Finance in China: A Review of Current Practice*, Hong Kong: Longman.
Yi, G. (ed.) (1986) *The Synopsis of Colleges and Universities in China*, Beijing: Chinese Higher Education Press.

Part IV

Developments in accounting practice

In Chapter 12, Chen and Yang identify the problems that currently hold back the development of the computerization of accounting in China, and offer some views on the opportunities that must be seized to overcome these obstacles. In Chapter 13, Carroll and Liu review the recent development of accounting research in China, identifying the need for better directed research to underlie the Chinese accounting reforms. Ren, Alexander and Kedslie, in Chapter 14, explore the broad economic and political developments that influence the Chinese economic reforms, while in Chapter 15 Scapens and Hao address the specific form that these changes have taken.

Chapter 12

The development of the computerization of accounting in China

J. Chen and D. C. Yang

INTRODUCTION

The application of computers and the introduction of a commodity (or market) economy have accelerated computerization of accounting in China. This computerization, which took off in the 1970s, has entered a new stage and is now deemed such a critical aspect of accounting that large amounts of capital and human resources are being spent on its development. As a result, comparatively sophisticated accounting software and systems have been produced.

CURRENT DEVELOPMENTS IN THE COMPUTERIZATION OF ACCOUNTING IN CHINA

The computerization of accounting in China has been a gradual process, from the use of a single microcomputer to the current wave of development of networking (see Coll 1988, Zhao 1988). Within 5,000 units (government units, enterprises and small businesses) which were investigated in 1988 (Accounting Society of China 1988), there were found to be microcomputers, 220 minicomputers and a few local area networks in use. Currently, national networking of the financing and banking system is being undertaken and significant progress has been made towards office automation in the national auditing profession. What we are seeing now is a simultaneous leap towards the application of microcomputers, mini-computers and networking. In terms of applications, the majority of the units under investigation tended towards a single function application: 74 per cent of them have implemented single and/or double function applications with an emphasis on management of wages and accounts; only 5 per cent have involved the complete accounting system; and very few of them have installed a combination of the accounting information system, the management information system and the decision support system. In terms of use of computer applications, departments in the State Council have the highest rate of 87.5 per cent; medium and large-sized enterprises have a rate of 40.3 per cent; and most of the small businesses have opted to forgo this technology. Two channels exist for developing the computerization project: in-house development, and contracts with universities or research institutes. With regard to programming languages, BASIC is the most frequently used, followed by COBOL and then other languages.

The organizational structure has developed fairly rapidly. In the early 1980s, research groups on accounting computerization had been established in many provinces, municipalities and associations of the accounting computerization genre and several fields of enterprises and academic exchange have begun. January 1988 saw the emergence of the China Accounting Computerization Research Group, and in April of the same year the Ministry of Finance established the Development and Research Centre of Accounting Computerization, a group put in charge of the research, extension and appraisal of software, the training of personnel, and the dissemination of information concerning accounting computerization. None the less, uniform national regulation is lacking and horizontal/vertical connections are non-existent.

Academic exchanges have become more frequent. Each province, municipality or field of enterprise has regular academic exchange activities. On 26 February 1988, the China Accounting Computerization Research Group convened its first enlarged conference in Beijing with the goal of clarifying the tasks of the group, such as the establishment of research projects, the sharing of experience and the co-ordination of the computerization process. On 10–14 June, a national research conference of accounting computerization was held in Chengde. The topics that were discussed at the conference were as follows:

1 The present stage of development of accounting computerization in China.

2 The standardization, interchangeability and commercialization of the computerization.
3 The macro-management of the computerization.
4 The impact of the computerization on the accounting system.
5 The division of the computerization system and the networking technology.
6 Other associated topics.

In August 1988, the National Symposium on Accounting Computerization was held in Beijing. Many papers, written by experts from all over China, were presented and these covered a wide range of subjects, such as: the basic structure, operational standards, internal control and coding techniques of the computerized accounting information systems; the use of networking in computerized accounting information systems; the standardization and compatibility of accounting software; the auditing of the computerized accounting information systems; the relationship between the computerized accounting information systems and the decision support systems; the principles of the computerization of accounting; the relationship between accounting software and the reform of the accounting system; the research on specialized computers and the language for accounting; and application and efficiency in the designing of accounting information systems.

CURRENT PROBLEMS IN THE COMPUTERIZATION OF ACCOUNTING INFORMATION IN CHINA

Lack of macro-management

Without a directing principle and development plan that can be applied to the unique situation in China, the process of accounting computerization is presently in a chaotic state of self-initiative and sporadic application.

Lack of qualified personnel plus limited availability and/or underuse of equipment

There is a lack of specialized staff in two areas: operations and software research and programming. A large amount of low quality and repetitious software has therefore been produced. Computer experts and accounting experts have not communicated with each other. While some units cannot utilize their computer experts because of lack of funds to purchase the necessary equipment, others cannot fully utilize their existing computers. The majority of the computers are simply used for word processing purposes.

Insufficient commercialization of accounting software

At present, there is no law that can be applied to protect the copyright of software. Software can be copied easily by others and this has drastically reduced incentives for programmers. The market for accounting software is yet to be established. As a result, there is no uniform price or place for the sale of software.

Lack of an internal control system

Many computer crimes have occurred in Dalian, Guangzhou and Xi'an in recent years. The sums involved range from thousands to millions (Chinese yuan). The techniques associated with these crimes are not very sophisticated. If appropriate measures were adopted, such cheating could certainly be prevented. However, this dire situation has not yet attracted sufficient attention owing to the fact that the accounting personnel concerned have not acquired sufficient computer knowledge.

Incompatibility of the traditional accounting system and computerization

The Chinese accounting system was established according to the needs of different types of enterprises, and was issued and regulated by the Ministry of Finance. This specifically detailed system cannot match the dynamic development of the market economy. The system is designed for manual processing and thus is not appropriate to the computing environment. To achieve the computerization of accounting, many new regulations must be set for the accounting system. For example, items need to be codified; the internal controls of accounting need to be applied to the computer; the storage medium needs to be regulated. The computerization of accounting must include modification of the traditional manual accounting system, with the assurance that the general principle of accounting will not be violated.

Lack of long-term planning in the application of accounting software

At present, the development of accounting software lacks any long-term planning with regard to the application of accounting software. This means that the future needs of rapid economic development cannot easily be met. The compatibility and the upgrading of software are both very limited; moreover, internal and external communication is very weak. These deficiencies have made it impossible to adapt to the scale of change in the nature of the business and to expand management information systems and decision support systems on the basis of accounting information systems.

Lack of attention to computer auditing

As a result of accounting computerization, auditing is now facing new difficulties. The existing auditing system cannot meet the need of the new computing environment, which not only complicates the way in which auditing is performed but also enlarges the content of auditing. This has, in turn, added more responsibilities to auditing personnel. Numerous units have asked for an audit of their computerized accounting system but the majority of the auditors are not qualified for this task. It is very rare for anyone to conduct a manual audit when there is a computerized accounting system available. Database auditing is yet to come.

Further measures

Research on security measures, EDP internal controls and the input of Chinese characters must be accelerated.

PROSPECTS FOR THE COMPUTERIZATION OF ACCOUNTING IN CHINA

The computerization of accounting in China is presently in a transitional period, the characteristics of which are:

1 Some regions and units are putting their efforts into research and development of a compatible system that is appropriate for them.
2 Some regions and units have already finished their research on

the check and acceptance criteria, application criteria and the concerned regulations.

3 The Ministry of Finance, which is in charge of accounting affairs, is considering establishing rules and regulations with the purpose of nationally regulating accounting software.

This will certainly give great impetus to the standardization and compatibility of accounting software in China.

Many points have been raised concerning the computerization of accounting. For enterprises the plan is that large and medium-sized enterprises should mostly use in-house computers and that small businesses should submit their accounting information to centres for the computerization of their accounting systems. These centres would focus their research on the accounting applications of computers, the business management of computers, and prediction/decision-making with computer systems. With regard to national financial and accounting affairs, it is proposed to establish national computer networks for processing financial data, with the aim of monitoring national financing and taxation activities. The networks would extend to regions, municipalities and counties, and, if possible, to individual enterprise networks, in order to provide a framework for the nation for making macro-decisions in the shortest time. Concerning economic predictions, the suggestion is to use computers to accumulate data and to link together manufacturing and commerce, foreign trade, finance, taxation and banking. The data accumulation and linkage will provide the decision-making department with data for making predictions and for formulating plans for reform.

Currently, universities and colleges are accelerating their training programmes for personnel who have knowledge of not only accounting but also computers. Accounting departments have already added to their list of required courses some type of course on accounting information systems. The undergraduate programme is geared to train students to become capable of managing computerized accounting systems. Local training centres are also actively involved in training software programmers and computer operators. Management units are training personnel for the computerization of their accounting affairs.

The potentially large market for software and the highly unified finance system have provided very favourable conditions for the computerization of accounting in China.

REFERENCES

Accounting Society of China (1988) *Accounting Research*, April, p. 44.

Coll, J. H. (1988) 'Computers in China: where the Chinese are; where they want to be', *Journal of Applied Business Research*, Spring, pp. 17–25.

Zhao, X. (1988) 'Present situation of OSI standards in China', *Computer Networks and ISDN Systems*, vol. 16, pp. 83–5.

Chapter 13

Accounting research in China

R. F. Carroll and F. Liu

INTRODUCTION

The purpose of this Chapter is to review and appraise the nature of accounting research which has occurred in China from the 1980s to the present. The focus will be on several general aspects which capture the essence of what has been happening with accounting research in China.

The Chapter consists of three parts. The first gives an appraisal of Chinese accounting research based on the general observations of the authors. The second provides some data based on all of the articles published in the magazine *Accounting Research*, which is considered in China to contain top quality papers. Articles from 1988 to 1992 have been chosen to demonstrate the trend of accounting research in China. The final part provides several recommendations for the improvement of accounting research in China.

GENERAL OBSERVATIONS

The basic features characterizing accounting in China after 1949 – the beginning of the so-called new China – can be divided into three phases chronologically. Phase one ranged from 1949 to the beginning of the Cultural Revolution in 1966. During this time the main achievements were threefold. Soviet accounting theory and methods were learned, absorbed and copied. Accounting theory and methods were established to serve a highly central-ized planned economy. Accounting research, heavily influenced by anti-capitalistic attitudes, also assumed the task of criticizing and negating the accounting theory and methods that had served the previous bourgeoisie. The approach to accounting research tended towards what might be called the 'unscientific' or perhaps even the 'anti-scientific'.

Phase two began in 1967 and ended in 1977. These ten years were a period of political struggle and turmoil for China. We refer to this period as the 'non-research' phase that represented ten lost years for accounting research.

After this rather bleak interval for China there came a period of significant change with respect to the perceived role of accounting and accounting research. What we classify as phase three, beginning in 1977 and continuing to the present time, is characterized by a dramatic shift towards a broader conception of the role of accounting research. In phase three accounting research aims:

1 To be more scientifically based.
2 To develop a more flexible and adaptive approach to accounting theory which would facilitate the establishment of accounting models that are most suitable for the Chinese economic system, which has been undergoing rapid internal change.
3 To develop accounting models to serve better China's growing and more open exchange economy.

Although phases one and two may be interesting from a historical perspective, the concern of this Chapter is the current phase three. This is a period of economic reform in China. Our interest is with how accounting research has changed in this era of reform and what paradigms are driving accounting research in China. The current trend in accounting research began in about 1985 but is most noticeable since 1988. Some basic features have been identified which reflect the current research mode.

The change from pure theoretical research to applied theoretical research

Accounting research in China has moved away from pure theoretical research to applied research. By theoretical research we mean: research which focuses mainly on the fundamental theoretical issues; research which has as its objective the perfection of theory and methodology of the subject with little attention being paid to practicability or immediate applicability of the research. Applied research, in contrast, is obviously very concerned with practical matters. Applied research focuses on those issues which serve to guide practice directly. It is less concerned with conceptual issues and more interested in real world applications.

The change from pure theoretical research to applied research in China occurred in the mid-1980s. In the early 1980s, it was fundamental concepts that most interested researchers. Issues such as the nature of accounting, the definition of accounting, the function of accounting, and the object of accounting weighed heavily on the minds of accounting researchers. Concepts were derived through the process of deductive reasoning. The formation of two schools, the school of information system and the school of management activities, essentially followed this paradigm.

During the latter half of the 1980s there was a gradual shift away from the theoretical model to more applied research. Researchers began to discuss practical concerns, such as accounting standards, accounting for changing prices, asset valuation, and income recognition and measurement issues.

It is notable that the Chinese Accounting Association (CAA) played a major role in this changing research orientation. The CAA formed several research groups in 1987. A most influential group known as the 'Accounting Theory and Standards Research Group' was directed by Professor Lou Er-Xing of Shanghai University of Finance and Economics, Professor Ge Jia-Shu of Xiamen University, and Professor Yan Da-Wu of the People's University of China. This committee concentrated its research on the formulation of accounting standards which they perceived to be most relevant to the economy and environment of China. It held its first symposium in 1989. Undoubtedly, the input of this group has had a significant role in affecting and shaping the contents and style of Chinese accounting research.

By 1990 applied research had gained considerable respectability. Three factors strongly support this assertion. First, the discussion and formulation of accounting standards had become a central topic to a majority of leading Chinese researchers. Second, the move away from purely state-owned enterprises to shareholding companies made it essential to establish new accounting methods. The old sectional accounting system, which may have suited the reporting needs of state-owned enterprises, had little relevance for a growing number of business enterprises. Third, 'truth' in accounting information had become a major concern across the entire country. In addition, issues such as changing prices, management models, and foreign currency translation had become hotly debated topics.

The minimal effects on practice of research results

Chinese accounting research in the past ten years or so may be divided into two fields, that is, financial accounting research and management accounting research. It is very difficult to obtain research data and it is also difficult to do rigorous quantitative analysis because of limited access to computers. Limited by the data, authors cannot determine empirically the effect of theoretical research on practice. There is a very serious implementation problem with respect to financial accounting research in China. Accounting practice must follow the unified sectional accounting system which is set by the Department of Administration of Accounting Affairs (DAAA) of the MOF. Any deviation from the system will be prohibited unless permission is applied for and received from the regulatory authorities. That is to say, even if imperfections are demonstrated by practice and it is clear that accounting problems exist, and even if strong suggestions for change come from accounting theorists, accounting practice will not be altered if the authorities decide not to listen. The past decade in China has demonstrated that the unified sectional accounting system is rigid and inflexible and has seldom attempted to implement proposals coming from academics.

With respect to management accounting, Chinese researchers knew little about management accounting before 1979. It has, however, gradually found its way into the accounting curriculum and by 1990 most universities were offering a course on this subject. Chinese scholars claim to have established a well-defined field of management accounting with accompanying methodological and theoretical support which is geared to the environment of China. But, as we perceive with financial accounting, there is a large gap between theory and practice. Two aspects lend credence to this phenomenon. First, much of Chinese managerial accounting is drawn from Western countries, especially from the USA and Canada. In these Western countries the assumptions underlying much of management accounting theory research, such as agency theory, assume perfect markets and costless information. This has created credibility problems even in the West, but in China, where the market mechanism is a long way from being fully developed, such management accounting theory may be interpreted as irrelevant. China is just in the initial stages of developing a market economy after assuming planned economy for some thirty years. The market mechanism is not yet in place. Second, although economic reform in the form of greater decentralization has been occurring in China for more than ten years, there is still much direction imposed by the central government. As a result there is low competitive pressure from the market. Therefore, most enterprises lack the impetus to apply the methods of managerial accounting in operating and decision-making.

On a more optimistic note, some critical factors deserve to be mentioned that may help to bring theory and practice closer together. One is that, in the process of formulating basic accounting standards for China, the accounting standards board within the MOF has recently invited comments from both academic scholars and practising accountants from enterprises throughout the country. This is a positive sign that theory may eventually find its way into practice and that the system may gain some flexibility.

Second, authorities in China have recognized that accounting changes are necessary to accommodate the information needs stemming from business activity in China's fast growing economy. New regulations in China specify that business accounting need not abide strictly by the unified accounting policy. There is encouragement to draw from Western accounting methodology where deemed appropriate. This, of course, gives enterprises greater freedom to choose accounting policies and raises the possibility for those enterprises of adapting research results to their accounting practice, which in the past would not have been possible.

Finally, several young scholars who have earned doctoral degrees in the field of economics have turned their research interests to the development of accounting standards. Familiar with accounting theory and theoretical research, they are well positioned to gather and interpret research data which are useful for the formulation of accounting standards.

Lack of sound methodology in accounting research

Methodology of accounting research can usually be separated into a priori methodology and empirical methodology. The former was popular before 1970 in the West, while the latter has been dominant in accounting research since the 1970s. A priori research refers to something which is believed without prior study or examination. Propositions are believed if they seem reasonable. General cultural outlook, for example, fixes belief a priori. Conclusions are stated but no attempt is made to verify these conclusions. At the core of empirical research is verification. Empirical observations, however, can change and so are not final. The tentative nature of scientific understanding means that it is not sufficient to verify or confirm a theory. As Popper (1961) has suggested, good theories, like good hypotheses, must be testable and every reasonable effort must be made to falsify or disconfirm the theory. The temporary nature of induction makes negative evidence more important than confirmatory evidence. One cannot say for sure that a theory is true if data confirm a prediction but if a theory leads to a prediction which is not supported by data one can argue that the theory is false and should be rejected. This so-called scientific method fixes belief on the basis of experience. If we define scientific accounting research as a repeatable, self-correcting mechanism which aims at understanding accounting phenomena on the basis of empirical observation then several advantages of the empirical method over a priori research become apparent. Having an empirical basis for beliefs means that experience rather than faith is the source of knowledge. In addition, empirical research has procedures in place for establishing the superiority of one belief over others. Persons holding different beliefs a priori have no way of reconciling their opinions but the scientific method allows for public observations which make it possible to compare old beliefs with new observations. Where they differ, the old beliefs can be discarded if they fail to fit the empirical facts.

Unlike the physical sciences, accounting is a social science and as such is full of methodological controversy with respect to research. Accounting research in the West, for example, makes heavy use of econometric models to predict human behaviour. Human beings can reflect on their actions and change their behaviour, rendering the model's predictions inaccurate. In spite of such difficulties and the recognition also that positivism has fallen out of favour in the social sciences, experimental approaches are vastly superior to a priori methods.

When we reviewed all of the accounting papers published in the main accounting magazines in China from 1988 to 1992, we could not find a single paper that used empirical methodology. We did find two papers that offered conclusions on the basis of empirical analysis but they were not empirical studies in themselves. One is entitled 'Some issues of accounting reform: a meaningful questionnaire' (C. Zongsun and Wang Ping, *Accounting Research*, June 1988). The other is 'Management of the accounting regulatory authority: strengths and weaknesses' (W. Zhang, *Finance and Accounting Communication*, August 1992). These studies simply stated the conclusions from questionnaires and no attempt was made to utilize or establish any analytical model.

We classified most of the other papers as a priori for the following reasons:

1 They make assertions or draw conclusions without the process of reasoning, analysing, or inferring. Most published research papers are merely introductions to new trends or new developments of the same field abroad. They tend to lack a point of view of their own.
2 No detailed citations and references accompany these articles. Accounting theory today is the product of the continuity of the theory developed in the past and it changes in response to altered conditions. Articles are more likely to benefit from previous research and literature reviews and they should list all citations and references that were used. This also helps to reduce the publishing of multiple papers which share the same viewpoint.

In China, there are more than 40 accounting journals and more than 3,000 articles are published each year. Because of the lack of sound research methodology, it is not possible to make a valid assessment of their assertions.

SOME DATA ON ACCOUNTING RESEARCH IN CHINA

This section provides details of how we classified accounting articles which were published in the journal *Accounting Research* from 1988 to 1992, in support of the assertions made earlier. We

Table 13.1 Number of papers published in *Accounting Research* 1988–92

	1988	1989	1990	1991	1992	Total
I	96	87	84	98	83	448
II	89	81	71	79	70	390
III	69	59	57	56	48	289

Note: The numbers in row I refer to all papers published in the journal. Non-academic papers are excluded. Row II excludes translated papers, reports of conference proceedings, etc. Row III includes only research papers and articles which introduce new trends or new schools of thought.

Table 13.2 Classification of all academic papers, 1988–92

Year	No. of papers	Theoretical			Applied		
		Accounting	Financial management & cost	Per-centage	Accounting	Financial management & cost	Per-centage
1988	69	28	9	54	19	13	46
1989	59	23	12	60	16	8	40
1990	57	16	4	35	19	18	65
1991	56	17	5	39	25	9	61
1992	48	14	4	37.5	25	5	62.5
Total	289	108	24	–	104	53	–

Note: The columns headed 'Accounting' consist of articles on financial accounting, management accounting, and computerized accounting. The columns headed 'Financial management & cost' include typical financial management, cost accounting, and management accounting articles. If accounting and finance are discussed in the same paper, we classify it as Accounting unless the accounting content is just incidental.

chose this publication because it is the official magazine of the Chinese Accounting Association. The magazine is one of the top academic accounting publications in China and articles within it are considered in China to have a high academic standard. Table 13.1 gives the total number of papers published in the journal over five years. Table 13.2 classifies all of these papers, while Table 13.3 examines the number of citations in the papers.

Table 13.3 Citations in papers, 1988–92

Year	No. of papers	Detailed citations %	No. of papers	Insufficient citations %	No. of papers	No citations %
1988	3	4.3	10	14.5	56	81.2
1989	1	1.7	14	23.7	44	74.6
1990	5	8.8	6	10.5	46	80.7
1991	5	8.9	4	7.1	47	84
1992	8	16.7	5	10.4	35	72.9
Total	22	7.6	39	13.5	228	78.9

Note: It is not yet common in China for published accounting articles to list references. We have classified those papers with more than five notes as having detailed citations and with five notes or less as having insufficient citations.

RECOMMENDATIONS FOR IMPROVING ACCOUNTING RESEARCH IN CHINA

The lack of sound research methodology is a major hurdle restricting the development of Chinese accounting research. We recommend that the editors of accounting research publications insist on including only those articles which meet higher research standards than is currently the case. Whether the studies are qualitative or quantitative, rigorous methodology is essential if standards are to improve. Editors should look for sound deductive reasoning, for example, for quantitative experimental studies which investigate hypotheses deducted from theories. For studies building on observation and measurement, editors should expect sound inductive reasoning. Critical to the improvement of accounting research in China is that the researcher's reasoning process be appropriate to the particular study. In addition, standards for bibliographies must be developed and consistently followed.

A greater emphasis needs to be put on empirical research. There is a role for descriptive research but China needs more prescriptive theory-building accounting research. Normative methods are needed to help to justify recommended accounting practices. Empirical observations are at the heart of the scientific method. They help to make accounting research self-correcting and lead to greater understanding.

Because China is undergoing dramatic economic change, creating a need for more sophisticated accounting information, an emphasis must be placed on utility. There are immediate practical accounting problems to be solved and to which accounting researchers are well positioned to contribute. There is also a need to encourage basic research to develop concepts to be tapped later by applied research. Ultimately, the quality of accounting research will be judged by its ability to help to interpret, explain and advance practice. In China, accounting researchers have an opportunity to bring theory and practice closer together and to lead rather than follow practice by focusing on China's current and future information needs.

BIBLIOGRAPHY

All papers published in the magazines *New Accounting* and *Industrial Accounting* in the 1950s and 1960s and in *Accounting Research* from the 1980s to the present.

Lin, C., Cai, Y. and Li, W. 'The framework for positive accounting research', *Journal of Accounting Research* (Taiwan), no. 83.

Liu, F. (1991a) 'A reappraisal of accounting theory of China', *Accounting Scholars*, 1 and 2.

—— (1991b) 'A comparative research of accounting theory between the USA and China', *Financial Research*, no. 2.

Popper, K. R. (1961) *The Logic of Scientific Discovery*, New York: Basic Books.

Yan, D. (1990) 'A review of accounting theory of ten years', *Accounting Research*, January.

Yang, J. and Yu, B. (1988) 'Brief introduction to the development of accounting theory and practice', in *Handbook of Modern Accounting*, Beijing: Chinese Financial and Economic Press.

Zhang, W. (1991) *Empirical Accounting: Introduction of New Schools of Accounting and Auditing*, People's Publishing Company of Henan Province.

Chapter 14

The trend of accounting reform in China
Issues and environment

M. C. Ren, D. Alexander and M. Kedslie

INTRODUCTION

The object of this chapter is to examine the trend of accounting reform in China. Since the subject is vast, it is necessary to define the parameters of this particular chapter. These are, first, to concentrate solely on financial accounting and, second, to direct our attention to the regulation rather than the practice of accounting.

ECONOMIC ENVIRONMENT

The most significant factor in accounting reform has been the economic reform which has taken place in China over the past fifteen years and which is still in a transitional stage. Economic reform will inevitably lead to accounting reform as the latter attempts to adapt to a fast changing socio-economic environment in which a centrally planned economy has been transformed into a socialist market economy.

The Chinese socialist market economy has not been a clearly defined concept but could be viewed as being the mid-point between the previous centrally planned economy and the free market economy of the West (Figure 14.1). It has emerged in China as a result of a trade-off between the socialist ideologies of the past and the requirements of economic development. If China wishes to achieve fast and steady economic development then it must establish a market mechanism. However, the socialist emphasis on economic security and equality, on public ownership of the means of production and on socialist comradeship have run counter to the market economy principles of free competition, private initiatives, accountability and responsibility.

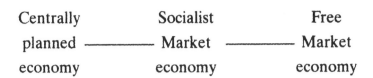

Centrally   Socialist   Free

planned ——————— Market ——————— Market

economy   economy   economy

Figure 14.1 Relative position of the Chinese socialist market economy

China's reform programme was launched in 1978. The period from 1949 to 1978 is generally regarded as the pre-reform period, in which a central plan was dominant in the national economy, and the period from 1978 to the present is regarded as a transitional period in which the importance of the plan has been gradually reduced and market forces gradually increased. Since the reform is still in an evolutionary process it is difficult to tie it down to a particular period and so this chapter relates to the model used during the centrally planned economy.

When we begin to examine the particular environmental elements driving accounting change there can be little doubt that the most significant are the dispersion of ownership and the transition of the economic mechanism.

Theoretically, the object of China's financial reporting in the past was to provide information to several outside user groups, including investors and creditors. However, because all organizations were owned exclusively by the public and driven by the economic mechanism of central planning, such reporting was inevitably designed to satisfy only one user, the government. Before reform began, public ownership was predominant and existed in two forms: 'state enterprises', theoretically owned by everyone, and 'collectives' owned by a defined group of workers. Private ownership was rigorously restricted (Table 14.1).

It can be seen from Table 14.1 that state enterprises were the predominant form of public ownership. Their equity capital came exclusively from the state through public financing, therefore the government, as the representative of all the people, was the sole investor in state enterprises. In addition, by owning and controlling all financial institutions, as well as restricting trade credit between firms, the government became the main creditor of state enterprises and consequently the main, if not the only, user of financial statements.

The other element which gave accounting its macro-economic focus was the comprehensive and compulsory economic plan. This

Table 14.1 Structure of industry by ownership

Year	Percentage of gross output value			
	State	Collective	Individual	Other
1978	80.8	19.2		
1979	81.0	19.0		
1987	59.7	34.6	3.7	2.0
1988	57.8	36.1	4.3	2.7
1989	56.1	35.7	4.8	3.4
1990	54.6	35.6	5.4	4.4

Source: China State Statistics Bureau 1991

was developed according to investigation of demand, which was converted into stipulated product mix and production output for different enterprises. Resources of capital, labour, equipment and materials were then allocated in line with the targets in the plan. Finally, the state determined prices and designated customers. This whole operation treated the national economy as a huge factory with each enterprise comprising a workshop of that factory. Resource allocation was determined by the plan rather than the price mechanism and, therefore, it is hardly surprising that the financial accounting system was designed primarily to assist government in planning, resource allocation and monitoring the success or otherwise of the plan.

Collective enterprises were theoretically owned by the group of people who operated them. However, the reality was that they were neither owned nor operated by a group of people. This was especially true for large and medium sized collectives since it was common practice to transfer them, administratively, into state ownership. The reason for this practice was that the ideal form of public ownership was ownership by all of the people, and ownership by a group of people only a primary objective. Thus, whenever a collective enterprise developed to a certain level, perhaps giving too much power to its owners, it would be transformed into a state enterprise. This reflects the ambiguity of the property rights operating in China at that time and also suggests that there were powerful disincentives to dissuade the owners of collectives from becoming too successful.

China's strategy for change from this system could be described as sequential and experimental rather than the type of comprehensive reform which has taken place in some Eastern European countries. Two dimensions of this decentralization strategy can be discerned: first, the transfer of state property rights to economic entities with a view to changing the behaviour of existing entities or creating new enterprises; second, the creation of a macro-economic environment within which these new economic entities could operate (Kuen 1991). As a result of these changes, the ownership structure has become more widely dispersed. Although public ownership still remains the dominant form, both domestic and foreign private enterprises have increased (Table 14.1). Official statistics show that, at the end of 1992, 139,000 domestic private enterprises were registered, accounting for 2,319,000 employees. In addition, some collectives and small or inefficient state enterprises have been leased or auctioned and some large and medium sized state enterprises have been reconstructed into shareholding companies or joint ventures. At the same time, measures such as the contracted management system have been introduced in an effort to help the remaining collectives and state enterprises to run more like entities.

The creation of a new macro-economic environment also involves the transformation of the resource allocation mechanism from that based on central planning to one with a market orientation. In line with this, the number of items controlled by the central allocation plan has been significantly reduced and the market mechanism is gradually being established. For example, there are now two national stock exchanges in China, in Shanghai and Shenzhen, and approximately 3,700 share-holding companies of which about 70 are presently listed (Zhu 1993). These changes have led to the emergence of additional users of financial information and to significant changes in accounting techniques arising from the introduction of such things as financial leasing, securities, business combinations, intangible assets and foreign exchange and the inevitable growth in bankruptcy.

POLITICAL INFLUENCES

Such enormous changes in the economic environment could not happen without political change, especially in China where political control is extremely powerful. It is true that Chinese policy makers are still conservative about political reform but there have been some changes regarded as essential for the implementation of economic reform.

Since 1978 the Party and the government's focus has moved from the ideological debate to economic development. Accounting, as a means to help to achieve effective management, has been provided with a favourable development climate. For example, in order to attract more foreign investment, steps have been taken to reduce the differences between China's accounting practices and internationally recognized practice. One aspect of this involved the reinstatement of China's Certified Public Accountant (CPA) system after its suspension for more than thirty years. At present there are more than 2,400 CPA firms and about 25,000 people engaged in public auditing, of which 10,733 are qualified CPAs (*People's Daily*, overseas edn, 26 August 1993).

The second notable aspect of this political change has been the move away from strict Marxism. During the Cultural Revolution (1966–76), all decisions were supposedly taken only after a detailed consideration of the relevant doctrinal principles. This led to the replacement of debit credit bookkeeping, which was seen to relate to capitalism, with a self-created bookkeeping concentrating on the state.[1] The selective and conditional deviation from Marxism has allowed the introduction into China of many accounting concepts and practices common in the Western world.

The third characteristic is that, as economic decentralization has progressed, political control has been gradually relaxed. Thus, by redefining Party and government functions, ownership, management and macro and micro-management, the range of activities regulated by the Party and government has been restricted and the remaining controls on certain activities have, with a few exceptions, become more predictable and less arbitrary. More importantly, the Party is now prepared to concede that many intellectual, scientific and technical questions can, and should, be addressed on their merits without regard to ideological considerations (Harding 1987). This policy has greatly encouraged professional bodies to become more involved in professional affairs.

Accounting cannot escape from the influences of culture. Even although China has had several million people employed in accounting activities at all levels, the cultural influences have been unfavourable to the development of accounting (Tang *et al.* 1992). Of all of the philosophies and religions influencing Chinese history, the most prominent has probably been Confucianism. Confucianism had a pro-agriculture, anti-commercial bias.

Peasants were considered to be the producers of wealth (i.e. food) and merchants were regarded as non-productive parasites on society (Dreyer 1993). Accounting, being seen as a commercial activity, had thus been awarded a low social status. After the foundation of the People's Republic of China (PRC) in 1949, Confucianism was criticized as a feudal philosophy but, without exception, was used for the purpose of ideological debate. Its influence still exists and is unlikely to disappear completely for the foreseeable future.

The advent of the PRC introduced Marxism to China. Marx's theory of political economics was officially accepted and, in common with Confucianism, had an anti-commercial bias. Marx stated that the wealth of society is created only by production activities such as agriculture, industry and construction along with some limited service activities such as communications and transport. The vast majority of service industries, including accounting, were excluded from the creation of wealth. Hence, from a policy making viewpoint, priorities were focused on industry, with particular emphasis on heavy industry, and service activities were taken lightly.

Just as it is impossible to eliminate the influence of Confucianism so it is impossible to eliminate the influence of Marxism, which still has official backing. However, the latter has now been determined to be a theory which is subject to a changing environment rather than the rigid teachings of the past. It is recognized that helpful theories and experiences can be transferred from the West. More importantly, the unrelenting development of market forces will gradually erode the base on which Confucianism rests. Reflections of this are already being seen in accounting where it is now socially and politically acceptable for intelligent young people to embark on a career in accounting.

ACCOUNTING REFORM

Accounting reform is the natural reaction to a changing socio-economic and political environment. This change has manifested itself in several ways.

Table 14.2 Comparison of main financial statements before and after July 1993

Pre-July 1993		Post-July 1993
1	Balance sheet	Balance sheet
2	Income statement	Income statement
3	Statement of commodity product cost	Statement of changes in financial position (or statement of cash flow)

Table 14.3 Simplified balance sheet, pre-July 1993

Fund applications:	Fund sources:
Fixed assets	Fixed fund sources
Original cost	State fixed fund
Less: depreciation	Enterprise fixed fund
Net book value	Fixed fund loans
Subtotal X	*Subtotal X*
Current assets	Current fund sources
Stocks	State current fund
Accounts receivable	Enterprise current fund
Cash & bank balance	Current fund loans
Subtotal Y	*Subtotal Y*
Assets set aside for special purposes	Special fund sources
Bank deposit	State special fund
Assets under special fund	Enterprise special fund
Subtotal Z	*Subtotal Z*
TOTAL	*TOTAL*

Source: Tang *et al.* 1992

Establishment of a socialist market economy

The establishment of a socialist market economy, although not the same as a market economy, has introduced a greater degree of market orientation than was previously evident. The immediate impact on accounting can be seen in comparing the contents of financial statements before and after July 1993 (Table 14.2). Prior to July 1993 the accounting system concentrated on demonstrating the efficiency of the enterprise in its cost-cutting activities. In addition, this cost information was useful to the state in setting prices. The move to the presentation of a statement of changes in financial position came in response to a change in some

Table 14.4 Simplified balance sheet, post-July 1993

Assets:	Liabilities:
Current assets	Current liabilities
Cash & bank balance	Short-term loans
Short-term investments	Notes payable
Notes receivable	Accounts payable
Accounts receivable	Advances on sale
Less: bad debt provision	Wages payable
Net book value	Taxes payable
Prepayments on purchase	Profits payable
Other receivables	Other payables
Deferred charges	Accrued expenses
Stocks	Long-term liabilities due
Long-term bonds due	within one year
within one year	
Subtotal	*Subtotal*
Long-term investment	Long-term liabilities
Shares	Long-term loans
Bonds	Bonds payable
Others	Accounts payable
	Other payables
Subtotal	*Subtotal*
Fixed assets	Owner's equities
Original cost	Paid-in capital
Less: depreciation	Capital surpluses
Net book value	Surplus reserves
	Undistributed profit
Subtotal	*Subtotal*
Intangible & deferred assets	
Intangible assets	
Patent	
Land-use right	
Goodwill	
Others	
Deferred assets	
Organizational expenses	
Subtotal	
Other assets	
Other long-term assets	
TOTAL	*TOTAL*

Source: MOF 1992

developed nations, although China still encourages enterprises to provide either a cash flow statement or a statement of financial position.

Table 14.3 outlines the contents of a pre-July 1993 balance sheet which is obviously fund oriented. Under a centrally planned economy some primary elements of production, such as land and intangible assets, were not recognized as commodities and thus were excluded from financial statements. Other productive elements, although included, were treated in an entirely different way. For example, since capital was allocated by the government on the basis of the economic plan, there was no requirement for a financial market. Therefore, many transactions relating to financial markets were replaced by other information. Sources of funds for state enterprises were divided into three parts, fixed, current and special funds, and were related to fixed, current and special assets. This provides us with a unique accounting equation:

$$\text{Fund applications} = \text{Fund sources.}$$

Regardless of any fund efficiency, all subtotals and totals were required to be equal but it was not uncommon to have an unbalanced account in practice which might be accepted by the financial authorities.

The 1993 changes in the format of the balance sheet can be seen in Table 14.4. Compared with the previous example, this is much easier to relate to a Western balance sheet, although it still requires some additional detail.

Increasing internationalization

The second influence on accounting reform has been that of increasing internationalization. China realized that isolation from the international community would be harmful to national development and decided that access to and from the outside world would be a critical aspect of reform. As far as accounting has been concerned, this has mainly resulted in the importation of Western practice, particularly from the USA and UK and via the IASC. China had abandoned the use of debit/credit bookkeeping but has reintroduced it, first in industry but now its use in every enterprise is advocated, regardless of the nature of its activities. This has led to the adoption of the Western accounting equation

$$Assets = Liabilities + Owner's\ equity$$

and to the need for a clear definition of the meaning of several terms such as asset, liability, revenue, expense, owner's equity and profit. In addition, it is now common practice to produce a capital account and manufacturing cost information.

The importation of accounting techniques is easier than the importation of accounting concepts and institutions (Parker 1989). It is noticeable that the socio-economic environment of a particular country has a considerable impact on what it chooses to import. In China, the most significant example is that of accounting standards. Prior to their introduction, accounting practice in China was determined by accounting regulations which differed for state, collective and foreign investment enterprises, that is, it varied according to the ownership of the enterprise. Each type of enterprise used different accounting policies which were detailed and mandatory. For example, large and medium sized state enterprises were taxed at a rate of 55 per cent but the rate for foreign investment enterprises was approximately 30 per cent. Consequently, comparison between different types of enterprises was difficult.

In contrast to accounting regulation, accounting standards will be applicable to all enterprises situated in the territory of China. This switch from regulations to standards will narrow the difference between Chinese and international practices and conventions and also will provide a greater necessity for professional judgement which should, in turn, help to improve the status of the accounting profession. Prior to 1978, some accounting concepts commonly used in the West were familiar to Chinese accounting academics and a few practitioners. However, only after 1978 did these concepts begin to have increasing influence on Chinese accounting practice. For example, although the accounting concepts of periodicity, money measurement, continuity, matching, accruals and materiality were embodied to some extent in accounting regulations, they were often dispersed throughout the regulations and were poorly defined. This made it easy to find contradictions between regulations for different enterprises and sometimes even in the same enterprise.

The publication of the first accounting standard by the Ministry of Finance (MOF 1992) has ended that situation. It consists of four basic assumptions – entity concept, continuity, periodicity, and money measurement – and twelve principles: objectivity, relevance, comparability, timeliness, clarity, accruals, matching, prudence, historical cost, revenue and capital identification, comprehensiveness, and materiality. Furthermore, although China's principles do not include substance over form, the spirit of it has been, to some extent, reflected in the standard. For example, financially leased fixed assets should be treated in the same way as an enterprise's own fixed assets and details disclosed in a footnote to the accounts. Also, if an enterprise owns more than 50 per cent of another company, or owns less than 50 per cent but effectively controls it, consolidated financial statements should be prepared.

Changes in legislation

The third influence on accounting development in China has been the change in legislation since the late 1970s. China's legal system, as detailed in the Constitution, consists of two different levels of legislation. At the higher level are the laws enacted by the National People's Congress (NPC) and, at the lower end, the administrative rules and regulations stipulated by the State Council (SC) in addition to those promulgated by Commissions and Ministries.

Prior to 1985, accounting was governed by administrative rules and regulations mainly enacted by the SC and the Ministry of Finance (MOF). From 1985 accounting law was dealt with by the NPC. The fact that legislation has been the main determinant of accounting practice has presented difficulties in that it is less flexible to a changing environment. The current law, now under revision, was prepared by reference to a centrally planned economy and is largely irrelevant for a socialist market economy. However, as the first law governing accounting practice, its significance cannot be underestimated (Nobes and Parker 1991).

In July 1986 the SC produced regulations for CPAs in the PRC and this has now been submitted to the Standing Committee of the NPC for reconsideration. The publication of the first accounting standard means that the regulation of accounting practice is taking on a wider view. This has resulted in an improvement in the quality of accounting regulation and, at present, accounting legislation is being reviewed to eliminate any

Table 14.5 Likely structure of accounting regulation in China

Regulation	Promulgator
Accounting Law	National People's Congress
Accounting Standards	Ministry of Finance
Accounting Policy	Enterprises

contradictions between it and the standard. It is estimated that the structure of China's accounting regulation (Table 14.5) will be similar to that in the West (Yan *et al.* 1993).

PROGRESS TO DATE

The result of fifteen years of reform efforts has been a substantial reduction in differences between China's accounting practice and internationally recognized practice. However, differences still remain.

First, China's accounting objectives are threefold, aiming to satisfy the information needs of:

1 Government, to assist in macro-economic management.
2 Investors and creditors, for investment decisions.
3 Managers, for operating decisions.

This is different from the situation in the USA and the UK where financial information is mainly aimed at assisting investors and, to some extent, creditors. Thus, in Chinese terms, accounting information has both macro and micro implications.

Second, although China's accounting principles include prudence, it is only conditionally applied, particularly in the case of taxation accounting which has not yet been disaggregated from financial accounting (Table 14.6). In addition, it is reflected in the fact that a bad debt provision is allowed but the valuation of securities and inventory at the lower of cost or market value is not permitted. They must be recorded at historical cost because of the combination of taxation and financial accounting.

Finally, unlike Western income statements, Chinese income statements show only income before taxation rather than net income. This difference results from the underlying Marxist economic theory on which accounting practice is based, which views income tax as an allocation of enterprise income to be

Table 14.6 An income statement

1 Revenue		**
Less: Cost of goods sold	**	
Selling expense	**	
Sales tax & surtax	**	
		**
	—	
2 Profit on sale		**
Add: Other revenue	**	
Less: Administrative expense	**	
Financial expense	**	
		**
	—	
3 Operating profit		**
Add: Investment income	**	
Non-operating income	**	
Less: Non-operating expense	**	
		**
	—	
4 Income before tax		**

Source: MOF 1992

shown, therefore, in a separate allocation statement. Close comparisons will reveal other differences and similarities.

It is perhaps interesting to note that the strongest influence in accounting change has come from the English-speaking world, particularly the USA and the UK, while the socio-economic environment of China has probably more in common with some of the continental nations, such as France and Germany, which share a similar legal system, that of status law.

Another similarity can be seen in the fact that France and Germany, like China, have accounting professions which do not have a significant influence in the development of accounting. In fact, government influence is stronger in China than in these countries and responsibility for accounting standard setting has been delegated, through accounting law, to the MOF. It is impossible for the Chinese accounting profession to obtain any kind of authoritative status such as the FASB in the USA (Tang *et al.* 1992). Finally, the Chinese interpretation of the 'true and fair view' is similar to that in France and Germany, that is, with strong emphasis on following regulations.

CONCLUSION

While being aware of the considerable achievements to date in China's accounting reform, there are several issues which should be emphasized. There is no doubt that China has a much more favourable international environment now in comparison to that of the early 1950s and this has greatly benefited its reforms. If China is to increase the market force in its economy, it could draw some invaluable lessons from the West. However, because of the particular stage of development of the market mechanism, China would be unwise to copy the model of Western countries. There are also some doubts as to the present suitability of International Accounting Standards (IAS) which are mainly influenced by the accounting practices of the USA and the UK. The best strategy for China would be to develop a flexible policy of reform which would endeavour to strike a balance between its present socio-economic environment and internationally accepted accounting conventions. The balance between China's socialist ideology and its capital economic structure will depend on economic reform which, in turn, depends on political reform.

Chinese accountants face a tough challenge. Besides the technical complications of accounting reform they will have to adjust to changes in the balance of socialist ideology and a changing economic structure. Thus, while introducing Western accounting practices, they must be careful not to run counter to current socialist ideology. It is difficult for China to import Western style institutions and any such importation is generally marked by China's particular socio-economic environment. For example, because China, compared with Western countries, still has overwhelming central control, the Chinese Institute of Certified Public Accountants (CICPA) acts as an independent professional body but is under the direct control of the government.

This difficult reform task is accompanied by a severe shortage of accounting practitioners and academics. Many were educated under the accounting system which operated in a centrally planned economy and desperately need to be re-educated to meet the rapidly changing needs of the Chinese economy. Both government officials and the accounting profession agree that accounting standards should take the place of accounting regulation. However, during the present transitional period, it is accepted that the accounting profession is not suitably developed to undertake this responsibility and so a system including both has been arranged, with the regulations being reviewed to eliminate any obvious contradictions with accounting standards.

To the outside world, it appears that China's move towards a market economy is accelerating. This is likely to bring continuing changes in accounting regulation and fresh challenges for its fast growing accounting profession.

NOTES

1 Increase/decrease bookkeeping is a double entry system, which is different from traditional double entry bookkeeping in that increase and decrease have the same meaning for both sides of the account, i.e. the assets and liabilities and owner's equity sides. For the operation of this system it is necessary to classify all accounts rigidly into one of these categories. It gives rise to many double sided entries and can consequently make balancing difficult. The figure for the trial balance can be extracted only by taking the difference between the increases and decreases on both sides.

REFERENCES

China State Statistics Bureau (1991) *China Statistical Yearbook*, Beijing.
Dreyer, J. T. (1993) *China's Political System: Modernisation and Tradition*, Basingstoke, UK: Macmillan.
Harding, H. (1987) *China's Second Revolution: Reform after Mao*, Washington, DC: Brookings Institution.
Kuen, L. (1991) *Chinese Firms and the State in Transition: Property Rights and Agency Problems in the Reform Era*, Armouk, NY: M. E. Sharpe.
Ministry of Finance (1992) *Accounting Standards, For Business Enterprises*, Beijing: Publishing House of Law.
Nobes, C. W. and Parker R. H. (eds) (1991) *Comparative International Accounting* (3rd edn), London: Prentice Hall International.
Parker, R. H. (1989) *Importing and Exporting Accounting: the British experience in International Pressures for Accounting Changes*, London: Prentice Hall International.
Tang. Y. W. Chow, L. and Cooper, B. J. (1992) *Accounting and Finance in China: a Review of Current Practice*, Hong Kong: Longman.
Yan, D. W., Jia, H. Z. and Xiao, W., (1993) *Principles and Practice of Accounting Standards*, Beijing: Publishing House of Popular Science.
Zhu, R. J. (1993) *People's Daily* (overseas edition), 14 May,

Chapter 15

Chinese accounting reform
Reasons and effects

R. W. Scapens and Z. Hao

INTRODUCTION

Of all the recent reforms of accounting in China, the 'Financial Guidelines for Business Enterprises' and the 'Accounting Standards for Business Enterprises', introduced in December 1992 and effective from 1 July 1993, will probably have the most far-reaching influence on Chinese finance and accountancy. These developments have followed more than ten years of economic reform and openness (to the outside world), and have been described as a 'revolution' in accounting reform (Yang 1993). Thus, the year 1993 may well represent the start of a new era in Chinese accounting history.

It is generally believed that a wide range of factors, such as politics, economy, culture, education and profession, exert an influence on accounting practices (Choi and Mueller 1984). In this Chapter we shall attempt to trace some of the factors which have exerted an influence on the process of accounting reform in China. In particular we will analyse the main reasons for the significant accounting reforms enacted in 1993 and their primary effects.

ANALYSIS OF REASONS

There are potentially very many factors which can have a role in the process of accounting reform. In this chapter we shall focus on the process of economic reform begun in 1978, the contribution made by academics and the education system, and the impact of legal and political factors.

Economic reform

Possibly the most important factor which influences accounting practices is the country's economic system, including the structure of ownership, the forms of enterprises, the stage of development, the form of management control, the relationship between owners and managers, the rate of inflation, and so on. In general, it may be expected that accounting practice will match the economic environment in which it exists and that changes in that economic environment will lead to changes in accounting practice.

China's economic condition has changed immensely since the policies of economic reform and openness were introduced in 1978.

> Looking back on the course of the past fourteen years, we can see that there have been two remarkable changes in China. One is the fact that the whole Party and the Chinese people have focused their attention on economic construction, rather than on 'political movements with class struggle as the key link'. The other is that in economic life, instead of the past highly centralized planned economy that operated in accordance with administrative instructions, market forces are now playing an increasingly important role.
>
> (Yuzhi Gong, quoted in Lin 1992)

The extent of these changes can be seen in the increasing diversity of ownership, the emergence of new types of business organizations, the rapid growth of the economy, the separation of ownership and management, the increasing amount of foreign investment, and the looseness of price control. In broad terms, the Chinese economy is now much more market oriented; it is now a socialist market economy.

Following more than thirty years of experience in government (since the formation of the People's Republic of China in 1949), the Communist Party of China has come to realize that the full development of a commodity economy is an indispensable stage in the economic growth of society (Communist Party of China 1984). The concept of the primary stage of socialism has been used by the Party in recent years to guide both economic and political development. As China established its socialist system on an undeveloped, semi-feudal and semi-colonial society, its economic development has been rather different from what Marx expected – he had assumed that socialism would be established on a developed capitalist society. It is argued that China is still in the primary stage of socialism and that a full market economy needs to be developed and the centrally planned economy reformed or abandoned. Thus, the primary stage of socialism covers a comparatively long period, starting in 1949 and still continuing; and not the rather short period in the early 1950s which it was previously believed to be.

An interesting feature of Chinese reform programmes has been the experimental, step-by-step, trial and error approach, using particular areas of the economy, regions of the country, types of enterprise, and so on to try out new ideas and new methods, to see what happens and to gain practical experience, and then to decide what to do next. One example is the Special Economic Zones (SEZs) which have been used to experiment with structural economic reforms. An example in the accounting field is the Joint Ventures Accounting System which was introduced in China ten years ago. This system was based on international accounting conventions and its success resulted in further accounting reform, such as the accounting system for enterprises experimenting with the shareholding system, and the accounting systems used in SEZs. Furthermore, the 1993 accounting reforms in general follow the model used for the Joint Ventures Accounting System.

Thus, it could be said that the 'Accounting Regulations for Joint Ventures Using Chinese and Foreign Investment', issued in 1985, was the precursor of the current accounting reforms. It was the first time since 1949 that China had established an accounting system based on international conventions. The new elements introduced at that time included:

1 Accounting principles such as matching, historical cost, and consistency.
2 A 'capital' concept; Chinese accountants had no notion of capital prior to that time.
3 The accounting equation

$$\text{Assets} = \text{Liabilities} + \text{Owner's equity}$$

which replaced the previous equation

$$\text{Fund applications} = \text{Fund sources.}$$

4 A distinction between capital expenditure and revenue expenditure.
5 Accelerated depreciation, but only if approved by local tax authorities.
6 Methods to record and account for intangible assets and organization expenses.
7 Methods to record and account for exchange gains and losses.
8 The classification of costs into direct materials, direct labour and manufacturing overhead.
9 A third financial statement: the statement of changes in financial position.

This joint ventures accounting system was regarded as very successful and was believed to have assisted in the promotion of foreign investment in China. In addition, it demonstrated that international accounting conventions, typically based on Western accounting procedures, could be applied in China. This prompted Chinese accountants to consider whether such an accounting system should be introduced into other Chinese enterprises, including the state-owned enterprises.

Possibly the most significant difference between the new accounting systems (such as those for joint ventures and for enterprises in SEZs) and the systems used until recently by state-owned enterprises could be found in the section dealing with 'owner's equity'. In the 'Accounting Regulations for Joint Ventures', for example, the concept of 'capital' was introduced, whereas in the accounting systems used by state-owned enterprises the term 'fund' was used. However, 'fund' and 'capital' are totally different concepts, both in definition and in bookkeeping. As the state allocates fixed assets to individual enterprises, it is the state which invests in and owns the enterprise. On receipt of fixed assets, a state owned-enterprise would make the following bookkeeping entry:

Fixed assets
    State fund source

When the enterprise provides depreciation, the following two entries would be recorded:

(1) State fund source
        Accumulated depreciation
(2) Depreciation expense

Special fund source: Fixed asset renewal and renovation fund.

Through entry (1) the state fund is reduced. Furthermore, the enterprise is not automatically permitted to retain the fund generated by the depreciation charge. If the state decides to withdraw the funds generated by the depreciation provision, the following entry would be recorded (see Tang *et al.* 1992: 29–33):

Special fund source: Fixed asset renewal and renovation fund
    Special fund bank deposits

In this case, the withdrawal of the depreciation fund actually means decreasing capital. There was no notion of 'capital maintenance' for state-owned enterprises under the old system. Whether all or a proportion of the 'fixed asset renewal and renovation fund' was or was not withdrawn was a government financial policy dependent on the economic situation and the requirements of state macro-administration. As a result, enterprises were dependent on further state funds to replace their fixed assets. However, as the state has been increasing the autonomy of state-owned enterprises in recent years, it has been allowing enterprises to retain larger proportions, and in some cases all of the 'fixed asset renewal and renovation fund'. Thus, these enterprises are now able to make decisions themselves regarding their capital investments.

The aim of diversifying the ownership of state-owned enterprises has gradually become more and more acceptable during the 1980s, whereas previously public ownership was widely recognized as the symbol of socialism. Furthermore, it is now accepted that during the primary stage of socialism various economic entities will exist simultaneously. Nowadays in China, in addition to state-owned and collective enterprises, there are individually owned enterprises, foreign investment enterprises, township enterprises, shareholder enterprises and other forms of mixed ownership.

However, these new ownership structures have served to highlight weaknesses in the existing systems of finance and accounting in China. In the centrally planned economy, ownership structures were relatively simple, and consequently did not create major problems for the accounting system. At that time accounting systems were principally designed for individual industries. Once new forms of ownership began to emerge (in addition to the state-owned and collective enterprises), new accounting systems had to be designed for each type of ownership, with the result that there were separate accounting systems for each type of ownership in each type of industry. There was, therefore, considerable complexity in the accounting systems, and a general lack of consistency and comparability (Zhang 1992).

In the Chinese economic reforms a key problem has been to invigorate the large and medium sized state-owned enterprises, which were generally believed to be very inefficient and lacking motivation. One important step in the reform process was the introduction of the contract responsibility system, which was first introduced on a trial basis for a number of urban enterprises in 1981 and was subsequently extended nation wide in 1987. Under this system, managers and employees of state-owned enterprises enter into contracts with the state for certain production tasks and, provided that they meet their production plans, profit targets and other contract terms, they can retain a proportion of their profits, subject to paying appropriate profits taxes. These retained profits can be used to expand the business, to pay bonuses and/or to improve the enterprise's collective welfare facilities. However, if the contracted tasks are not completed, the enterprise must make up any short fall in payments to the state from its own funds. The contract responsibility system was intended to increase the managerial autonomy of enterprises and to improve the motivation of both managers and workers; it is widely believed to have been very successful.

In addition to the contract responsibility system, now in widespread use, it was proposed in the mid-1980s that a shareholder-based system should be introduced as the next step in the reform process. However, since the first shareholder enterprise in China, the Beijing Tian Qiao Department Store, was registered in July 1984, there had been no accounting regulations for shareholder enterprises. Prior to the recent accounting reforms, most shareholder enterprises adhered to the accounting regulations for state-owned enterprises, supplemented with some special amendments. However, these amendments varied among enterprises and caused unnecessary complications in financial reporting. For instance, some enterprises divided all classes of share capital into two separate elements (a fixed fund and a current fund) and treated share capital as they had previously treated the state fund (Tang *et al.* 1992).

As might be expected, enterprise groups[1] have more accounting problems than single enterprises. By the beginning of the 1990s there were around 2,000 groups of all kinds in China. Within a group there could be subsidiaries and branches in different industries, with different types of ownership. These subsidiaries and branches might use quite different accounting systems. As a result, major problems appeared when consolidated financial statements were prepared. To cope with such situations, some groups have set up their own accounting systems. For instance, the China International Trust and Investment Corporation designed and introduced, with the approval of the Ministry of Finance (MOF), an accounting system for use by all of the subsidiaries in its group.

The development of management accounting in China also created a need to reform accounting systems. Since Western accounting ideas were introduced into China in the early 1980s, management accounting has become increasingly popular. Various management accounting techniques have been tried in a number of Chinese enterprises (Scapens and Meng 1993), but a number of problems have been encountered. A major problem was that management accounting techniques did not fit easily with Chinese accounting systems. In order to promote management accounting in Chinese enterprises, and to encourage its use in business decision making, the old accounting systems had to be reformed.

The introduction of Western financial accounting into China is likely to be rather more difficult than the introduction of Western management accounting. In the case of management accounting, there was no such separate discipline in China prior to the 1980s, although some similar techniques and methods did exist (see Shanghai University 1987, Scapens and Hou 1994). However, in the case of financial accounting, various systems of financial reporting already existed and were compulsory for state-owned and collective enterprises. Furthermore, financial accounting was the main course in accounting departments of Chinese universities. When 'Western financial accounting' was taught, the term 'Western' was always used, whereas such a term was not used for 'management accounting' courses, although the contents were predominantly Western.

However, since much of the data used in management accounting comes from the financial accounting system, management accounting techniques cannot be used properly unless both systems use the same concepts and terminology. When Western management accounting was first introduced into China, the existing financial accounting systems used quite different concepts and terminology. One major difference was the cost classi-fication systems. Whereas Western management accounting draws distinctions between fixed and variable costs, and between period and product costs, Chinese cost classifications distinguished raw materials, fuel and power, wages and workers' welfare, workshop administrative expenses, and enterprise administrative expenses. Furthermore, all expenses, including administrative expenses and selling expenses, were included in the product costs, there being no notion of period costs at all. Thus, if management accounting techniques were to be used, the accountants had to recalculate and reclassify costs. As can be imagined, this led to considerable duplication of effort. Such tasks are not easy in enterprises in which the accountants deal with the transactions without computers, relying only on the abacus.

As the government is gradually reducing its direct interference in the day-to-day business administration of most state-owned enterprises, accountants will begin to play a more extensive role in their operation and decision-making. As a result, it is likely that management accounting will become increasingly important. This is creating further pressure for Chinese accounting reform, since a suitable financial accounting system is needed so that accountants can use management accounting techniques in enterprise administration.

Academic research and education

Academic research and education have made substantial contributions to the Chinese accounting reform process. The direction of the reform, its content and the particular accounting measurements to be used were widely debated in academic circles, and various proposals for accounting reform were advanced. Furthermore, through higher education, secondary vocational education and adult education, a large proportion of the accountants in China have, in recent years, studied both Chinese accounting and Western accounting and have gradually gained knowledge of international accounting conventions. This education process laid the foundations for the current accounting reforms.

Chinese accounting academics have undertaken various activities to promote research on accounting standards. In 1987, the Accounting Society of China (which comprises Chinese accounting academics and is similar to the American Accounting Association) set up a Research Group on Accounting Theories and Standards to undertake studies and to make recommendations on accounting standards. The Group has established for itself a set of working procedures, launched investigations, convened conferences, and put forward recommendations on such subjects as the structure of Chinese accounting standards and accounting for changing prices.

Numerous articles about the process of setting up Chinese accounting standards were published in the course of the debate on accounting reform. In general, academics argued in favour of introducing accounting standards in China. Their arguments included:

1 Responding to economic reform and openness.
2 Catching up with economic development.
3 Improvement of macro-administration of economic activities.
4 Strengthening micro-business management.
5 Expansion of international exchange.

There was also general agreement that Chinese accounting standards should consist of two levels: fundamental standards and applied standards. Fundamental standards are the general principles of accountancy which should be comparatively stable over time. Applied standards are the specific requirements that particular procedures and methods should be used, and they would need to be issued and revised from time to time. Also discussed were the relationships between accounting standards and the various accounting systems used in different industries and by different types of enterprise, the various steps needed to set up accounting standards, and the guiding ideology.

Following the rejection of the extreme leftist thinking which had dominated the country in the 1960s and 1970s, both academics and practitioners gradually came to favour Western accounting theories and methods.

In looking at accounting as a discipline we tend to view it as having no national boundaries, in the sense that accounting principles and practices as they exist in different countries have much in common because they are the result of human wisdom and experience accumulated over centuries. However, we must acknowledge that accounting in many respects does have national or regional boundaries, in that the political, social and economic environment is bound to have a far-reaching impact.

(Lou 1987:1)

There was an extensive international exchange of accounting ideas between Chinese and foreign academics during the 1980s. Professors from universities in the USA, UK, Japan, Germany, Australia, Canada, as well as other countries visited China to present lectures and to attend symposia. International accounting firms, which were expanding their businesses in China at that time, held training seminars for Chinese accountants and students. In addition, Chinese scholars went to Western countries to study Western accounting theories and practices, and to do research. Thus, Western accounting theories and practices were introduced into China, and gradually these new ideas became generally accepted and provided the underpinning for the current accounting reforms.

Accounting education has also played an important role in the reform process. Students who graduated during the 1980s learned both Chinese accounting and Western accounting, including both financial accounting and management accounting. Now, after a period of five to ten years, many of these students hold relatively senior management and accounting positions in the government and in enterprises and other organizations. As a result of their exposure to Western ideas during their education, they have found it quite easy to accept the accounting reforms. A number of them have actively advocated reform. Generally, it is such former students who carry out the accounting reforms in practice. Consequently, they are a key force in Chinese accounting reform; without them it would have been impossible to have carried out the major accounting reforms of 1993.

Legal and political influences

Legal and political factors have also influenced Chinese accounting reforms. The new accounting systems have had to accord with the existing but evolving framework of laws, and certain political events have had a considerable influence on the reform process.

A law on 'Joint Ventures Using Chinese and Foreign Investment' was adopted by the Second Session of the Fifth National People's Congress on 1 July 1979. There followed a series of laws and regulations on joint ventures, including a law on the income tax of joint ventures. However, such developments urgently required the establishment of appropriate accounting systems. After initial study and discussion, the MOF issued a draft 'Accounting Regulations for Joint Ventures Using Chinese and Foreign Investments' in 1983. This was the first accounting system in China to reflect international accounting conventions since the foundation of the People's Republic of China in 1949. It was eventually approved and published, together with a list of the accounts to be used, in March 1985.

In April 1991, the National People's Congress promulgated a new law on the Income Tax of Enterprises with Foreign Investment and Foreign Enterprises which replaced the previous law on the income tax of joint ventures. This new law used the term 'enterprises with foreign investment', which included not only Sino-foreign equity joint ventures and Sino-foreign contractual joint ventures but also foreign-capital enterprises established in China. Thus, it became necessary to replace the 'Accounting Regulations for Joint Ventures' with the 'Accounting Regulations for Enterprises with Foreign Investment', and this was issued in June 1992.

Although there are differing opinions on the shareholding system, the government's current position is to encourage experimentation. According to an article in the *Beijing Review*,

> the shareholding system will help to promote the separation of the functions of the government from those of enterprises, the change in the way enterprises operate, and the accumulation of social capital. We should therefore try it out in selected enterprises, reviewing our experience regularly and formulating laws and regulations to ensure that the system develops in a sound and orderly manner.
>
> (Jiang 1992)

It has been suggested by academics in China that the contract responsibility system should be replaced by the shareholding system. Thus, it is quite possible that the shareholding system will become widely adopted. However, it is also very likely that the government will maintain a majority holding in the former 'state-owned' enterprises in order to maintain the socialist character of the Chinese economy.

Nevertheless, the introduction of a shareholding system will mean that the state is no longer the sole user of the financial statements, and so the objectives and methods of financial reporting will have to be revised to meet the needs of a wider group of users. Furthermore, the absence of appropriate financial reporting regulations could hinder the development of the shareholding system. For instance, it could limit the extent to which Chinese shareholder enterprises will be able to access world stock markets, and it could discourage foreigners from purchasing Chinese stocks.[2] The potential problems were well recognized by both the government and the managers of shareholder enterprises. In May 1992, the government (through the MOF and the State Commission for Restructuring the Economic System) promulgated an 'Accounting System for Experimental Enterprises with the Shareholding System', which was designed in the light of international accounting conventions.

At the beginning of the 1990s, accounting practices in China could be divided into two categories: those which followed international accounting conventions (such as those used in enterprises with foreign investment, enterprises with the shareholding system, and enterprises in certain Special Economic Zones) and those following traditional accounting procedures (such as those which continued to be used in state-owned enterprises, collective enterprises and township enterprises). At that time, the influence of international accounting conventions was extending rapidly, while traditional practices were also changing, albeit gradually. It was the period of most 'uneven' accounting practices since 1949. In each of the above two categories, there were numerous accounting systems based on both types of ownership and industrial groups. In total, more than forty accounting systems were in use at that time. This complicated picture pointed to a need for a unified set of national accounting standards. Nevertheless, there was some resistance to extending the accounting practices in the first category to the enterprises which were then using the traditional accounting practices in the second; some people feared that the introduction of too many capitalist ideas would mean that they were following the 'capitalist road'.

However, the speed of accounting reform was significantly increased by an important political event: namely, remarks made by Mr Deng Xiaoping during his tour of South China in the Spring of 1992. According to Zhong (1992):

> While in South China, Deng repeatedly expressed his hope that the people would be bolder in undertaking reform and in bringing about change, would open dare to experiment and would not act like bound-feet women [i.e. walk haltingly]. When one is sure of the worth of an endeavour, one should have a go at it boldly and dare to make breakthroughs'.

With the encouragement given by Deng's speech, the Ministry of Finance, which is responsible for the administration of accounting affairs in China, decided to hasten its steps towards accounting reform.

The MOF had actually started work on accounting standards in 1987, and had drafted standards for discussion and comment several times since then (Hao 1992). During this process, however, the general line of thinking was that existing accounting practices should be changed gradually in order to avoid confusion in the economic order, and that accounting standards would be set up only when conditions matured. Such thinking seemed too slow when compared with the requirement for bold reform. When, following Deng's speech, the MOF decided to act more quickly, it had two possible approaches. First, it could introduce both fundamental and applied accounting standards as soon as possible, which would achieve the goal of accounting reform in a single step and reduce the possibility of duplicating work. Second, it could issue fundamental accounting standards first. At the same time it could begin the necessary alterations and improvements to existing accounting systems, which would continue through a period of transformation, and ultimately it could issue applied and detailed accounting standards to replace existing accounting systems at a suitable time in the future. After discussion and consideration, the MOF decided to adopt the second approach (see Zhang 1992). The result was the two statements issued in December 1992, the 'Accounting Standards for Business Enterprises' and the 'Financial Guidelines for Business Enterprises', plus a general reduction in the wide variety of accounting systems (from more than forty to just nine).

ASSESSMENT OF EFFECTS

As the new Chinese accounting standards have only recently been introduced, it is difficult to assess in detail their effects but it is possible to give an initial assessment of some apparent impacts and influences.

Financial reporting

Following the reforms, Chinese financial statements should be more easily understood by the various users in different countries. Foreign business executives used to complain that they had great difficulty in understanding the records kept and the statements prepared by Chinese accountants. But now more familiar formats for the balance sheet, income statement and statement of changes in financial position are to be used by Chinese industrial enterprises (see appendix).

The main changes which the reforms have made to the financial statements are outlined below:

1 Generally accepted accounting terms are now used. As can be seen from the appendix, Chinese financial statements are similar to the statements widely used by companies all around the world.
2 The system of 'fund accounting' (typical of accounting systems in centrally planned economies) has been abandoned. Previously, separate funds had to be maintained for fixed assets, current assets, and other specific purposes. The assets representing each of these funds had to be shown separately on the balance sheet and, in each case, the assets and the fund had to balance. This reflected the strict controls imposed on enterprises in the centrally planned economy, which stipulated that funds could be used only for specified purposes.
3 An equity section has been added to the balance sheet and the concept of 'capital' has been introduced. As the economic reforms have made state-owned enterprises independent, autonomous entities, it is no longer possible for the state simply to withdraw enterprise funds at will. Enterprises are now expected to maintain their production capability and to keep a minimum registered capital.
4 The income statement has been simplified. Previously, the income statement was intended primarily for internal and

central planning purposes. The new income statement is more oriented towards external readers, with obvious international features.

5 A third statement has been added: the statement of changes in financial position.

The pattern of accounting administration has also changed. Previously, accounting and financial regulations were laid down according to both industry and type of ownership. The new accounting standards, however, apply to all enterprises established in China. As a result, the financial statements of enterprises with different types of ownership are now produced on the same basis. This change will undoubtedly increase the comparability of the accounting information produced by different enterprises. Furthermore, it may be expected that accounting practice in China will become more unified.

The reform of financial reporting in China should assist further economic reform and development. Standardized accounting practices will create a certain order in the national economy and the single system of financial reporting will benefit investors and creditors whose better informed decision-making should promote the flow of economic resources, both internally and from abroad. Since it will be much easier for foreign investors to understand Chinese accounting information, foreign investment into China will be encouraged. With the development of a stronger national economy, Chinese enterprises should also find it easier to enter world markets and to conduct business on a multinational basis. Furthermore, as the new financial reporting regulations are based on international accounting conventions, such enterprises should not find it difficult to do business in accordance with international business practices. In particular, they should find it easier to raise funds on international financial markets, for instance through issuing corporate stocks and bonds.

Management control

The introduction of 'Accounting Standards for Business Enterprises' will also assist the process of reforming the management control of state-owned enterprises. Under the socialist market economy, all enterprises (including state-owned enterprises) are independent economic entities; in other words, they are corporate bodies, responsible for their profits and losses.

> By straightening out the relationships between the ownership and management of enterprises, separating the functions of the government from those of the enterprises and granting the latter more autonomy, we should turn them into legal entities responsible for their own decisions about their operation and expansion, and for their own profits and losses.
>
> (Jiang 1992)

As a result of the new responsibilities being placed on state-owned enterprises, they must strengthen their internal management control and improve their operating efficiency and effectiveness in order to survive and grow in what are increasingly competitive markets. In the last few years Chinese state-owned enterprises have been transformed from simple extensions of the state planning apparatus into independent operating mechanisms with comparatively autonomous management. The new accounting standards should provide a basis for systems of internal financial control.

Furthermore, as the financial reporting responsibilities of enterprises have been clearly set out in the accounting standards, the government, through the various Ministries, should no longer be in a position to request enterprises (especially, state-owned enterprises) to supply considerable amounts of financial data, as it did under the old system. This should prevent the government from interfering directly in the management of enterprises. However, this does mean that enterprises, having gained increased managerial autonomy, will need management accounting systems which fit alongside the external reporting requirements of the new accounting standards.

In practice, accounting for decision-making is becoming an increasingly important part of the management control of Chinese enterprises. Previously, the construction of fixed assets, the purchase of raw materials and the sales of final products were all determined by the government through the state planning system. The enterprise management simply organized the manufacture of the products required by the state plan. The funds generated by the depreciation of fixed assets were handed over to the appropriate state agencies, to whom requests had to be made for all new fixed assets. Raw materials were allocated to enterprises and finished goods delivered to the state (or its distribution agencies). These procedures have changed gradually over the last ten years. Nowadays most enterprises make their own decisions regarding the purchase and sale of fixed assets, raw materials and final products. Thus, there is a need for management accountants to investigate markets, forecast demand, assess proposals, and make proper analysis and comment.

As a result of the reforms, enterprises have had to strengthen their control of corporate finance. The strict principle that specific funds had to be used for specific purposes no longer applies. The application of that principle under the centrally planned system meant that funds which had been provided for fixed assets, current assets, and other specific purposes could not be used interchangeably. However, enterprises must now plan their utilization of all kinds of economic resources and must prepare effective budgets. They can raise additional financial resources; indeed, some enterprises can issue corporate bonds and share capital. Thus, there is a need for enterprise managers and accountants to develop techniques for evaluating the potential uses of financial resources.

An important change brought about by the accounting reform is that cost statements are no longer required external information. However, this does not mean that enterprises do not need cost statements internally. With the development of a socialist market economy, especially the reduction in the extent of price controls and the changes in the government's economic administrative function, the state will be less dependent on cost information supplied by individual enterprises. Thus, enterprise cost information will no longer be 'publicly' available and it will become more of a business secret. However, with the increasing autonomy of enterprise management and the new intensity of market competition, the level of cost will become a vital element with which to measure business performance and to decide future strategy. Accordingly, all enterprises have to strengthen their systems of cost responsibility in order to improve their internal cost management. According to Chen (1992), one result of the accounting reform is that cost management should be conducted in more detail, and consideration given to cost prediction, cost decision, cost control and cost supervision.

Cost management will certainly be a significant link in the management control of Chinese enterprises. The previous system of cost classification gave much more attention to cost essence,[3] and less to cost control. Under that system, Chinese accountants did not analyse the relationship between costs and volume of output. Therefore, they had no concepts or effective measurements of cost behaviour for purposes of cost control. However, the situation gradually began to change at the beginning of the 1980s.

For over thirty years Chinese enterprises have used systems of responsibility accounting (see Scapens and Hou 1994). The typical internal responsibility units in state-owned enterprises were workshops or sections. However, the extent of their economic responsibilities and rights were frequently unclear. Consequently, it was difficult to tell which costs and revenues were controllable and which were not (Qiu 1992). Classifying costs into fixed and variable elements, according to concepts of cost behaviour used in the West, might be a first step to greater cost control but it must be recognized that both fixed costs and variable costs require control. Although certain costs (i.e. fixed costs) do not vary with the level of output, decisions are taken which affect the level of such costs in the long term. Thus, it is important that responsibility centres should be established to control both fixed and variable costs.

International influence

As pointed out above, Chinese accounting reforms have been influenced by international accounting practice. Chinese accounting academics and practitioners have studied foreign concepts and techniques, and experts and professors from other countries were invited into China to give their opinions and suggestions on Chinese accounting reform. Furthermore, the International Accounting Standards Committee (IASC) has had an important influence on Chinese accounting standards, even though China has no representative on the IASC.

In February 1992, some ten months before the 'Accounting Standards for Business Enterprises' were issued, the MOF convened an International Symposium on Accounting Standards in Shenzhen, the biggest Special Economic Zone in China. The Chairman and Secretary-General of the IASC and other experts from the USA, Singapore and Hong Kong attended the Symposium, during which discussions were held with Chinese accounting experts on setting Chinese accounting standards. Many IASC standards and procedures are reflected in the Chinese accounting reforms.

The Chinese accounting standards are a further step towards international harmonization of financial reporting. Since China opened itself to the outside world, it has become a significant part of the world economy and promises to become an even more important part in the future. The Chinese government and the management of Chinese enterprises have gradually come to realize the importance of adopting international business practices. At the same time, foreign investors and business people are coming to expect Chinese enterprises to carry out their businesses in the manner that is generally acceptable worldwide, which includes accounting practice and financial reporting. However, since China remains a socialist country, there continues to be doubt as to whether China can harmonize its accounting practice with Western countries. But, as we have seen, the political and legal structures have not formed an obstacle to the process of accounting reform in China. As a result, Chinese accounting practices can be harmonized with international financial reporting.

This reform of Chinese accounting has to be seen in the context of some significant changes in world accounting. Much has happened since the end of the 1980s. The upheavals in Eastern Europe have created a need for major accounting changes in these emerging market economies. Furthermore, the Fourth and Seventh Directives have been implemented in most EU countries, and the IASC has now issued thirty-one standards. The Chinese accounting 'revolution' of 1993 adds another dimension to this process of accounting change. In various attempts to classify international accounting practice (e.g. AAA 1977 and Nobes 1992), the Communist (centrally planned) accounting model had appeared as a separate cluster. Now, however, that cluster has lost virtually all of its members and so it is probably time to reclassify international accounting practices.

There are certainly clear indications of a move towards the international harmonization of financial accounting and reporting. The differences in accounting among different countries are narrowing, but the course of harmonization remains quite slow. Nevertheless, China has reformed its accounting system and begun to adopt international accounting conventions. As we discussed above, this was done in part to provide the understandable financial information which is needed to promote an international flow of economic resources.

CONCLUSION

The year 1993 was one of major accounting reform in China. The 'Accounting Standards for Business Enterprises' which came into effect on 1 July 1993 form an important stage in the process of accounting and economic reform in China, which also has substantial implications for the rest of the world. China, the country with the largest population in the world, has the potential to be the world's largest market and a significant player in world economic relations and trade. The accounting reforms are a major step towards internationalizing China's economy. They will make it easier for foreign investors to invest in China, and for Chinese enterprises to access world markets.

In this chapter we have explored a number of the factors which have played a role in the process of accounting reform. First, we argued that economic reform is possibly the primary reason for Chinese accounting reform. The process of economic reform in China necessitates reform of the accounting system. Second, the academic community has made valuable contributions both in demonstrating the need for accounting reform and in setting accounting standards. Furthermore, the accounting education system in China has prepared Chinese accountants to implement the accounting reforms. Finally, Mr Deng's speech during his tour of Southern China was a major political factor which gave considerable impetus to the reform process and led to the introduction of Chinese accounting standards.

Accounting reform in China is expected to benefit the country's economic development. By following international accounting conventions it is hoped to improve the prospects for foreign investment, to expand international economic exchanges with multinational businesses setting up production facilities in China, and to assist Chinese enterprises to enter world markets. Finally, accounting reform in China is an important element of the international harmonization of accounting practices.

NOTES

1 Enterprise groups comprise combinations of a number of enterprises. A large state-owned enterprise might be authorized to act as a parent company (and to control a number of other enterprises) and to set up new subsidiaries and joint ventures, with both domestic and foreign investors, by a government decree, or through the purchase of other enterprises, or by agreement between the interested parties.
2 Foreign investors are permitted to buy certain Chinese stocks, known as B shares. Shareholder enterprises in China issue two types of shares: A shares which are quoted in RMB (the local currency) and available to Chinese investors, and B shares which are quoted in US dollars and available to foreign investors.
3 Cost essence is the actual composition of cost. According to Marxist theory, cost is the amount of labour consumed during production. Accountants had to measure the amount of labour consumed as accurately as possible. That was the task of costing in the centrally planned economy. However, in a market economy, cost can be measured by the monetary units exchanged.

APPENDIX

The balance sheet format is shown in Chapter 14 p. 252 above.
The income statement format is shown in Chapter 14 p. 258 above.
The statement of changes in financial position format is shown in Table 15.1 below.

REFERENCES

American Accounting Association (1977) 'Report of the Committee on International Accounting Operations and Education, 1975–1976', *Accounting Review: Supplement to Vol. 52.*
Chen, Y. (1992) 'Ten questions should be cleared up after finance and accounting reform', *A Supplement to Finance and Accounting*, no. 12, pp. 60–63, Beijing.
Choi, F. D. S. and Mueller, G. G. (1984) *International Accounting*, Englewood Cliffs, NJ: Prentice-Hall.
Communist Party of China (1984) 'Decision of the Central Committee of the Communist Party of China on reform of the economic structure', *Beijing Review* 27 (44).
Hao, Z. (1992) 'The development of accounting standards in China', *International Accounting Comparison and Development*, Cheng Du [ed.]: Southwest University of Finance and Economics.
Jiang, Z. (1992) 'Accelerating reform and opening-up', *Beijing Review* 35 (43): 9–32.
Lin, L. (1992) 'Dialogue on socialist market economy', *Beijing Review* 35 (43): 33–7.
Lou, E.-Y. (1987) 'Accounting and auditing in the People's Republic of

China', in E.-Y. Lou, S. N. Wang and A. J. H. Enthoven [eds], *Accounting and Auditing in the People's Republic of China. A Review of its Practice, System, Education and Development*, Dallas: Centre for International Accounting Development, University of Texas. Chapter 1.

Nobes, C. W. (1992) *International Classification of Financial Reporting* (2nd edn), London: Routledge.

Qiu, Z. (1992) 'Contrasting the Western style with the Chinese style of responsibility accounting', *International Accounting Comparison and Development*, Cheng Du [ed.]: Southwest University of Finance and Economics.

Scapens, R. W. and Hou, B. (1994) 'The evolution of responsibility accounting systems in China', *Research in Third World Accounting*, London: JAI Press.

Scapens, R. W. and Meng, Y. (1993) 'Management accounting research in China', *Management Accounting Research*, (4): 321–41.

Shanghai University of Finance and Economics and the University of Texas at Dallas (E.-Y. Lou, S. N. Wang and A. J. H. Enthoven [eds]) (1987) *Accounting and Auditing in the People's Republic of China: A Review of its Practice, System, Education and Development*, Dallas: Centre for International Accounting Development, University of Texas.

Tang, Y. W., Chow, L. and Cooper, B. J. (1992) *Accounting and Finance in China: A Review of Current Practice*, Hong Kong: Longman.

Yang, J. (1993) 'Review and preview of accounting system reform', *Finance and Accounting*, no. 6: 3–8.

Zhang, D. (1992) 'Implementing Accounting Standards for Business Enterprises, serving better the process of reform and openness', *A Supplement to Finance and Accounting*, no. 12: 22–6.

Zhang, Y. (1992) 'Considerations on several matters about the setting-up and implementation of the General Rules and the Standards', *A Supplement to Finance and Accounting*, no. 12: 11–14.

Zhong, S. (1992) 'Fresh impetus from Deng's message', *Beijing Review* 35 (15): 4–6.

Table 15.1 Statement of Changes in Financial Position

Year:_____	*Monetary unit: Yuan*

Sources and Applications of Working Capital	*Changes of Working Capital Items*

I. Sources of working capital:
  1. Current year profit:
    Add: Items not affecting working capital:
      (1) Depreciation of fixed assets
      (2) Amortisation of intangible assets and
           deferred assets
      (3) Shortage of fixed assets (less excess)
 	
      (4) Loss from disposal of fixed assets (less gain)
 	
      (5) Other expenses and losses not affecting
           working capital
    Subtotal
 	
  2. Other sources:
    (1) Proceeds from disposal of fixed assets
    (2) Increase of long-term loans
    (3) Decrease of long-term investments
    (4) Decrease of fixed assets for investment
    (5) Decrease of intangible assets for investment
    (6) Net increase/(decrease) of capital
    Subtotal
    Total Sources of Working Capital
	I. Increases of Current Assets in the Year:
	    1. Cash
	    2. Short-term investments
	    3. Notes receivable
	    4. Net of debtors
	    5. Prepayment to suppliers
	    6. Other debtors
	    7. Stocks
	    8. Deferred and prepaid expenses
	    9. Long-term bond investments matured within one year
	   10. Net losses of current
	   11. Other current assets
	
	    Net Increase of Current Assets

Table 15.1 continued

Year: _____   Monetary unit: Yuan

Sources and Applications of Working Capital	Changes of Working Capital Items

II. Applications of Working Capital:
1. Distribution of profit:
  (1) Income tax payable
  (2) Surplus reserve provided (compensating losses with ' — ')
  (3) Dividends
  (4) Special fund payable
  (5) Adjustment to decrease last year's profit (adjustment to increase with ' — ')
  Subtotal
2. Other applications:
  (1) Net increases in fixed assets and construction in progress
  (2) Increases of intangible assets, deferred assets and other assets
  (3) Repayment of long-term loans
  (4) Increases of long-term investments
  Subtotal
	II. Increases of Current Liabilities in Year:
	1. Short-term loans
	2. Notes payable
	3. Creditors
	4. Advances from customers
	5. Other creditors
	6. Accrued payroll
	7. Welfare payable
	8. Unpaid taxes
	9. Dividends payable
	10. Other unpaid accounts
	11. Provision for expenses
	12. Taxes deductible
	13. Long-term liabilities matured within one year
	14. Other current liabilities

Total Application of Working Capital	Net Increases of Current Liabilities
Net Increases of Working Capital	Net Increases of Working Capital

Part V

Developments in the accounting profession

In Chapter 16, Mo, Tam, Lui and Shum review the development of the Institute of Certified Public Accountants in China, placing this in its historical context, exploring the certification process, and comparing this with the position of the longer established Hong Kong profession. Gao, in Chapter 17, offers a wide-ranging discussion of the university system of accounting education in China, making some comparisons with the UK situation, and reporting a survey of Chinese accounting students' attitudes. In Chapter 18, Chong and Vinten offer a comparison of the way in which the auditing approach is currently developing in China with the UK experience, identifying the relevance of problems in the UK for China.

Developments in the accounting profession

Chapter 16

China's CPA examination
Preparing for the expanding profession

P. L. L. Mo, W. H. Tam, G. M. C. Lui and C. M. Y. Shum

INTRODUCTION

Since the adoption of the open door policy in 1979, China has moved from an agricultural-based society to a society where trade and manufacturing enterprises play a more significant role. The turn of the century is characterized by the flooding in of foreign investments, the listing of Chinese enterprises on foreign markets and the development of share capital systems. Two stock exchanges – the Shanghai Stock Exchange and the Shenzhen Stock Exchange – opened on 19 December 1990 and 3 July 1991 respectively. However, in the first year of operation, the two stock exchanges were opened only to domestic Chinese investors. In December 1991, the issuing of B shares (shares in Chinese companies reserved for non-PRC investors) in Shanghai Stock Exchange marked the first trading of shares by foreign investors. Since then, the B-share market has been undergoing rapid development. By the end of 1992, a total of eighteen companies which have issued B shares were listed on the two stock exchanges. In 1993, a third type of stock issued by Chinese state-owned enterprises, H shares, joined the Hong Kong Stock Exchange. There are currently fourteen H shares listed on the Hong Kong Stock Exchange.

The securities market does not operate in a vacuum. The support from other professionals, such as legal experts and qualified accountants, is essential for the successful development of a macro financial market. However, the accounting body in China is under the jurisdiction of the Chinese government, and lack of independence has been the major criticism levelled against the Chinese accounting profession. In order to face the challenges of the future, resulting from the rapidly changing financial market, it is time for the accounting profession to establish its own autonomous institute, examination structure and internationally recognized qualification. The purpose of this chapter is to delineate the current certified public accountants' (CPA) examination in China. A comparison is also conducted between the CPA examination in China and the Chartered Association of Certified Accountants (ACCA) examination in Commonwealth countries.

HISTORICAL DEVELOPMENT

The first CPA regulations were announced in 1918 by the Northern Warlords government (1912–27). Three years later, the first Chinese CPA firm was established in Beijing. In 1925, the first Accounting society was founded in Shanghai. After the Nationalist government had wholly taken over China by 1928, two new sets of regulations – 'Certification of Public Accountants' and 'Regulations for Accountants' – were issued. These regulations were very similar to those of China's Western counterparts and covered areas of business, qualification requirements, legal responsibilities and codes of professional ethics.

After the Communist government assumed power in 1949, the CPA system was suspended until 1980. Following the open door policy, China began to reestablish the institutional framework for the CPA system. In December 1980, the Ministry of Finance announced the 'Provisional Regulations on the Setting Up of an Accounting Consultancy'. This announcement marked the first stage in the re-establishment of the CPA profession. In July 1986, the government issued 'Regulations of the People's Republic of China on Certified Public Accountants', the first legal framework covering issues such as national examinations, education and experience requirements, rules of work, and the required affiliation to a public accounting firm.

Up to 1986, there were only 500 CPAs and 80 accounting firms in China. In addition to consultancy, the major services rendered by these firms included attestation of the financial records of Sino-foreign joint ventures. The period between 1986 and 1988 can be considered as the second stage of the CPA development. The number of CPAs in China increased to 3,000 while the number of CPA firms increased to 250 during this time.

The third stage began in November 1988, with the establishment of the Chinese Institute of Certified Public Accountants

(CICPA). The CICPA, which is currently under the jurisdiction of the Ministry of Finance, is recognized as the body in charge of all affairs relating to CPAs, such as registration of CPAs and CPA firms, and CPA examinations. Specifically, CICPA has responsibility for enforcing self-education and self-regulation of CPAs and CPA firms. In addition, CICPA acts as a liaison between CPAs and government agencies. By the end of 1992 there were 10,733 CPAs and the number was expected to increase to 15,000 at the end of 1993 (CICPA, 1993 Regulations – Explanatory Notes). Despite this significant increase, the demand for qualified CPAs still cannot be met within a short period and the Ministry of Finance has estimated that 300,000 CPAs will be needed by the end of this decade.

In October 1993, the announcement of new 'Regulations of the People's Republic of China on Certified Public Accountants' (the Regulations; MOF 1993) marked a new era for CPAs in China. This set of regulations aims to create an environment to prepare Chinese CPAs for anchorage in the international accounting arena while also allowing foreign CPAs to enter the Chinese accounting market.

CHINA'S CPA CERTIFICATION

Certification by evaluation

Before the promulgation of the Regulations (1986), CPAs in China were certified according to experience and educational background. Candidates could apply to be evaluated by local regulatory agencies through their affiliated CPA firms. Owing to the lack of standardized evaluation criteria, the granting of CPA qualifications was not consistently applied throughout different provinces. Under this certification system, practically all certified accountants were retired accounting or financial officers of government agencies (Office of the National Examination Board, MOF 1993b)

In view of the deficiencies of the above system, the Regulations (1986) specified the criteria for certification by evaluation. Article 6 of the Regulations (1986) stated that applicants for evaluation should have accounting experience and they should be senior accountants, accounting professors, associate professors, researchers or assistant researchers. Futhermore, candidates with a college degree (or equivalent) and at least twenty years of financial accounting experience could also apply for evaluation. The evaluation process was centralised and became the responsibility of the Office of National Examination Board. Three kinds of certificates and documents had to be presented for verification; academic certificates, which included graduation certificates and testimonials; documents concerning work experience; and the applicant's publications and testimonials in his/her area of specialization. Oral examinations might also be required if deemed necessary.

Effective from 1 January 1994, the Regulations (1993) stipulate that the CPA qualification can only be obtained by examination. There is no more certification by evaluation. However, the new regulations allow candidates to apply for partial exemption, i.e. on an individual paper basis.

Certification by examination

In order to upgrade and ensure the standards of CPAs, the Regulations (1986) introduced a new certification process in China. According to Article 6, of the 'Regulations on CPAs' (the Regulations; MOF 1986), the candidate sitting for the national examination, administered by a national board approved by the MOF, must be 'a Chinese citizen who loves the PRC and supports the socialist system'. In addition, the candidate should possess a college degree (or equivalent) plus three years of accounting or auditing related work experience. However, this prerequisite as examination candidate has been modified in the Regulations (1993). According to Article 8 of the Regulations (1993), a candidate must be a Chinese citizen who has completed tertiary technical education (not necessarily studying accounting), or has a work title indicating that the candidate is at middle level accounting or accounting related areas of work.

The examination is in written form and is divided into four papers, namely accounting, auditing, tax law and other regulations, and financial management. Under special circumstances, however, oral examination may be administered. The first national examination was held in 1991 and the second in October 1993. To ensure a steady increase of entrants into the profession, CICPA expects the examination to become a regular event which takes place annually.

Candidates are not required to take all four papers in one

sitting. Two kinds of certificates will be issued to successful candidates. A 'pass-all' certificate will be granted upon passing all four papers in one sitting. On the other hand, a certificate will also be granted on an individual-paper basis and then the candidate has to pass the remaining papers within the next two consecutive sittings. After passing all four papers, a candidate must be affiliated to a CPA firm to meet the practising requirement. Failure to fulfil the practising requirement within five years of passing the examination will result in the voidance of the certificate previously obtained by passing the examination.

The issuing of a practising certificate is uniformly administered by the MOF. A CPA's practising certificate will be relinquished upon his/her departure from a CPA firm, but it can be reinstated at a later date.

CERTIFICATION PROCESSES IN HONG KONG AND CHINA

In Hong Kong, CPAs obtain their qualification by examination, which is administered by the Hong Kong Society of Accountants (HKSA). The examination follows the structure of the Chartered Association of Certified Accountants in the UK through a joint scheme. Candidates passing the joint scheme examination are eligible to be admitted as members of both associations. As the certification process of CPAs in Hong Kong is similar to that in other Commonwealth countries, we use Hong Kong as a basis for comparison with the process in China (Table 16.1). Owing to the close economic ties between Hong Kong and China, it is worthwhile analysing the differences between their certification processes in order to gain an insight into the future development of China's accounting profession.

ANALYSIS AND RECOMMENDATION

Generally speaking, CICPA conforms to the certification process in other parts of the world. A university degree is a common prerequisite for certification. However, social demands play a significant role in the formation of requirements. One of the goals of CICPA is to generate 300,000 CPAs by 1999 in order to meet the demand from the rapidly developing financial markets. Realization of this goal is doubtful for two reasons.

Table 16.1 Comparison between the new examination schemes of ACCA/HKSA (from June 1994) and CICPA (from January 1994)

Criteria for comparison	ACCA/HKSA	CICPA
Prerequisite as examination candidate	1 Aged 18 years or above and of good character. 2 Academic achievement: (a) 2 Advanced and 3 Ordinary Level passes or 3 'A' and 1 'O' passes in distinct and separate subjects including English and Mathematics; or (b) a recognized degree or equivalent.	According to Article B, a candidate must be a Chinese citizen who has: 1 completed tertiary technical education (not necessarily studying accountancy), or 2 a work title indicating that the candidate is at middle level acounting or accounting related areas of work (educational requirement not specified in this case).
Structure of examination	The examination is divided into 3 stages, with 2 modules in each stage, covering a total of 14 papers. The stages are: Foundation, Certificate, and Professional.	The examination covers 4 papers: 1 Auditing. 2 Tax laws and other regulations. 3 Accounting. 4 Financial management.
Exemption policy	Exemption will be granted on a subject basis up to a maximum of 10 papers. Papers non-exemptible: *Module E* 1 Accounting and audit practice. 2 Tax planning *Module F* 3 Financial reporting environment. 4 Financial strategy.	The 1993 Regulations abolish the exemption policy on waiver of examination requirement by evaluation. However, partial waiver of examination can be granted to candidates on an individual basis. To apply for partial examination waiver, applicants should have a high-ranked work title in accounting, or in an accounting-related profession (Article 8).
Examination format	Integrative approach: different subjects are integrated in one paper. Examination has mainly problem-solving questions (objective questions can be found in Foundation stage).	Distinct subject approach. Examination includes objective (e.g. multiple choice and true/false) problem-solving and open-ended questions.

Table 16.1 Continued

Criteria for comparison	ACCA/HKSA	CICPA
Pass requirements	A pass will be granted only if papers in the same module are passed at the same sitting. The examinations must be completed within 10 years of the first eligible sitting.	Certificates will be granted on papers passed. Remaining papers must be passed within the next 2 consecutive sittings.
Professional membership	Two types of membership: 1 Qualified accountant, with 3 years of accounting related work experience. 2 Certified Public Accountant, with 4 years of full-time approved auditing experience (or 30 months in the case of post qualification experience).	With two years' experience in auditing, candidates passing the examination can file for CPA certification (Article 9).
Renewal of practising certificate	Subject to annual renewal.	According to Article 13, CPA practising certificate will be revoked if one of the following occurs: 1 civil incapacity. 2 conviction of criminal offence. 3 serious misconduct. 4 voluntary relinquishment of CPA practice for up to one year. However, reinstatement can be applied for.
Continuing professional education (CPE)	HKSA recommends to all members to attain a minimum of 20 structured and 20 unstructured hours per annum.	CPAs are required to report on a minimum of 2 weeks of full-time CPE per year. Cumulative full-time CPE must total at least 2 months within 3 years.

Table 16.1 Continued

Criteria for comparison	ACCA/HKSA	CICPA
Professional body	An independent and self-regulatory entity governed by Professional Accountants Ordinance in Hong Kong.	Ministry of Finance remains the final arbiter but active administration is handed to the CICPA (Chapter 5).
Areas of work	Tax, accounting, auditing and consultancy services.	1 Tax, accounting, auditing and consultancy services. 2 Verification of capital injection.
Reciprocity	Full members of a total of 12 approved institutes will be admitted as members of HKSA.	According to Article 44, non-PRC citizens can apply for the CICPA examination as well as the CPA certification under the Principle of Mutual Reciprocity.

First, competition for a university education is very fierce in China. Restricting the entrance requirement to degree holders only would severely limit the number of potential prospective CPA candidates who are permitted to sit the examination. Second, the pass rate of only 4 per cent (i.e. 600 candidates) in the first round of the CICPA examination in 1991 indicates that most of the candidates were not up to the standard required by CICPA.

It is obvious that CICPA is in a catch-22 situation. Increasing the number of CPAs without lowering the standard, all within a short period, is difficult to accomplish. The entry requirements under the Regulations (1993) have been relaxed to allow more non-university degree holders to sit the examination. Although this measure has the effect of increasing the number of prospective candidates and CPAs to meet the shortage problem quickly, it raises serious concern about the quality of future CPAs. Owing to the extensive scope of accounting and auditing and audit-related knowledge and its complex underlying issues, the global trend is to ask for more formal accounting education requirements of a potential candidate. For instance, the American Institute of Certified Public Accountants (AICPA) now recommends that all its member states adopt a 150-hour rule, representing a five-year university education, as one of the entry requirements to sit the Uniform CPA Examination. The new entry requirements being adopted by China seem to be going in the opposite direction.

The authors suggest that CICPA should gradually raise the entry requirements to university-degree level in the future. In addition, CICPA can consider adopting a college equivalency examination for non-degree holders. On passing such an examination, candidates can be regarded as meeting the prerequisite to sit the CPA examination. As a result, CICPA can accelerate the rate of granting CPA certificates while at the same time maintaining the standards of CPAs.

One positive step being taken in the new Regulations (1993) is the termination of certification by evaluation permitted under the Regulations (1986). It indicates the Chinese authorities' intention to strengthen the quality of existing CPAs. Furthermore, in the new regulations, the Chinese government shows a progressive liberalisation in allowing foreigners to apply to participate in the uniform national examination and their registration under the principle of reciprocity. This move can increase the supply of CPAs in meeting its dramatic demand and at the same time Chinese CPAs can share the experiences and technical knowledge of professionals from other countries – a type of technology transfer. In addition, China should quickly establish specific procedures for granting non-citizens certification of CPAs in order to facilitate its re-admission to the General Agreement on Tariffs and Trade (GATT).

Changes in the CPA examination

Changes have been made in the examination syllabuses of both CICPA and ACCA/HKSA. A significant modification was implemented in the October 1993 CICPA examination. Though the subject areas remained unchanged, the content of individual papers was different.

According to the *Official Questions and Answers* for the first CPA examination, issued by the Office of the National Examination Board (1992), emphasis was placed on the content of the particular rules and regulations governing enterprises. For example, the old syllabus for the Accounting paper was divided into five parts. The first part was compulsory and covered general accounting guidelines. The remaining four parts covered accounting for specialized industries, namely industrial accounting, commercial accounting, construction accounting and joint-venture accounting. Candidates could choose one of the four parts to answer. In general, the questions required memorization of the accounting treatments for specific industries according to the rules and regulations set down by the Chinese government. Previous accounting guidelines in China were developed along the socialist model in which accountability of funds rather than profits was stressed. As a result, the basic accounting theory and conceptual framework that were generally covered in the Western CPA examinations were not tested in the CICPA examination.

As China continues to open up to the world, offering unrivalled business and investment opportunities, accounting practices within the country will need to be in harmony with the international standards that speak the global language of cross-border investment. The Chinese government issued the 'Accounting Standards for Business Enterprises' and 'Financial Guidelines for Business Enterprises', which became effective on 1 July 1993. These two standards and guidelines are close to Western standards and are more geared than before to profitability and performance. The standards and guidelines were incorporated into the new examination syllabus and were included in the October 1993 examination. However, the format and structure of the examination were similar to the 1991 examination.

Regarding the ACCA/HKSA examination, a new scheme will be implemented in June 1994 (ACCA 1993a). The previous structure employed a distinct subject approach. The syllabus for individual papers was confined to the respective areas of knowledge. By contrast, the reform of the syllabuses reflects the integration of supporting knowledge, such as quantitative techniques and economics, into core topics. In addition, management information technology and soft-skills such as communication are stressed under the new scheme. As reflected in the ACCA/HKSA (1993) pilot papers, the examination will have an international context. For instance, candidates are expected to know about the European markets and about international trade agreements such as the General Agreement on Tariffs and Trade (GATT).

In summary, both CICPA and ACCA/HKSA respond to the changing environment. The CICPA examination switched from a socialist model to one that conforms with international standards.

Likewise, the expanded scope of examinations can also be found in ACCA/HKSA through its integration of subjects.

CONCLUSION

Economic changes in China led to changes in accounting concepts as evidenced by the issuing of the 'Accounting Standards for Business Enterprises'. Under a project funded by the World Bank, Deloitte Touche Tohmatsu International is working with a Chinese team of experts to develop accounting standards and financial reporting formats. New accounting standards are expected to be promulgated gradually within the next three years (Kohut 1993).

The establishment of CICPA and the CPA examination comprise an important step towards the further development of accounting infrastructure. However, given the dynamic global business environment, featuring rapid changes in information technology (IT), and swift development of new financial instruments in capital markets, CICPA should always be forward looking. In preparing accountants to meet future challenges, CICPA should strengthen the existing mandatory continuing professional education (CPE) programme by requiring Chinese CPAs to acquire IT skills and to enhance their management ability and professional judgement. In addition to technical skills, ethical issues should be duly considered by CICPA as a requirement for certification and CPE.

To conclude, the current efforts of CICPA to enhance the international professional image signifies a giant step for China into the global business arena.

REFERENCES

Barrett, G. R. (1992) 'Is accounting becoming the first truly international profession?', *Journal of Accountancy*, October, pp. 110–13.
Chartered Association of Certified Accountants (1993a) *The New Examination Scheme*, London: ACCA.
—— (1993b) *ACCA Examination Pilot Papers*, London: ACCA.
Kohut, J. (1993) 'Deloitte to train China auditors', *South China Morning Post*, 6 February.
Lau, A. H. L. and Yang, J.-L. (1990) 'Auditing in China: historical perspective and current developments', *International Journal of Accounting*, vol. 25, pp. 53–62.
Ministry of Finance (1986) *Regulations on Certified Public Accountants*, Beijing.

—— (1992a) *Accounting Standards for Business Enterprises*, Beijing: Publishing House of Law.

—— (1992b) *Financial Guidelines for Business Enterprises*, Beijing: Publishing House of Law.

Office of the National Examination Board, Ministry of Finance (1992) *The First National CPA Examination: Official Questions and Answers*, Beijing.

—— (1993a) *Accounting: Official Teaching Guides for 1993 CPA Examination*, Beijing.

—— (1993b) *Auditing: Official Teaching Guides for 1993 CPA Examination*, Beijing.

—— (1993c) *Financial Management: Official Teaching Guides for 1993 CPA Examination*, Beijing.

—— (1993d) *Tax Law and Other Regulations: Official Teaching Guides for 1993 CPA Examination*, Beijing.

Winkle, G. M., Huss, F. H. and Tang, Q. (1992) 'Accounting education in the People's Republic of China: an update', *Issues in Accounting Education* 7(2): 179–92.

Chapter 17

Accounting education and practice in China
Perceived problems and solutions

S. S. Gao

INTRODUCTION

The economy of China has grown rapidly in the last decade since the economic reform of the 1980s. This is evidenced by the annual growth rate of GNP of 7–15 per cent. The deepening economic reform and expansion in China has resulted in a growing demand for both qualified accountants and accounting educators. There is, however, an acute shortage of qualified accountants in the country. Although Chinese accounting education programmes are, for the most part, well developed and reflect the progress made to date in economic reform (Winkle *et al.* 1992: 189), there are many problems facing Chinese educators, particularly in terms of the current adaptation to the 'Accounting Standards for Business Enterprises' (MOF 1992). More specifically, Chinese educators are facing significant challenges both in developing new curricula and in meeting the demands for professional accountants (e.g. certified public accountants, CPA) who are needed in the development of the market economy. The main aims of this chapter are to provide evidence of some of the practical problems facing accounting education in China and to present possible solutions to these problems.

Knowledge of accounting education in China is generally scarce among Western counterparts. The few studies that have appeared in Western accounting literature have described the general context of accounting education in China (e.g. Guo 1988, Watne and Baldwin 1988, Wong and Wong 1988, Yam 1988, Lin and Deng 1992). Studies providing descriptions of Chinese accounting programmes have usually relied on information from only a single accounting programme at a Chinese university (e.g. Watne and

Baldwin 1988). Although Winkle *et al.* (1992) provided more comprehensive coverage of Chinese accounting programmes, based on a survey of fourteen Chinese universities, major problems in Chinese accounting education and practice were not the focus of the study and so were not discussed. Several other papers have provided information on the general status of accounting in China (e.g. Zhou 1988, Fang and Tang 1991), management accounting (e.g. Bromwich and Wang 1991), financial accounting (e.g. Lefebvre and Lin 1990, Skousen *et al.* 1993), and government accounting (Aiken and Lu 1993). The main focus of these papers was generally the Chinese accounting system, accounting reforms, or the internationalization of Chinese accounting, but not the problem of accounting education in China.

Gao (1992) discussed China's accounting education under the economic reform, and highlighted the responsibility of the Chinese educators and reformers and their possible contributions to China's accounting education. The main accounting education problems discussed in Gao's paper were related to the accounting system or model, the educators, the students' attitude, and the way of teaching. In this chapter we discuss other issues which are important to the current accounting education in China. They include the accounting curriculum, the links between China's accounting education and the accounting profession, the issue of political accounting,[1] and students' expectations about prospective employers.

BACKGROUND

The education system in China has long been linked to the centrally planned economy in which universities served the state and the central government. On the one hand, as mentioned in Watne and Baldwin (1988), educational authority in China remained highly centralized, and was controlled and administered by the State Education Commission (SEC). On the other hand, different types of universities existed, with different funding channels and administrative bodies, at several levels. The higher education system in China is shown in Figure 17.1. Under the Chinese system, the SEC under the direct leadership of the State Council is responsible for the policy and macro/central-control of higher education institutions in the whole country. Local higher education bureaux or departments are under dual-leadership, in that they have to report to both the SEC and their local government or the affiliated Ministry. Under the current higher education system, there are different kinds of universities which are managed and funded by different bodies. Individual universities administratively belong either to the SEC, Ministries, provinces, local prefectures/cities or to a combination of two of these. There are key universities which are directly under the control of the SEC, Ministry-affiliated universities which belong to an individual Ministry,[2] provincial universities which are funded and administrated by provinces, and local universities which belong to cities and prefectures.[3] In addition, there are some universities which are jointly funded and controlled either by a Ministry and a province or by a province and a local prefecture/city. They are called universities under dual-leadership. Because of the variety of funding and administrative authorities, universities differ significantly in terms of academic teaching and research, finance and size. Most importantly, there is a lack of competition among universities because they are at different levels and are funded by different channels. Nevertheless, ten years of education reform in China have dramatically changed the structure of universities, giving greater authority and responsibility to both universities and faculties.

Accounting in developing countries has been regarded as weak and in need of improvement for quite some time (Wallace and Briston 1993). China as a developing country is no exception. Although contemporary accounting education has existed in China for more than half a century (Lou 1992: 469), its development under the market-oriented economy has just begun, associated with the economic reform of the centrally planned economy dating from the early 1980s. Accounting education in China, since the Communists took power in 1949, has experienced different phases: 1949–57, 1958–77, 1978–91 (Gao 1992). A fourth phase started in 1992 when the 'Accounting Standards for Business Enterprises' was first issued. This phase is different from the third, although both come under the economic reform programme. The fourth phase is the period of educating accounting faculties, students and practitioners according to the new accounting standards, which are fairly similar to the GAAPs in the West. After this phase, Chinese accounting education will most likely be the same as its Western counterparts, and the level of accounting education will reach Western standards. However, current

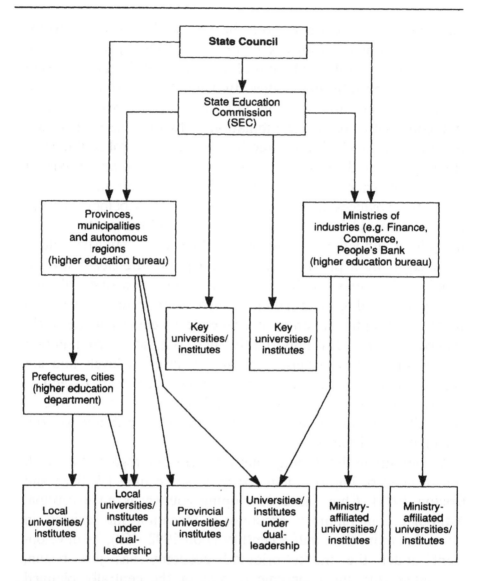

Figure 17.1 The higher education system in China

accounting education in China is still constrained by the whole higher education system, particularly with respect to university funding, university independence, and academic freedom.

At present there are about 100 institutes and universities in China offering undergraduate programmes in accounting, with a total enrolment of over 10,000 students. The undergraduate accounting programmes at Chinese universities are four-year programmes, one year more than universities in the UK. The Master's programme in accounting consists of about two years of prescribed learning and about one year of research, including writing a thesis and teaching practice. The doctoral programme in accounting takes 2–3 years of individual research. There is a severe shortage of qualified doctoral staff in faculties in China. The reasons include central government control of the authority to grant doctoral programmes, with respect to the number of both faculties and supervisors. A doctoral supervisor in China must be designated as being 'very distinguished' among professors in the same area. Unlike in the West (e.g. the USA, the UK, The Netherlands, Germany), where professors are usually qualified to supervise doctoral students, in China less than 10 per cent of professors can be authorized by the SEC to be a supervisor of doctoral students. The typical teaching load of an accounting professor or lecturer at a Chinese university is 4–6 hours per week, usually one class which meets for two hours twice or three times per week.

PROBLEMS IN ACCOUNTING EDUCATION

Three areas are usually identified as problematic by Chinese accounting educators:

1 A shortage of instructional equipment, such as computers for students' use, projectors, and seminar rooms.
2 The relative importance of accounting as perceived by the public.
3 Low motivation of students.

Clearly, the first problem is common to all developing countries, because it depends upon the country's economy. The second and third problems are linked to the traditional, centrally planned system (Gao 1992). There is still a majority view in China that accounting is no more than glorified bookkeeping. In this section we will focus on other practical issues facing Chinese accounting educators.

Accounting curriculum

The accounting curriculum is one of several components of accounting education and is perhaps the most important because it is the medium through which the objective of accounting education is implemented and achieved. There have been many changes in accounting curricula at Chinese universities since 1980 (cf. Watne and Baldwin 1988, Lin and Deng 1992, Tang *et al.* 1992 and Zhang 1993). For example, managerial accounting at many universities has been changed to reflect more of the Western control techniques. Agricultural accounting and other industry-specific courses have been eliminated at most universities. Table 17.1 presents the accounting curriculum offered by Shanghai University of Finance and Economics (SUFE) and Table 17.2 shows SUFE's category of courses. For the sake of comparison, the accounting curriculum of a Western university, that offered by the University of Central Lancashire (UCL) in the UK, is given in Table 17.3.

The undergraduate programme (i.e. BA degree in accounting) at the UCL takes three years, that is, one year less than at SUFE. However, many courses at SUFE are not wholly relevant to the accounting discipline. If we remove those unrelated courses from the curriculum,[4] the rest of the programme is only two-thirds of the total programme in terms of credits, and about half of the total teaching hours. As for the specialized core courses and the specialized courses, they are fewer in number than the courses offered at the UCL. Also, less options are available to students, particularly in the final year at SUFE. Not included are several courses which are believed to be very important to an accounting programme, such as corporate finance, taxation, organizational and behavioural aspects of accounting, and international accounting. Corporate finance has long been ignored in accounting programmes at Chinese universities.[5] This may be because of the lack of real stock markets and a system of private ownership. The lack of complexity in the Chinese taxation system may help to explain the omission of taxation (Winkle *et al.* 1992). Other subjects (international accounting, behavioural accounting, etc.) are quite new to China, with the result that most faculties are not able to offer them.

SUFE recently proposed major changes to its curriculum. The new experimental accounting curriculum, which is presented in Table 17.4, clearly is an advance on the old one in many respects. For example, it adds many new accounting related courses, such as foreign investment accounting, joint venture accounting, and accounting history. The courses in the proposed curriculum are generally comparable to the UCL's in terms of numbers of units and subject areas covered. They cover most of the subjects that were suggested in the 1988 Statement of 'Education Requirements

Table 17.1 Distribution of courses and credits at SUFE, China

Courses	Total credits	Year 1	Year 2	Year 3	Year 4
Political theory	28				
Political economics	10	*			
Philosophy	6			*	
History of the Chinese Communist Party	4		*		
Education of Communist ideology and ethics	8	*	*	*	*
General basic courses	39				
English	12	*	*	*	
Higher mathematics	8	*			
Computer applications	1	*			
Programming language	4		*		
Chinese	6	*			
Physical culture	8	*	*	*	*
Basic courses in finance and economics	13				
Statistics	3		*		
Industrial business administration	4	*			
Public finance and credit	3			*	
Economic laws	3		*		
Specialized core courses	27				
Elementary accounting	4	*			
Financial accounting	8	*			
Cost accounting	8			*	
Management accounting	3				*
Auditing	4				*
Specialized courses	16				
Western accounting	3				*
Accounting theory	2				*
Comparative accounting	3				*
The design of accounting systems	2				*
Application of computers in accounting	6			*	*
Social survey	2		*		
Year-end thesis	2		*		
Graduate thesis	8				*
Total credits for the compulsory courses	135				
Total credits for elective courses	28				
Grand total	163				

Source: Tang et al. 1992: 213

Table 17.2 Category of courses at SUFE, China

Category of courses	Courses	Credits	%	Hours	%
Political theory	4	28	18.5	465	17.0
General basic courses	6	39	25.9	821	30.0
Finance and economics	4	13	8.6	225	8.2
Specialized courses	10	43	28.5	734	26.8
Elective course (min.)	16	28	18.5	494	18.0
Social survey and thesis	–	12	–	–	–
Total	40	163	100.0	2739	100.0

Source: Tang *et al.* 1992: 214

for Entry into the Accounting Profession', which was published by the American Institute of Certified Public Accountants (AICPA 1988). However, taxation is still excluded from the programme. The major problem with the proposed programme lies in the international area. There are too many items on international topics, such as foreign investment accounting, Sino-foreign joint venture accounting, foreign exchange accounting, foreign trade accounting, and international accounting. These topics should be incorporated into a course on international accounting rather than be named as separate courses.

Chinese accounting education must be developed within the whole structure of China's education system. Subjects must not be introduced and taught in isolation, but placed in a wider context. Efforts should be put into designing an accounting curriculum which reduces duplication in the coverage and teaching at different levels of the system. The accounting curriculum for undergraduates must be flexible enough to include only subjects which are basic and essential to accounting and should leave the other subjects in the specialized areas to be taken at Master's or doctoral level. Specialization must not be encouraged at undergraduate level, as this will limit the students' mobility in the employment market. The curriculum must be flexible enough to ensure that necessary adjustments can be made to incorporate any developments that will enhance the quality and knowledge of students. Furthermore, accounting education university level should be theoretically and conceptually oriented; and technical knowledge and procedures should be acquired on the job and/or through continuing education. The emphasis on teaching accounting as a technical subject at Chinese universities must be

Table 17.3 BA accounting degree course units at the UCL, UK

Course units	Credits	Year 1 I	Year 1 II	Year 2 I	Year 2 II	Year 3 I	Year 3 II
Introduction to economics	5	*					
Business operation	5	*	*				
Introduction to financial accounting	5	*	*				
Introduction to management accounting	5	*	*				
Computing for accounting & financial services	5	*	*				
Legal obligations in business	5	*	*				
Quantitative methods for business	5	*	*				
(Intermediate) financial accounting	6			*	*		
(Intermediate) management accounting	6			*	*		
Financial control and information technology	6			*	*		
Industrial economics	4			*			
Business decision analysis	4			*	*		
Organizational studies for accountants	3				*		
The company and the law	6			*			
Introduction to research methodology	3				*		
Core subjects							
Advanced financial accounting	7					*	*
Advanced management accounting	7					*	*
Corporate finance	7					*	*
Options							
Public sector accounting	3			*			
Public sector economics	4					*	*
Social aspects of accounting	3			*			
Behavioural aspects of accountants	3				*		
Theory and practice of auditing	6					*	*
Theory and practice of taxation	6					*	*
Financial services I	5			*	*		
Financial services II	6					*	*
Project/dissertation	6					*	*
International accounting I	3					*	
International accounting II	3						*

Source: Department of Accounting and Financial Services, University of Central Lancashire

Table 17.4 Proposed accounting course structure (undergraduate programme) at SUFE, China

Course units	Year 1 I	Year 1 II	Year 2 I	Year 2 II	Year 3 I	Year 3 II	Year 4 I	Year 4 II
Core units								
Introductory accounting	4							
Principles of financial accounting		4	4					
Special topics in financial accounting					3	3		
Cost accounting					5			
Management accounting						3		
Auditing							3	
Major units								
Financial management					3	3		
Applying computers in accounting						4		
English for accounting							3	3
Special topics in accounting theory								3
Accounting electives								
Foreign investment accounting								
Sino-foreign joint venture accounting								
Banking accounting								
Foreign exchange accounting								
Foreign trade accounting								
Capital construction accounting & finance								
Government or budget accounting								
International accounting								
Accounting history								
Accounting system design								

Source: Translated from Zhang 1993

changed, and future accountants must be educated and trained as professionals and as managers not followers. Thus, the accounting curriculum and the accounting programme must be designed in such a way that students will not only be knowledgeable about their subjects but will also have a broad understanding of the realities of the economic, social and legal environments in which any business operates. Although no one model of accounting curriculum may be appropriate for all universities and colleges in China, it would be desirable to have a minimum coverage of economic, business and accounting topics by all of the universities and colleges there.

It will be interesting to see how Chinese educators cope with the new accounting standards in their curriculum. It is likely that these will replace much of the current contents regarding the principles of financial accounting and special topics in financial accounting. This is because most of the financial accounting presently taught at Chinese universities is based upon the socialist accounting framework, which differs widely from the accounting framework under a market economy. Undoubtedly, the continued development of the accounting curriculum in China is vital to the success of economic reforms (Winkle *et al.* 1992: 189).

Links between accounting education and the accounting profession

Western experience shows that university accounting education has (and must have) direct links to the accounting profession.[6] However, the link between the two has not been appreciated by many Chinese educators. Very few universities in China have so far established such a link, owing to the fact that the accounting profession in China is in its initial stage and is underdeveloped. Also, the services provided by the accounting profession have not fully been recognized by the public. Accountants are mostly regarded as bookkeepers in enterprises.

Since it is believed that the major shift from traditional accounting to modern accounting may best be illustrated by having practitioners change from being purely company accountants to being professional accountants, it is necessary to develop and strengthen the accreditation of certified public accountants (CPA) and to expand their ranks. It is initially planned that the numbers of CPA in China will be increased from the present 2,000 to 300,000 by 1999, while accounting firms will increase from about 500 to 2,000 and will be prepared to co-operate with some international accounting firms to set up joint ventures using Chinese and foreign investment. Obviously, university education plays a major part in achieving such a goal. Universities have to produce sufficient numbers of graduates to enter the profession directly or to be trained further as qualified accountants. However, this cannot simply rely on the change of curriculum at the universities by shifting the emphasis from theoretical aspects to technical. Universities also have to improve the knowledge and quality of current accountants. It is the quality not the number of accountants that represents the level of service in accountancy. Academic studies of other developing countries (e.g. Bangladesh by Parry and Groves 1990, Panama by Rivera 1990, and Tanzania by Abayo and Roberts 1993) have suggested that the training of more accountants does not necessarily raise the quality of accounting.

To achieve a proper balance between teaching graduates and training current accountants is not an easy task. This is partially because of the lack of a labour market system in China and the fact that the social status and salaries of professional accountants are relatively low. Many accounting graduates want to exchange their future accounting career for others, such as marketing or general management.[7] Also, many of the accounting profession want to transfer to other areas when the opportunity arises.[8]

The links between accounting education and the accounting profession are usually determined by the development of the latter. Mature accounting professions in developed countries have significantly influenced accounting education there. As a result of such influence, the links between the two were established accordingly. In the Chinese case, however, where the accounting profession is underdeveloped, the effective way to develop these links lies in the hands of the educators. What they can do is to add to their accounting curriculum professional functions, professional codes of ethics and professional practice, and so provide professional training as an optional part of the accounting programme for those students who would like to pursue accounting as a career. One possibility would be to change the current four-year model to five. The final year would concentrate on professional training and after the five years graduates would gain professional recognition. On the other hand, universities should attempt to recruit more staff from practising accountants. Current recruitment policy in China needs to change. At present, almost all new members of staff in accounting faculties are recruited directly from the university's own graduates or postgraduates. As a result, very few staff have had professional experience or have personal links with the accounting profession. Some faculty members did recently start up their own accounting firm, but the range of services that they can provide is quite limited.

'Political accounting'

Cheng (1980) described accounting in China as 'political accounting', accounting that is dominated by political influences. Political influence is evident throughout China's accounting education, from the university system as a whole to the accounting degree programme, from degree regulations to accounting research. Like other organizations in China, a university is politically influenced and serves ideological as well as social purposes. This is facilitated by the Communist Party of China (CCP) structure at the university, which operates parallel to the administrative structure. The CCP branch serves as a vehicle for educating academics in party beliefs, as a source of internal control to ensure that decisions at all levels within the university are consistent with the goals of the state and the party, and as a 'union safeguard', helping to protect the rights of teachers and students by providing an appeal mechanism in any disputes with other parties (e.g. rectors).

Another example of political accounting lies in the area of accounting research. Accounting research in China has rarely embraced scientific methods and is largely based on government policy and simple-minded descriptions of 'what is' and 'what to do'. Many published articles in both academic journals and professional magazines are no more than political propaganda. In other words, the writers of these articles behaved simply as propagandists for the CCP, socialist ideology or government policies. For example, *Accounting Research*, the official journal of the Chinese Accounting Association and the Chinese Costs-Research Association, which has been highly regarded as the 'pure' academic journal in China, published many politically oriented papers as well as speeches by Communist and government officers. These papers and speeches were usually considered to provide the theoretical background to accounting research in China.

Article 2 of the 'Regulations Concerning Academic Degrees in the People's Republic of China' states: 'all citizens who support the leadership of the Communist Party of China and the socialist system and who attain a certain academic level may apply for appropriate academic degrees in accordance with the requirements stipulated by the Regulations' (SEC 1986). Clearly, support of the CCP and the socialist system is a prerequisite for anyone who wants to apply for accounting and other degrees. In order to

show their support, students must study the 'political theory' that
occupies almost all of the academic year. Correspondingly, universities and faculties have to show their interest in political subjects
by offering such courses. (This may explain why 'political theory'
was a major part of the accounting curriculum at SUFE; see Table
17.1.) At the same time, accounting researchers must write 'political accounting' papers.

An effective solution to such problems is not easy to find, particularly in the current situation. For the moment, the best plan
would be to strengthen the links between Chinese universities and
foreign universities and to promote university exchanges based
on purely academic activities. Such international links will surely
weaken the domestic political influence on accounting education.

Students' expectations of prospective employers

The main objective of accounting education is to produce qualified accounting graduates who will be capable of undertaking
accountancy. Before they graduate, what views do students hold
about the types of jobs and employers that they wish to have
later? Our research shows that, since the economic reforms,
students in China have greatly changed their views on the ranking
of future employers. Prior to reform, the top-rated group of
employers included government administration departments,
industrial departments within Ministries, and large state-owned
companies. Now the majority of accounting students wish to be
employed by foreign or private firms. These findings will help, to
some extent, to develop a new syllabus for many course units
which will meet students' requirements.

A questionnaire-based survey of accounting students at two
Chinese institutes was carried out. The Chinese-language questionnaire was pilot tested by three Chinese exchange students at
a UK university before being sent to the two institutes in China:
a Ministry-affiliated institute belonging to the People's Bank of
China and a provincial institute. The provincial institute is a polytechnic where science and engineering are the main subject areas.
Accounting degree courses are administered by the department
of management engineering. There was not much difference
between the responses from the two institutes. The questionnaire
required the participants to indicate on a scale ranging from
1 (the lowest) to 15 (the highest) their perception of prospective

employers for whom they would like to work. For the purpose of analysis, the sample was initially classified into two groups by gender. There were 46 male students with an average age of 22.1 years and 69 female students with an average age of 21.9 years. The results are presented in Table 17.5. The overall mean scores for each employer were computed for the 115 students and the prospective employers were then ranked accordingly: the higher the mean score, the higher the rank of the employer.

The findings show that there is no difference in the ranking of the first four employers between male and female students. Foreign-owned firms were ranked highest. Most students indicated that foreign owned-firms pay better than any other employers. Also, foreign-owned firms are more efficient than Chinese firms. Joint-venture firms were ranked second. Although most Chinese CPA firms are small, recently established without any reputation as yet, they were ranked third. These results provide the following conclusions:

1 Chinese accounting firms, which have recently been developed, have gained increasing recognition from accounting students.
2 CPA accounting firms are currently attracting accounting students and the potential is large.
3 Most Chinese accounting students will be likely to pursue accountancy as their career in an accounting firm.
4 The accounting profession will be respected in society and will be developed to high standards.

The bottom five rankings are small state-owned enterprises, the non-academic sector of universities/institutes, further education and training for MA and PhD, collective-owned companies and, finally, large state-owned companies. There are some differences between the male and female students' perceptions of this group. The male students regard further education and training for MA and PhD as the final option, preceded by the academic sector of universities/institutes.[9] This poses another serious challenge for Chinese accounting education. The major reason for the bottom ranking of further education and training may be economic, since the educational sectors are usually low paid. The females ranked this ninth, after the academic sector of universities/institutes. Collective-owned firms were ranked last by the females but eighth by the males. Surprisingly, female students ranked small companies at fourteen, whereas males ranked them at seven. It may be

Table 17.5   Ranking of prospective employers by Chinese undergraduates

Employers	Overall ranking	Ranking by male	Ranking by female
Foreign-owned firms (e.g. the Big Eight)	1	1	1
Joint-venture firms	2	2	2
Chinese CPA firms	3	3	3
Private companies	4	4	4
Banking, insurance firms	5	6	6
Government tax bureaux	6	9	5
Local administration departments	7	11	7
Medium enterprises*	8	5	12
Universities/Institutes (academic staff)	9	14	8
Industrial departments within Ministries	10	10	11
Small enterprises*	11	7	14
Universities/Institutes (non-academic staff)	12	13	10
Further education and training (for MA, PhD)	13	15	9
Collective-owned companies	14	8	15
Large enterprises*	15	12	13

* These enterprises are state-owned: small enterprises employ under 1,000 employees; medium 1,000–5,000; and large over 5,000.

that female students rely more on job security than their counterparts. In terms of the middle ranks, from six to ten, there are some variations between the male and female students. Although it is not clear what factors cause such variation, individual factors, such as family background and personal preference, and social factors, such as culture and tradition, may hold the key.

These findings do indicate that jobs at universities and higher degrees are no longer regarded as superior to other careers, as they were ten years ago. As a result, universities will face staffing problems in the future unless salaries and benefits in the higher education sectors are improved significantly. Also, the findings indicate that from the students' point of view, the private sector is preferred over state-owned companies and government administration departments in terms of employment. This provides an alternative measure of the success of China's economic reform, since the reform has changed people's perception of the state-owned system *vis-à-vis* private ownership. Its political and economic significance is quite obvious. Further, the findings provide a basis for further research into the gender issue in both accounting education and the accounting profession in China. We believe that some interesting results will be found.

CONCLUSION

This chapter provides evidence of underlying problems facing accounting education and practice in China under the current economic reform and the application of enterprise accounting standards. Accounting has a significant role in the provision of information for the economic growth of China. Accountability for economic activities along with reliable, timely, and relevant accounting reports are essential for attracting foreign investors. Thus, identifying and resolving problems in accounting education and practice may prove useful for the economic development of China. This chapter has addressed four issues facing Chinese accounting educators: the accounting curriculum, the links between accounting education and the accounting profession, political accounting, and students' expectations about prospective employers. Other related issues have already been discussed by Gao (1992).

Several conclusions may be derived from this study. First, there have been many changes in accounting curricula at Chinese universities since 1980. The proposed curriculum at SUFE is for the most part equivalent to the curricula in the UK and the USA, although taxation has not been offered as a major course at SUFE. Second, links between accounting education and the accounting profession are not well established, and professional influences on accounting education have not been significant. Third, political accounting still predominates in Chinese accounting and accounting education. A realistic solution to this issue is to develop and strengthen international links between Chinese universities and their foreign counterparts. Fourth, China is liable to face a serious staffing shortage in accounting education: graduates, particularly male students, regarded being on the academic staff at universities and pursuing further education (for MA and PhD) as final options. Fifth, state-owned companies, which currently dominate the Chinese economy, are no longer considered superior to the private sector in terms of employment, as far as Chinese accounting students are concerned.

Generally, changes in accounting education in China are linked to the economic reforms of the last decade which moved the country towards a market-oriented economy and away from the completely centralized economic plan (Winkle *et al.* 1992). There is no doubt that both Chinese accounting and accounting education are changing, and will continue to do so for the foreseeable future.

NOTES

1 Cheng (1980) first named part of the accounting system in China as 'political accounting'. In this chapter political accounting generally refers to the political influence on accounting education and research.
2 Most accounting programmes in China are taught at universities belonging to a Ministry (e.g. the Ministry of Finance, the Ministry of Commerce, the People's Bank of China, the Ministry of Foreign Trade). After 1985, many local universities offered accounting training and undergraduate programmes. A few key universities also offered accounting programmes to postgraduate or doctoral levels. As Winkle et al. (1992: 187) found, there were fewer accounting courses offered at key universities than at schools affiliated to the Ministry of Finance (e.g. SUFE).
3 Currently there are some private universities funded by local individuals and foreigners. These universities are generally very small, and are administrated by a local higher education authority. Thus, they are classified as local universities.
4 Units in the political theory sector and in the general basic courses are not wholly relevant to the accounting programme, although some of them may be quite useful to Chinese students (e.g. English, Computer applications).
5 Some programmes may include corporate finance or financial management (e.g. the accounting programme at Shaanxi Institute of Finance and Economics in Xian). However, the contents of these courses differ from the contents taught in the West, since they usually cover only part of management accounting.
6 Accounting education in the UK may be a good example. Most accounting programmes in the UK are validated by the accounting bodies (e.g. ACCA, CIMA) to some extent. Graduates with an accounting degree from most UK universities can gain some exemptions from some professional examinations.
7 Gao (1992: 406) found that many Chinese students in the accounting programme did not like accounting subjects (e.g. principles of accounting, financial accounting). Students usually took less courses in accounting and more in related business courses and other general courses.

8 For example, 20 of the 30 accounting graduates from Shaanxi Institute of Finance and Economics in 1983 were directly employed as accountants in companies and industries. After three years the number still in accounting was down to 11, and after five years, the number was down to 3.

9 Findings indicate that in the third world male students usually perform better in accounting subjects at universities than female students (Karim and Ibrahim 1992). This is applicable also to China, according to our experience.

REFERENCES

Abayo, A. G. and Roberts, C. B. (1993) 'Does training more accountants raise the standard of accounting? Further evidence from Tanzania', in R. S. O. Wallace, J. M. Samuels and R. J. Briston (eds) *Research in Third World Accounting*, vol. 2, London: JAI Press.

Aiken, M. and Lu, W. (1993) 'Chinese government accounting: historical perspective and current practice', *British Accounting Review* 25(2) 109–29.

AICPA American Institute of Certified Public Accountants (1988) *Education Requirements for Entry into the Accounting Profession* (2nd edn), New York.

Bromwich, M. and Wang, G.-Q. (1991) 'Management accounting in China: a current evaluation', *International Journal of Accounting* 26(1): 51–66.

Cheng, P. C. (1980) '"Political" accounting in China: what the West should know', *Journal of Accountancy*, January, pp. 76–82, 85.

Fang, Z. and Tang, Y. (1991) 'Recent accounting developments in China: an increasing internationalization', *International Journal of Accounting* 26(2): 85–103.

Gao, S. S. (1992) 'Accounting education under the economic reforms: the Chinese case study', in M. P. B. Bonnet *et al.* (eds) FMA Kroniek, The Netherlands: Samsom, pp. 395–413.

Guo, D.-Y. (1988) 'The past, present, and future of accounting education of China', in K. Someya (ed.) *Accounting Education and Research to Promote International Understanding*, New York: Quorum Books, pp. 105–11.

Karim, R. A. A. and Ibrahim, A. M. (1992) 'The performance of male versus female accounting students: evidence from the Third World', *Advances in International Accounting*, vol. 5, pp. 255–62.

Lefebvre, C. and Lin, L.-Q. (1990) 'Internationalization of financial accounting standards in the People's Republic of China', *International Journal of Accounting* 25(3): 170–83.

Lin, Z. and Deng, S. (1992) 'Educating accounting in China: current experiences and future prospects', *International Journal of Accounting* 27(2): 164–77.

Lou, E.-Y. (1992) 'Accounting education in the People's Republic of China', in K. Anyane-Ntow (ed.) *International Handbook of Account-*

ing Education and Certification, Oxford: Pergamon Press, pp. 469–75.

Ministry of Finance (1992) *Accounting Standards for Business Enterprises*, Beijing: Publishing House of Law.

Parry, M. J. and Groves, R. E. (1990) 'Does training more accountants raise the standards of accounting in Third World countries? A study of Bangladesh', in R. S. O. Wallace, J. M. Samuels and R. J. Briston (eds) *Research in Third World Accounting*, vol. 1, London: JAI Press, pp. 117–40.

Rivera, J. M. (1990) 'The accounting profession and accounting education in Panama', in B. E. Needles and V. K. Zimmerman (eds) *Comparative International Accounting Educational Standards*, Urbana-Champaign: Centre for International Education and Research in Accounting, University of Illinois, pp. 175–92.

Skousen, C. R., Brackner, J. W. and Ren-Kuan H. (1993) 'Financial accounting in state-owned enterprises in China', in R. S. O. Wallace, J. M. Samuels and R. J. Briston (eds) *Research in Third World Accounting*, vol. 2, London: JAI Press, pp. 313–32.

State Education Commission of China (1986) *Regulations Concerning Academic Degrees in the People's Republic of China*, Beijing: SEC.

Tang, Y. W., Chow, L. and Cooper, B. J. (1992) *Accounting and Finance in China: A Review of Current Practice*, Hong Kong: Longman.

Wallace, R. S. O. and Briston R. J. (1993) 'Improving the accounting infrastructure in developing countries', in R. S. O. Wallace, J. M. Samuels and R. J. Briston (eds) *Research in Third World Accounting*, vol. 2, London JAI Press, pp. 201–24.

Watne, D. A. and Baldwin, B. A. (1988) 'University-level education of accountants in the People's Republic of China', *Issues in Accounting Education* 3(1): 139–55.

Winkle, G. M., Huss, F. H. and Tang, Q. (1992) 'Accounting education in the People's Republic of China: an update', *Issues in Accounting Education* 7(2): 179–92.

Wong, T. C. and Wong, F. W. (1988) 'Accounting education in China: a case study', in K. Someya (ed.) *Accounting Education and Research to Promote International Understanding*, New York: Quorum Books, pp. 260–7.

Yam, S. C. (1988) 'Accounting education and training in China today', in K. Someya (ed.) *Accounting Education and Research to Promote International Understanding*, New York: Quorum Books, pp. 124–36.

Zhang, W. (1993) 'Initial idea for deepening the reform in the teaching of accounting', *Accounting Research*, no. 2, pp. 35–41.

Zhou, Z. H. (1988) 'Chinese accounting systems and practices', *Accounting, Organizations, and Society* 13(2): 207–24.

Chapter 18

The auditing system in China and the UK
A critical comparison

H. G. Chong and G. Vinten

INTRODUCTION

History has shown that auditing has long been practised in China. However, internal political turmoil and the closed-door policy severely hindered the continuing practices of auditing. The audit emphasis was all the while on detecting fraud and irregularities, but the open-door policy in 1979 saw the country importing a large volume of foreign ideas and technology, including audit and accounting practices. To cope with this immediate change, China needs to reassess its traditional aims of auditing to meet the world challenge. The readiness and openness of the Chinese to foreign practices on the accounting perspective can be found in Aiken and Lu (1993). They note that:

> The [accounting] method used by the Warlords government [in China] was taken from Japan; the system introduced by the Nationalist government was borrowed from Europe and America; while current government accounting practice was mainly influenced by the [then] Soviet Union.
>
> (Aiken and Lu 1993: 124)

In view of this, it is the aim of this chapter to assess the possibility of applying UK auditing practices in China. Of course, careful modifications of the UK auditing model are needed before its being implanted in China, mainly because of the different socio-economic and political backgrounds of the two countries. The chapter will look first at the historical perspective of audit practices and of the profession both in China and the UK and then it will address and compare the issues and problems faced by current auditing practices in both countries.

HISTORICAL PERSPECTIVE

There are different views on the exact date at which auditing was first practised.[1] Written records have shown that China was the first country in the world to establish an auditing system (Shuo and Yam 1987). Auditing during that time was mainly focused on checking the completeness of financial records of the imperial kingdom, the honesty of government officials in handling public money and properties (Tang *et al.* 1992), and the accuracy of receipt and expenditure (Tai and Yang 1988). Auditors were actively involved in searching for errors and irregularities, and reported the results of their findings directly to the emperor. Death was the only sentence for offenders (Lu 1988: 132). Auditors in those days were personally selected by the emperor and commanded a prestigious and powerful position. However, both the degree of responsibility and authority and the form of audit varied from one dynasty to another.[2] Despite this, auditing remains the main vehicle to detect fraud and irregularities.

The Revolution of 1911 by the Nationalist government brought in the idea of capitalism, together with auditing and accounting theory and practices, from the West. At that time, auditing was emphasized largely because of the government's intention of eradicating corruption, and improving the country's efficiency and productivity. An Audit Section was set up by the government,[3] and in the meantime the establishment of private certified public accounting firms was encouraged, although their number was small.[4] This idea was short-lived. When the political movements took place in the 1949 Communist Revolution, the government was preoccupied with economic and social reforms, foreigners were expelled,[5] and audit practice came to a halt. The country fell into another cycle of political turmoil. During the Mao regime (1949–76), auditing was emphasized and valued only when the government introduced the 'Movement Against the Three Evils' (1951–2),[6] and the 'Four Clean-up Movements' (1963–6);[7] but these were overshadowed by set-backs caused by ultra-leftist political movements, such as the Great Leap Forward (1959–61), and the Cultural Revolution (1966–76). In 1956–7, all enterprises, including audit practices, became jointly owned by the state and private individuals, and shortly thereafter were converted into state-owned enterprises. The programme of nationalization brought all enterprises, including audit practices, under state control, and auditors no longer enjoyed the status of independence, since they had similar interests and ideologies to those of the government. Eventually, by 1958, all auditing firms closed owing to a 'lack of clients' (Lu 1988: 133).

The departure of Mao saw the ideas of economic reform and the open-door policy being brought into China, starting in 1979. It is the only period in Chinese history that could see auditing staying on the government's agenda. On 15 September 1983, at the Fifth National People's Congress, the government approved a new Constitution of China to set up an Audit Administration. The Administration was to be led by an Auditor General,[8] whose objectivity and independence came under the protection of the Constitution. The Administration reports all audit findings to the National People's Congress. Various audit departments were gradually set up within the Administration, provinces, cities and self-governing areas. The open-door policy brought in huge foreign investments and technology.[9]

Auditing has again become an essential mechanism in the move to restore confidence in foreign investors, particularly the World Bank, to provide a constant flow of financial aid and funds. It acts as an independent vehicle to ensure that funds are properly channelled and are used effectively and efficiently. The whole process, focus and needs of auditing have now changed from the traditional practices of meeting the internal needs of emperors in earlier dynasties to catering for external users' driven demand. This dramatic change has been a great cultural shock to the Chinese as a whole and the government in particular. To cope with these sudden needs, external assistance was required.

Audit practice in the UK has a relatively shorter history than in China. The appointment of independent auditors took place in the 1840s (Edwards 1989). In 1880, the Institute of Chartered Accountants of England and Wales (ICAEW) was formed, in conjunction with the requirements of the Companies Act of 1862 and the Banking and Joint Stock Companies Act of 1879, which required company auditors to report to shareholders on whether or not, in their opinion, a company's balance sheet was full and fair, and properly drawn up. The standing of auditors did not match public expectations (Littleton 1966), especially in the case of the audit failure in the spectacular collapse of the City of Glasgow Bank in 1878. By overvaluing assets, undervaluing debts and misnaming balance sheet items, the Bank's directors had for years hidden its insolvency while continuing to pay dividends (see Chatfield 1977). During this time they escaped audit attention. Subsequently there was a large public outcry and much debate on the exact roles and responsibilities of auditors.[10]

The audit profession in the UK was quick to respond by introducing the word 'opinion' to replace 'certify' in audit reports, to emphasize that the auditor's certificate was an opinion not a guarantee (Chatfield 1977: 132). The audit profession in the 1890s was tinged with educative tones, not only to reassure the public as to the profession's desire to operate in the public interest but also to ensure that they held more realistic expectations of what auditors could deliver. In this century, the 1970s were characterized by a series of investigations undertaken by the Department of Trade and Industry which again criticized the inadequacy of auditors' responsibilities: failure to detect errors, failure to collect specific pieces of evidence, failure to act adequately and diligently on evidence collected, inadequate reporting, and forming erroneous judgements on accounting treatments adopted by companies (Russell 1991). The publication of the Cross Report (1977) and the Grenside Report (1979) led to the setting up of a Joint Disciplinary Scheme to investigate cases of public interest concerning auditors. This was succeeded by the Auditing Practices Committee (APC),[11] which was to develop Auditing Standards and Guidelines.

The next section of this chapter looks at selected problems and issues which face the auditing profession in the UK, in comparison with the situation in China.

EXPECTATION GAP

The expectation gap may be defined as the gap between the expectation of the general public and the duties that auditors need to perform (Porter 1988, 1992).[12] There is no strong empirical evidence that the expectation gap exists in China, compared to the audit environment in the UK. This could be because of the relatively limited awareness of the actual role of auditors in China. Also, auditors in China are mainly engaged in governmental audits, the main aims of which are to detect fraud and report on irregularities, and to evaluate the effectiveness, efficiency and economy of government units. By comparison, external auditors in the UK need to comply with a larger number of Auditing

Standards and Guidelines,[13] and have to meet the needs and expectations of a larger proportion of users of financial statements than do their Chinese counterparts. Lack of empirical evidence to support the existence of an expectation gap in China should not prevent the Chinese auditing profession from taking the necessary precautionary actions at present, in order to avoid similar shameful litigation and audit failure happening in the East.

Various surveys[14] have shown that financial statements nowadays need to serve a wider range of users, who have different interests in the disclosed information. This accounts for the widening of the expectation gap. In an attempt to narrow the gap, both the ICAEW, in 1986, and the APC, in 1987, set up working parties to develop auditing guidelines because, as the ICAEW (1986) admitted, 'there appears to be a considerable gap between the public's perception of the role of the audit and auditors' perception of that role'. Despite their efforts, the gap remains obstinately unbridged and appears to be as large in the 1990s as it was 150 years ago.

Litigation cases in the UK show that the general public is greatly concerned about the responsibilities and duties of auditors. Allegations involving auditors have attracted considerable attention from the financial press and the media. Cases including the Bank of Credit and Commerce International (BCCI),[15] Barings Bank, Barlow Clowes, DeLorean, Ferranti, the Johnson Matthey Bank, the Levitt Group, Polly Peck, the Maxwell Communications Corporation, and Mint and Boxed, to name but a few, not only have provided ammunition for unfavourable press comment, seriously questioning auditors' responsibilities, but also have undermined the credibility and professional integrity of auditors.

Users of financial statements perceive auditors to have a wider function than that which is performed or required by legislation. Concerted criticism has called upon auditors to extend their audit sampling[16] to ensure the accuracy of financial statements, to improve the quality of internal control systems, to reflect truly in the financial statements the financial position of the audited enterprise (Turley 1985, Gwilliam 1987, Holt and Moizer 1990), and even to detect and report fraud and irregularities.[17] The APB, instead of leading the audit profession, persists in remaining in the line of defence, under constant and enormous pressure to meet users' demands. The actual responsibilities and procedures of the profession have become blurred and, instead of standing firm on its decisions concerning audit procedures, the profession's defence tends to prevaricate. For instance, it thrusts the burden of detecting fraud and irregularities on to management, and claims that, 'because of the characteristics of fraud and other irregularities, particularly those involving forgery and collusion, a properly designed and executed audit may not detect a material fraud or other irregularities' (APB [1990, para. 14]). It then argues that any additional duties and responsibilities will bring additional costs to clients and might even delay the issuing of annual reports and auditors' reports.

The argument attracts mixed feelings. Jenkins (1990) reckoned that:

> Deep seated fraud with wide collusion may be virtually impossible to identify, given the limitations of audit techniques ... the auditor is already required to do all that is probably reasonable to detect it. His [her] work is planned so that he [she] has a reasonable expectation of detecting material mis-statements, whether intentional or not. However, he [she] cannot be expected to offer a guarantee since, with management collusion and effective disguise, fraud can be almost impossible to detect using accepted audit techniques.
>
> (Jenkins 1990: 22)

This notion was supported by Cooke (1990), despite calls by the general public to extend auditors' responsibilities to detect fraud:

> In a MORI survey commissioned by KPMG Peat Marwick McLintock, it was found that 75 per cent of the public considers that an auditor has a responsibility to detect fraud of all kind and 61 per cent considers the auditor should actively search for fraud. This is impossible to do. Fraud is, by its nature, concealed. Often management with an intimate knowledge of the business cannot detect fraud that has occurred for some years in their own company, and if the auditors find it, it is usually by chance.
>
> (Cooke 1990: 24)

However, Sikka et al. (1992: 35) argued that, 'to win public support, auditors should have a duty to detect/prevent material fraud.' There seems to be no straight answer to these calls, but the audit profession should consider extending its duties, as part of the accountability exercise, to detect material fraud and irregularities. Singleton-Green (1990) correctly pointed out:

> the real issue is fraud. We cannot get away from the fact that the layman expects the auditor[s] to discover all serious frauds ... The fact is that if auditors did not have a responsibility to find fraud, people would not waste time and money suing the ones who fail to find it.
>
> (Singleton-Green 1990: 34)

Indeed, Gracia-Benau and Humphrey (1992) claim that

> there are those who would willingly embrace such an additional detection responsibility if only the problematic issue of remuneration could be sorted out for the additional work required.
>
> (Gracia-Benau and Humphrey 1992: 322)

A thorough review of the exact responsibilities of auditors needs to be carried out (Swinson 1991, 1992), in order to restore users' confidence. Without this, there seems to be no straightforward solution to narrowing the ever-widening expectation gap. Educating the public is on the agenda of the APB, in an attempt to highlight the 'true' responsibilities of auditors: Changing the wording of the audit report and publishing professional statements describing in general terms what auditors do are two favoured options.

AUDIT REPORTS

Standardized short form audit reports have also been blamed for the emergence of the expectation gap. Users were misled by the particularly arcane phraseology appearing in them. The short, standardized audit reports were in favour in the 1970s. It was hoped that they would reduce the inconsistency and complexity of audit reports, generate at-a-glance understanding (Holt and Moizer 1990), and narrow the expectation gap eventually. The outcome of the exercise proved quite the opposite. Research findings support the need for change in the form and content of audit reports (CICA 1988, Craswell 1985, Holt and Moizer 1990). The ICAEW (1986) called for more consideration of positive reporting, and the inclusion in the audit report of explicit statements of assurance regarding each aspect of audit responsibilities.

The stylized, short form reports were seen as a rather complex codification system; the emphasis now should be on adopting a language more understandable to non-expert readers of reports. Longer versions of audit reports were introduced in the 1990s. Once again, indecision on the part of the audit profession in the UK served to confuse not only the users but also the profession itself.

A survey carried out by Innes et al. (1991) showed that a longer version of the report is favoured by users and could narrow the expectation gap. In line with this, the APB (1993) issued Statement 600 requiring all audit reports issued on or after 30 September 1993 to comply with the new reporting version. The longer form of audit reporting, which consists of five sections,[18] emphasizes the provision of information on generalized audit responsibilities rather than the detailing of specific considerations and findings affecting the enterprise that has been audited. The intention, therefore, appears to be to provide readers with 'a fuller understanding of some of the limitations of the financial statements and of the scope, nature and limitations of audit work' (Innes et al. 1991: 12). Rather than furnishing more information about the results of the audit, this form of report tends to focus on information about auditing. The longer audit report does not always mean a better report, since it neither refers to the inherent limitations of financial reporting and audit procedure nor mentions that financial statements 'are not intended to be a statement of a company's net worth and that there cannot be a guarantee that the company will survive as a going concern' (Jones and Lim 1992:90). As long as users are not fully aware of the exact role of audit reports, confusion will not subside. Changing the audit report is merely an excuse, as this will result not in unselfish, socially orientated concessions on the part of the auditors but in a self-serving retreat from responsibility by the audit profession (Neebes and Roost 1987).

PUBLICATION OF PROFESSIONAL AUDITING STATEMENTS

By the end of July 1993, the Chinese Institute of Certified Public Accountants (CICPA) has issued a total of nine professional standards,[19] in contrast to the Ministry of Finance's publication of accounting regulations which are 'much less detailed and comprehensive, and mainly for governing accounting, enterprises and institutions' (Skousen *et al.* 1990: 167). In the UK, the then APC had issued a series of Auditing Standards and Guidelines, and had commissioned reports, known as Audit Briefs, which serve as guidance to auditors in discharging their duties, and are intended to clarify the real responsibilities of auditors. However, many of these publications have been regarded as having a protective, legitimating spirit, with no real effect on either expanding the boundaries of audit practice or providing clearer depictions of the precise nature of audit performance (Booth and Cocks 1989, Sikka *et al.* 1989). Even the APC itself, in an Audit Brief entitled '*What is an Audit?*', admitted that, instead of focusing on the varying possibilities as to what an audit could comprise, it described the audit responsibilities derived from companies legislation, as interpreted by the profession, and the favourable approaches adopted by the profession to discharging their responsibilities (Buckley 1980). The existing Auditing Standards and Guidelines merely serve as the codification of the auditing practices of the largest audit firms in the UK (Moizer *et al.* 1987), rather than actively pursuing high quality professional standards, the rationalistic basis of audit expertise (Booth and Cocks 1989), and protecting the public interest. Till now, no disciplinary action has been taken by the professional accounting institutions against individual partners of major firms or the firms themselves that failed to carry out adequate audit procedures; they have not been barred from public practice in the UK (Sikka *et al.* 1989, Mitchell and Sikka 1993: 30). The vagueness of auditing guidelines has also caused incalculable damage to the credibility of the audit profession (Hopwood 1990: 84). This inadequacy on the part of the APB has given audit firms enormous room to manoeuvre, to interpret the guidelines at their own discretion, and to use audits as an initiative to attract further consultancy services,[20] as long as they operate within the accepted parameters of the social, economic and political climate. After all, these guidelines are not deemed to be mandatory by the professional accountancy bodies.

Codification of audit practice and professional pronouncements on the audit function, if applied with care, could to a certain extent improve communications with and understanding by users; if applied unwisely, they might undermine the mystical qualities of professional behaviour and judgements in each situation (Robson and Cooper 1989, Hopwood 1990). These pronouncements, and even annual corporate audit reports, have a limited circulation and readership, and the publicity attached to them is frequently far outweighed by dramatic corporate failure or by the unearthing of a major fraud missed by the auditors[21]. The deeply ingrained, heartfelt nature of the users' expectations of the audit as an early warning system of impending financial failure has been persistently reflected in investigations of the performance of the audit profession. Little effort has been expended by the APB on subjective areas such as adequacy, going concern,[22] judgement, materiality and audit risk,[23] reasonableness, relevance, reliability, substance over form,[24] sufficiency, true and fair view,[25] and understandability. Undoubtedly, different audit situations need different degrees of judgement and decision-making. Guidelines in these areas would set the maximum tolerance limit within which auditors are allowed to manoeuvre without any fear of facing possible legal prosecutions at a later date. Synchronizing auditors' decision-making on judgemental issues could gradually reduce users' confusion over financial statements, caused by auditors arriving at different treatments or results in a similar situation. The elimination of confusion would prevent the expectation gap from intensifying but would not entirely remove the gap, even when the general public were given the chance to know the full extent of the work performed by auditors.

MATERIALITY AND AUDIT RISK

Standardizing decision-making on judgemental issues in auditing is one of the ways to narrow the expectation gap. Materiality is one such judgemental issue. In the planning stage of an audit, auditors need to consider carefully the tolerance level of material items that they allow to take place, and the extent of audit work. In the evaluation stage, materiality serves as the yardstick for evaluating the sufficiency of audit evidence. Commentators have expressed strong feelings and concern about materiality.[26] It has been described as the 'cornerstone of accountancy' (Frishkoff 1970: 116), the 'Achilles' heel of the accounting profession' (O'Glove and Olstei 1977: 19), the 'fundamental tenet of securities law and accounting literature' (Hutchinson 1980: 942), a 'grey area in auditing' (Jennings et al. 1991: 100), the 'norm which determines the nature, timing and extent of audit work' (Chong 1992: 9), the 'norm of auditing' (Chong and Vinten 1993:

18), and the 'degree of importance of an item(s) to users of accounting information' (Chong 1993: 25). As a concept it has been variously referred to as: core, critical, elusive, ill-defined, illusive, important, mysterious, nebulous, psychological, and unknown.[27] It is, indeed, an inexplicable concept; the lack of a guideline on materiality has caused extensive confusion and concern to both the accounting and auditing professions.[28] Auditors are faced with a dilemma: they must meet the increasing needs and expectations of users while being cost effective in their auditing techniques. Too much auditing work not only causes undue distress to both auditors and their clients but also risks ending up with too much detail to be disclosed in the financial statements. This could distract users from focusing attention on information which is crucial to decision-making. Too small a sampling for testing would worry auditors in case their clients were to go into liquidation within a short time of clean audit reports being issued. A balance must be struck between the two extremes. Not surprisingly, auditors may still arrive at different opinions in similar situations,[29] and so cause worry and confusion to users. Materiality is definitely one of the judgemental areas that the APB needs to resolve before the expectation gap expands any further.

Materiality is closely linked with audit risk. Too high a threshold of materiality in an audit could lead to an increased level of audit risk, and to the chance of being sued for negligence. The audit risk model recommended by the APB itself has attracted a lot of criticism as a result of its lack of practicality (Brown and Solomon 1990, Peters 1990), its failure to consider the weighting of each component (that is, inherent risk, control risk and detection risk) of the model (Skerrat and Woodhead 1992, Strowser 1990, 1991) and its lack of emphasis on the effects of materiality on audit risk (Cushing and Loebbecke 1983, Skerratt and Woodhead 1992). Survey results severely criticize the validity of the model for causing increased uncertainty in the audit process (Daniel 1988, Jiambalvo and Waller 1984). The definition of the individual components of the model receives an equally hostile reception (Peters 1990, Gwilliam 1987). Despite this, materiality and audit risk are yet to receive priority in the guidelines of the APB.

AUDITORS' INDEPENDENCE

The independence of auditors is an important principle in auditing. Without true independence, reliance on the work and opinion of the auditor is compromised (Arens and Loebbecke 1988). Auditors need to 'be, and be seen to be, free ... of any interest which might detract from objectivity' (CACA 1984: para. 1b). Nothing should appear in the course of an audit which would cast doubt on the impartiality of the auditor. This means that independence, despite its importance, will always be difficult to measure (Dunn 1991: 19). Again, the APB is yet to issue guidelines on auditors' independence.

As far as the Chinese are concerned, economic reforms require the separation of economic functions from politics, in order to make enterprises self-reliant and self-developing economic units. At present, most major enterprises are still, to some extent, economic extensions of government authorities.[30] Local government authorities may exercise indirect control over an enterprise by virtue of tax planning. By falsifying the amount of tax payable to the central government, enterprises enjoy the benefits of paying less tax and of higher retained profits. In return, these enterprises pay a proportion of the benefits to the local government. As Skousen et al. (1990) noted, auditing bureaux are under the supervision of local government

> the auditors' promotion and salary increases depend on recommendations from administrative officials. The former tend to follow the instructions given by local government officials to protect the local interest rather than to follow the requirements set by the central government.
>
> (Skousen et al. 1990: 165)

This has seriously undermined the credibility of auditors and their independence in discharging their duties.[31]

The 1985 UK Companies Act protects auditors from unfair dismissal by allowing them to submit written representation in general meetings. Additional help comes from the rotation of auditors, the setting up of audit committees, and the appointment of internal auditors. The setting up of the Joint Monitoring Unit (JMU) and the presence of an independent regulatory agency (Mitchell et al. 1991, Humphrey et al. 1992a, which oversees the appointment, the fee determination, and the practices of auditors of large companies, also combine to secure the image of independence of external auditors. However, this does not safeguard auditors against being blackmailed by corporate management over their (re)appointment or their taking on further consultancy services in exchange for clean audit reports (Cousins and Sikka 1993). The behaviour of external auditors is almost never researched and rarely commented on (Vinten 1988, 1992a). The setting up of the JMU by the accounting institutions was intended to ensure that proper professional duties are carried out. Eighteen inspectors were appointed to visit 250 audit firms of public limited companies every five years and to call on another 150 every year. Each visit is made by prior arrangement (usually with eight weeks' notice) and the inspection normally takes less than four days. The purpose is to sample-check three audit client files. Under this arrangement, it will take 57 years to visit all auditing firms in the UK (Mitchell and Sikka 1993: 45). As far as the independent regulatory agency is concerned, its components remain open for discussion.[32]

The above commentary may reflect the inability of the audit profession to regulate itself. Instead of projecting a better image, it looks as if the APB will stay on the defensive. Auditors should seriously review their present roles and responsibilities, including the possibilities of detecting and reporting fraud as part of their audit services (Sikka *et al.* 1992). In order for the audit profession to perform its existing duties and any others, it must secure public trust and confidence, in part by promoting an ideology of professional independence, objectivity, neutrality, and impartiality (Willmott 1989).

PERSONNEL SHORTAGES

The audit profession in China is facing an acute shortage of trained and experienced personnel (Shuo and Yam 1987, Skousen *et al.* 1990, Tai and Yang 1988, Tang *et al.* 1992, Wang and Qian 1987. Rapid economic growth has created plenty of opportunities for both local and foreign qualified auditors (Evans 1992: 20). The training of accountants and auditors was formalized only in the early 1980s,[33] and the first examination set by the Chinese Institute of Certified Public Accountants (CICPA) was held in 1991.[34] Despite this, CICPA had 10,700 members by the end of July 1993 (Zhang 1993). This contrasts with 1985, when the Chinese government had to transfer more than 28,000 people, who had only limited basic accounting and auditing training, to various audit departments. Many of these people were relatively old, had varying educational backgrounds and lacked practical experience in auditing. Extensive in-house and on-the-job training was warranted (Tai and Yang 1988). The quality of these auditors was gradually upgraded and many were replaced by newly trained accountants. Auditing has become part of the teaching curriculum at various levels of education, from colleges to universities. The supply of auditors has also been augmented by those who have graduated or trained overseas, particularly in the West.

The shortage of trained personnel might also result from the nature and extent of audit procedures carried out by individual audit assignments. However, this should not constitute an excuse for not being able to serve all clients to the full. Proper planning, selection of audit sampling, audit techniques, evaluation of the relevance and reliability of audit evidence, and types of audit reports[35] could enhance the efficiency, effectiveness, and conclusions of audits. The co-operation of factory managers[36] and other management and an understanding of the purposes of auditing could also expedite completion dates.

Major audit firms in the UK have internal audit manuals and supporting checklists to ensure that all audit assignments are properly planned and carried out. Close supervision of audit trainees is emphasized. This practice merits serious consideration by auditing firms in China.

CONCLUSION

In the UK it is now time for the APB to reassure the public that auditors are independent of the stewards of a company who are responsible for recommending to shareholders, the auditors' (re)appointment as well as the fee determination. The whole auditing profession in the UK needs to undergo a fundamental reform of its accounting institutions (Mitchell and Sikka 1993: 30), including major surgery to improve its image so as to reflect selfless, disinterested auditors; to reassure financial statement users and regulators that, despite perceptions to the contrary, auditors are independent and are not prepare to knuckle under to, or act as the 'paid servants' of, corporate management (Humphrey et al. 1992b: 150).

Not surprisingly, Lee (1992) observed that, while major audit firms are not afraid of assuming new responsibilities, such as tax planning and management advisory services, the profession as a whole seems to deny responsibilities, and concluded that:

> attempts to limit the economic consequences of being professionals are not very convincing to a public that can observe auditors in a position of power dominated by economic self-interest ... rather than being a professional service, auditing is a business product whose economic viability is now in question ... firms need to face up to the question of whether they want to be professionals or commercial profit-maximising organisations. They cannot be both.
>
> (Lee 1992: 102)

Denial of responsibilities, limited (or no) proper supervision and punishment by the APB and accounting institutions of defaulting members (and audit firms), lack of proper guidance, and confusing objectives of audit services all account for the continuing growth of the expectation gap. What goes on in the UK and the West today has a habit of repeating itself in the East tomorrow. Zhou (1988), however, sees the problem differently:

> the rigidity of the Chinese economy system, the mandatory and detailed nature of its accounting regulations, as well as the lack of a set of complete and coherent accounting theories and methodologies, has made it difficult for Chinese accounting to adapt to the changing economic environment.
>
> (Zhou 1988: 220)

This notion is not supported by Skousen and Yang (1988: 203): 'current Chinese cost centre accounting and control techniques are similar to those used by the United States and other Western countries.' This reinforces the Chinese readiness to adopt Western practices and techniques. However, the Chinese need to ensure that accounting and auditing techniques adopted from the West are properly modified to meet the local socio-economic and political needs. Close collaboration between East and West should be encouraged to help to construct useful audit models which are self-regulating, in order to withstand the ever increasing challenges of modern societies.

NOTES

1 Different commentators have different opinions on the exact date at which the first auditing system was established in China. Shuo and Yam (1987: 11) argue that it started off in the year 700 BC; Zhao (1987: 173) reckons that it was about 2000 years ago; while Chen (1991: 4), Fu (1971), Gao (1982), Lau and Yang (1990: 54), Lu (1988: 131), Skousen et al. (1990: 157), Tai and Yang (1988: 226), and Tang et al. (1992: 180) seem to agree that this practice took place during the Western Zhou Dynasty, about 3000 years ago.

2 Refer to Zhao (1987) for a detailed summary on the history, development, varying degree of importance, and authority of auditors over each of the 29 dynasties in China.

3 The Audit Section was changed to an Audit Department in 1931, primarily responsible for the internal audit function of the government.

4 In 1921, there were only 13 Certified Public Accountants (CPAs) in the entire nation. The number gradually increased in subsequent years. In 1948, there were over 500 CPAs in the city of Shanghai alone (Tai and Yang 1988: 226). The Certified Public Accountants Society was established in 1925. By April 1935, 1,662 CPA licences were issued (Lu 1988: 133).

   In September 1983, there were more than 70 CPA firms with approximately 1,000 CPAs (Huang 1987: 52).

   The total number of Chinese CPAs had risen to 10,700 by the end of July 1993 (Zhang 1993).

5 Prior to 10 June, 1993, foreigners were treated as 'foreign devils' by bosses in the Communist Party (Editorial, *Financial Times*, 25 August 1993, p. 13).

   On 10 June 1993, Zhu Rongji, China's Vice-Premier in charge of the economy, acted to slow the rapid growth of the economy, after he had received recommendations from international advisers, including the World Bank, whom he considered as 'foreign monks'. This openness shows that China is prepared to accept foreign advice (Nicoll 1993).

6 These 'evils' are corruption, waste and bureaucracy.

7 That is, cleaning up politics, economy, organization, and ideology.

8 The Auditor General's appointment and dismissal is based on the majority decision of the National People's Congress (NPC) upon the recommendations of the Premier. The NPC is the highest elected governing body in China.

9 The Tiananmen Square massacre in 1989 seriously undermined the credibility of the Chinese leadership and raised the question of human rights in China. This event later led to China's losing in the bidding for the Year 2000 Olympic Games.

   Several attempts have been made by the Chinese government to improve its image. These include introducing in August 1993 an anti-corruption communiqué to reflect 'clean government', in order to win the confidence of foreign investors (Walker 1993:4).

10 Similar concern was also reflected in the USA. Cases such as Ultramares Corporation v. Touche, Niven and Company in 1931 and McKesson and Robbins in 1939 seriously undermined credibility.
11 It was changed to the Auditing Practices Board (APB) in 1991.
12 There exists a wide range of descriptions on the notion of the expectation gap. Apart from Porter, Gaa (1991) considers it 'a game played by regulators and the auditing profession'; Willmott (1991) calls it an 'auditing game'; while Snyder and Woolf (1993: 80) say that it is 'the real discrepancy between what auditors claim they will achieve and what they actually deliver . . . [and] is therefore performance-related'.

Innes et al. (1991: 3) analysed the expectation gap in more detail and divided it under six different headings:

1 Positive perceptions gap: between what auditors perceive that they are doing and what users perceive that auditors are doing.
2 User perceptions gap: between what users perceive that auditors are doing and what users perceive that auditors should do.
3 Normative perceptions gap: between what users perceive that auditors should be doing and what auditors perceive that they should be doing.
4 Auditor perceptions gap: between what auditors perceive that they should be doing and what auditors perceive that they are doing.
5 Normative auditor-positive user perceptions gap: between what auditors perceive that they should be doing and what users perceive that auditors are doing.
6 Normative user-positive auditor perceptions gap: between what users perceive that auditors should be doing and what auditors perceive that they are doing.

13 By the end of 1992, the APB in the UK had issued 3 auditing standards, 38 auditing guidelines and 6 exposure drafts; while the Chinese Institute of Certified Public Accountants had published 9 auditing guidelines by the end of July 1993.
14 For example, Arrington et al. (1983), Arthur Andersen & Co. (1974), Baron et al. (1977), Beck (1973), Humphrey et al. (1992a), Lee (1970a) and Porter (1992).
15 Refer to Vinten (1992b) and Warman (1993) for detailed discussions on the deficiency of audit functions in the cases of BCCI and the Maxwell Corporation.
16 See Carpenter and Dirsmith (1993) and Power (1992) for detailed discussions of audit sampling techniques.
17 For example, refer to Matsumura and Tucker (1992) and Tombs (1993) for discussions on auditors' responsibilities regarding fraud detection and reporting errors.
18 Auditors' reports on financial statements should include the following matters:

1 A title identifying the person or persons to whom the report is addressed.
2 An introductory paragraph identifying the financial statements audited.

3 Separate sections, appropriately headed, dealing with:

(a) respective responsibilities of directors (or equivalent persons) and auditors;
(b) the basis of the auditors' opinion;
(c) the auditors' opinion on the financial statements.

4 The manuscript or printed signature of the auditors.
5 Date (with address) on which the auditors' report was signed.

19 The CICPA standards are:

1 Guidelines on audit of financial statements.
2 Guidelines on capital verification.
3 Guidelines on audit planning.
4 Guidelines on preparation of audit work papers.
5 Guidelines on issuance of audit report.
6 Guidelines on the offer of management letter.
7 Code of professional ethics for Chinese CPAs.
8 Guidelines on educational requirement and vocational training.
9 Rules on practice review.

20 A survey shows that firms in the UK were found to be practising the 'low balling' system whereby audit firms, in particular the Big Six, offer big reductions in their professional audit fees, in order to win business and/or other consultancy services` from the company concerned (Brinn and Peel 1993: 37). This practice should be discouraged, as it seriously confuses users as to the actual level of input by auditors in discharging their duties.

21 The public will point their fingers at the profession and ask the favourite question, 'Where were the auditors?'

22 Refer to Constantine (1992) and Sherwood (1993) for further discussions on the treatment of the problem of going concern in auditing.

23 The APB issued exposure drafts on audit materiality (Statement of Auditing Standards 220) and audit risk assessment (Statement of Auditing Standards 300) in August 1993. These drafts failed to mention the bases of measuring materiality thresholds and audit risk.

24 Refer to Hopwood (1990) and Martens and McEnroe (1992) on the controversial issue of substance over form in the auditing context.

25 It is described as a 'mythical concept' by Mitchell and Sikka (1993: 36). Refer to Nobes and Parker (1991), Parker and Nobes (1991), and Walton (1991) for detailed discussions on the implications and importance of the 'true and fair' view in the accounting and auditing context. Refer to McGee (1991) on the legal perspective of the concept. The European context may be seen in Alexander (1993), Ordelheide (1993), and Walton (1993).

26 As early as 1933, Gordon defined materiality as 'a fact, the untrue statement or omission of which would be likely to affect the conduct of a reasonable man with reference to the acquisition, holding or disposal of the security in question' (Gordon 1933: 438). Chetkovick (1955: 48) considered materiality as a concept which is useful for

'separating those important from unimportant items', while Ghatalia (1984: 500) refers it as 'what is important and what matters'.

Compared with the definitions of the various accounting bodies, all of these definitions aim at meeting users' needs. Interested readers should refer to definitions of materiality in the Institute of Chartered Accountants in England and Wales (1968: para. 1), Australian Accounting Research Foundation (1974: para. 6), (South African Institute of Chartered Accountants 1984: para. 89), New Zealand Society of Accountants (1985: para. 3.1) and Canadian Institute of Chartered Accountants (1987: para. 4).

27 The ten adjectives were used respectively by: Hewitt (1975: 892); Jennings et al. (1985b: 338); Pattillo (1975: 20) and Lee (1970b: 19); Jennings et al. (1985a: 640); Barnes (1976: 19); Study Group on Audit Technique (1965) and Jeffries (1981: 13); Rose et al. (1970: 139); Jennings et al. (1985a: 667); Moonitz (1961: 2); and Reininga (1968: 31).

28 Refer to Chong (1992) for a summary of materiality thresholds recommended by accounting bodies, academia, and audit manuals; also for the pros and cons of having rigid guidelines on materiality for the profession.

29 This could be because auditors may consider not only the quantitative effects but also the qualitative aspect of the items. Chong and Vinten (1993) discuss the qualitative aspect of materiality.

30 By May 1993, more than 100,000 private firms, from trading companies to real estate developers, were doing business in Hainan, an island the size of Taiwan, which is situated off the southernmost tip of China. Hainan is 'travelling faster down the free-market road than almost any other region in China' (Walsh 1993: 34).

31 Skousen et al. (1990: 165) also noted that enterprise directors even told auditors, 'Don't come and audit our accounts ... This is the greatest help you can be to us.'

32 Sikka et al. (1992: 35) argued that 'all aspects of auditing should be regulated by an agency independent of the [audit] profession and the DTI.'

33 The Accounting Society of China was set up in January 1980, while the Auditing Society of China was created in 1984.

34 Evans (1992: 21) observed that 'CICPA held its first examination for Chinese accountants last year [1991]. But of the 25,000 applicants, only half actually took the exams and of these only 4 per cent passed. Zhang De-Ming, Secretary-General of CICPA and director of the Department of Administration of Accounting Affairs at the Ministry of Finance, said the low pass rate was because ... it was the first exams and applicants were not clear on what the exams would entail ... [There was] inadequate time [for students] to prepare for the exams and poor training ... this would improve with time.'

35 Despite the existence of a guideline on auditors' reports, Bai (1988: 48) noted that 'there is a wide variation in the format of audit reports [in China]. Some contain a list of adjustments that, in the auditors' opinion, should appear in the working papers, while some provide a

full assessment of the business operations of the year under review.'

This practice not only will waste considerable time in the preparation of audit reports but also will definitely confuse users of financial statements as to the real meaning of audit reports and the reliability of the financial statements.

36 Shuo and Yam (1987: 12) reported that, 'from 1984 to 1986, the Audit Administration had carried out many kinds of audit in the administrative organs and state enterprises. Despite the problems of understaffing and lack of training, the Administration had audited more than 120,000 units and enterprises across the country. The Administration had discovered many cases of fraud, error, waste and tax evasion valued at about Rb4.3 billion (equivalent to £540 million). By the middle of 1986, the Audit Administration had 3,000 audit offices and a total audit staff of 34,000.

In 1986, in order to prevent factory managers leaving their position before their books were audited, a new rule was implemented. 'All managers of enterprises are not allowed to retire or leave their office unless the enterprise's books are audited by the Administration.'

Later, in 1991, Chen noted that, 'from 1986 to 1989, . . . the amount of fraudulent gains, wrong bookkeeping and value for money audited out by internal auditors is respectively: Rb700 million, Rb3.5 billion, Rb5 billion, and Rb7.2 billion (equivalent to £87.5 million, £700 million, £625 million, and £900 million respectively)' (p. 30), while 'internal auditing departments of Shandong Province audited about 26,000 projects in 1989, found out and corrected more than Rb250 billion (equivalent to £31.3 billion) that related to frauds; found out more than Rb75 billion (equivalent to £9.4 billion) that related to losses and wastes; raised more than Rb180 billion (equivalent to £22.5 billion) . . . for organisations from operational audit . . . money relating to unseasonable loans and tax, and infringement of the state's financial regulations, and value for money had accounted for Rb2,200 billion (equivalent to £275 billion)' (p. 46).

Knowledge of proper accounting, of adequate accounting control systems, and of the purposes of auditing should be made widespread in order to reduce similar happenings in the future.

REFERENCES

Aiken, M. and Lu, W. (1993) 'Chinese government accounting: historical perspective and current practice', *British Accounting Review* 25(2): 109–29.

Alexander, D. (1993) 'A European true and fair view?' *European Accounting Review* 2(1): 59–80.

Arens, A. A. and Loebbecke, J. K. (1988) *Auditing: an integrated approach* (4th edn), Englewood Cliffs, NJ: Prentice Hall.

Arrington, C. E., Hillson, W. A. and Williams, P. F. (1983) 'The psychology of the expectations gap: why is there so much dispute about auditor responsibility?', *Accounting and Business Research* 13(52): 243–50.

Arthur Andersen & Co. (1974) *Public Accounting in Transition: American shareholders view the role of independent accountants and the corporate reporting controversy*, Chicago, Ill: Arthur Andersen & Co.

Auditing Practices Board (1993) *Auditing Reports on Financial Statements*, Statement 600, London: APB.

Auditing Practices Committee (1990) *The Auditor's Responsibility in relation to Fraud, Other Irregularities and Errors*, Statement 418, London: APC.

Australian Accounting Research Foundation (1974) *Materiality in Financial Statements*, Statement of Accounting Standards no. 5, DS 7, Melbourne: AARF, pp. 531–3.

Bai, Z. L. (1988) 'Accounting in the People's Republic of China: contemporary situations and issues', in B. E. Needles and V. K. Zimmerman (eds) *Recent Accounting and Economic Developments in the Far East*, Urbana-Champaign: Centre for International Education and Research in Accounting, University of Illinois, pp. 27–50.

Barnes, D. P. (1976) 'Materiality: an illusive concept', *Management Accounting*, October, pp. 19, 20, 32.

Baron, C. D., Johnson, D. A., Searfoss, D. G. and Smith, C. H. (1977) 'Uncovering corporate irregularities: are we closing the expectations gap?', *Journal of Accountancy*, October, pp. 14–24.

Beck, G. W. (1973) 'The role of the auditor in modern society: an empirical appraisal', *Accounting and Business Research* 3(10): 117–22.

Booth, P. and Cocks, N. (1989) 'Power and the study of the accounting profession', in D. J. Cooper and T. M. Hooper (eds) *Critical Accounts*, Basingstoke, UK: Macmillan.

Brinn, T. and Peel, M. (1993) 'Low-balling and the small firms', *Certified Accountant*, January, pp. 37–9.

Brown, C. E. and Solomon, I. (1990) 'Auditor configural information processing in control risk assessment', *Auditing: A Journal of Practice and Theory* 9(3): 17–38.

Buckley, R. (1980) *What is an audit?*, Audit Brief, London: Auditing Practices Committee.

Canadian Institute of Chartered Accountants (1987) *Materiality and Audit Risk in Conducting an Audit*, Auditing Standards Committee, Toronto: CICA.

—(1988) *Report of the Commission to Study the Public's Expectation of Audits* (MacDonald Commission), Toronto: CICA.

Carpenter, B. and Dirsmith, M. (1993) 'Sampling and the abstraction of knowledge in the auditing profession: an extended institutional theory perspective', *Accounting, Organizations, and Society* 18(1): 41–63.

Chartered Association of Certified Accountants (1984) *Professional Independence*, London: CACA.

Chatfield, M. (1977) *A History of Accounting Thought*, Huntington, NY: Robert E. Krieger.

Chen, H. (1991) 'A feasibility study of the modern internal auditing system in the People's Republic of China', unpublished MSc dissertation, London: City University Business School.

Chetkovich, M. N. (1955) 'Standards of disclosure and their development', *Journal of Accountancy*, December, pp. 48–52.

Chong, H. G. (1992) 'Auditors and materiality', *Managerial Auditing Journal* 7(5): 8–17.

—(1993) 'Materiality in UK financial statements: an empirical investigation', *Journal of Accounting and Finance* 7(1): 23–47.

Chong, H. G. and Vinten, G. (1993) 'Materiality: the norm of auditing?', *Executive Accountant* 20(1): 18–20.

Constantine, J. (1992) 'The APB and going concern: the way ahead', *Accountancy*, November, p. 89.

Cooke, R. (1990) 'It takes two to do the audit tango', *Accountancy*, October, pp. 23–4.

Cousins, J. and Sikka, P. (1993) 'Accounting for change: facilitating power and accountability', *Critical Perspectives on Accounting* 4(1): 53–72.

Craswell, A. (1985) 'Studies of the information content of qualified audit reports', *Journal of Business Finance and Accounting*, Spring, pp. 93–116.

Cross Report (1977) 'Report of a committee under the chairmanship of the Rt Hon. the Lord Cross of Chelsea', *Accountancy*, December, pp. 80–86.

Cushing, B. E. and Loebbecke, J. K. (1983) 'Analytical approaches to audit risk: a survey and analysis', *Auditing: A Journal of Practice and Theory* 3(1): 23–41.

Daniel, S. J. (1988) 'Some empirical evidence about the assessment of audit risk in practice', *Auditing: A Journal of Practice and Theory* 7(2): 174–81.

Dunn, J. (1991) *Auditing: Theory and Practice*, London: Prentice Hall International.

Edwards, J. R. (1989) *A History of Financial Accounting*, London: Routledge.

Evans, L. (1992) 'Reds cut the tape', *Accountancy Age Magazine*, October, pp. 17–21.

Frishkoff, P. (1970) 'An empirical investigation of the concept of materiality in accounting', in *Empirical Research in Accounting: Selected Studies*, supplement to *Journal of Accounting Research*, vol. 8, pp. 116–37.

Fu, P. (1971) 'Governmental accounting in China during Chou Dynasty (1122 BC–256 BC)', *Journal of Accounting Research* 9(1): 40–51.

Gaa, J. C. (1991) 'The expectations game: regulation of auditors by government and the profession', *Critical Perspectives on Accounting* 2(1): 83–107.

Gao, D. Y. (1982) *History of Chinese Accounting* (in Chinese), vol. Beijing: Chinese Finance and Economics Publishing House.

Ghatalia, N. S. (1984) 'Materiality for auditors: a US–UK approach', *Chartered Accountants (India)*, February, pp. 500–503.

Gordon, S. (1933) 'Accountants and Securities Acts' *Journal of*

Accountancy, November, p. 438.

Gracia-Benau, M. A. and Humphrey, C. G. (1992) 'Beyond the audit expectations gap: learning from the experiences of Britain and Spain', *European Accounting Review* 1(2): 303–31.

Grenside Report (1979) 'Report on the Joint Committee appointed to consider the Cross Report and related matters', *Accountancy*, June, pp. 124–32.

Gwilliam, D. R. (1987) *A Survey of Auditing Research*, London: Prentice Hall International.

Hewitt, J. O. (1975) 'Developing concepts of materiality and disclosure', *Business Lawyer*, April, pp. 887–956.

Holt, G. and Moizer, P. (1990) 'The meaning of audit reports', *Accounting and Business Research* 20(78): 111–22.

Hopwood, A. G. (1990) 'Ambiguity, knowledge and territorial claims: some observations on the doctrine of substance over form; a review essay', *British Accounting Review* 22(1): 79–88.

Huang, H. Q. (1987) 'Auditing', in Shanghai University of Finance and Economics and the University of Texas at Dallas (E. -Y. Lou, S. N. Wang and A. J. H. Enthoven [eds]), *Accounting and Auditing in the People's Republic of China: A Review of its Practice, System, Education and Development*, Dallas: Centre for International Accounting Development, University of Texas, pp. 53–73.

Humphrey, C. G., Moizer, P. and Turley, S. (1992a) *The Audit Expectations Gap in the United Kingdom*, Research Board, London: Institute of Chartered Accountants in England and Wales.

—— (1992b) 'The audit expectations gap: *plus ça change, plus c'est la même chose?*', *Critical Perspectives on Accounting* 3(2): 137–61.

Hutchinson, J. L. (1980) 'Materiality and internal accounting controls under the Foreign Corrupt Practices Act', *Arizona State Law Journal*, vol. 40, pp. 931–51.

Innes, J., Brown, T. and Hartherly, D. (1991) 'The audit expectation gap: a UK perspective on the expanded audit report' *Discussion paper ACC/9107*, University of Dundee, Scotland.

Institute of Chartered Accountants in England and Wales (1968) *The Interpretation of 'Material' in relation to Accounts*, Accounting Recommendation 2.206, Statement V10, London: ICAEW.

—(1986) *Report of the Working Party on the Future of the Audit*, London: ICAEW.

Jeffries, K. R. (1981) 'Materiality as defined by the courts', *CPA Journal*, October, pp. 13–17.

Jenkins, B. (1990) 'The auditor's guide to bridging the gap', *Accountancy*, October, pp. 22–3.

Jennings, M. M., Reckers, P. M. J. and Kneer, D. C. (1985a) 'A source of insecurity: a discussion and an empirical examination of standards of disclosure and levels of materiality in financial statements', *Journal of Corporation Law*, vol: 12, pp. 639–88.

—— (1985b) 'Concept of materiality and disclosure: can the disciplines and practitioners agree?', *Securities Regulation Law Journal* 12(4): 337–66.

—— (1991) 'The auditor's dilemma: the incongruous judicial notions of the auditing profession and actual auditor practice', *American Business Law Journal*, vol. 29, pp. 99–125.

Jiambalvo, J. and Waller, W. (1984) 'Decomposition and assessment of audit risk', *Auditing: A Journal of Practice and Theory* 3(2): 80–88.

Jones, M. and Lim, C. H. (1992) 'The expanded auditors' report: could do better', *Accountancy*, November, pp. 90–91.

Lau, H. L. and Yang, J. L. (1990) 'Auditing in China: historical perspective and current developments', *International Journal of Accounting*, vol. 25, pp. 53–62.

Lee, T. (1992) 'The audit liability crisis: they protest too much' *Accountancy*, December, p. 102.

Lee, T. A. (1970a) 'The nature of auditing and its objectives', *Accountancy*, April, pp. 292–6.

——(1970b) 'Materiality: the elusive concept', *Singapore Accountant*, December, pp. 19–25.

Littleton, A. C. (1966) *Accounting Evolution to 1900* (2nd edn), New York: Russell & Russell.

Lu, T. G. (1988) 'Governmental accounting and auditing in China: evolution and current reforms', in J. L. Chan and R. H. Jones (eds) *Governmental Accounting and Auditing: International Comparisons*, London: Routledge, pp. 122–48.

McGee, A. (1991) 'The "true and fair" view debate: a study in the legal regulation of accounting', *Modern Law Review* 54(6): 874–88.

Martens, S. C. and McEnroe, J. E. (1992) 'Substance over form in auditing and the auditor's position of public trust', *Critical Perspectives on Accounting* 3(4): 389–401.

Matsumura, E. M. and Tucker, R. R. (1992) 'Fraud detection: a theoretical framework', *Accounting Review* 67(4): 753–82.

Mitchell, A. and Sikka, P. (1993), 'Accounting for change: the institutions of accountancy', *Critical Perspectives on Accounting* 4(1): 29–52.

Mitchell, A., Puxty, A., Sikka, P. and Willmott, H. (1991) *Accounting for Change: Proposals for Reform of Audit and Accounting*, London: Fabian Society.

Moizer, P., Turley, S. and Walker, D. (1987) 'Reliance on other auditors: a UK study', *Accounting and Business Research* 18(72): 343–52.

Moonitz, M. (1961) *The Basic Postulates of Accounting*, Accounting Research Studies no. 1, New York: American Institute of Certified Public Accountants.

Neebes, D. L. and Roost, W. G. (1987) 'ASB's ten "expectations gap" proposals: will they do the job?', *CPA Journal*, October, pp. 23–5.

New Zealand Society of Accountants (1985) 'Materiality in financial statements', Statement of Standard Accounting Practice no. 6, *Accountants' Journal* (New Zealand), August, pp. 67–8.

Nicoll, A. (1993) 'Zhu heeds foreign advice to slow China's growth', *Financial Times*, 25 August, p. 3.

Nobes, C. W. and Parker, R. H. (1991) 'True and fair view: UK auditors' view', *Accounting and Business Research* 21(84): 349–61.

O'Glove, T. L. and Olstein R. A. (1977) 'How well do accountants understand materiality?', *Journal of Portfolio Management*, vol. 3, pp. 19–25.

Ordelheide, D. (1993) 'True and fair view: a European and a German perspective', *European Accounting Review* 2(1): 81–90.

Parker, R. H. and Nobes, C. W. (1991), 'True and fair view: a survey of UK financial directors', *Journal of Business Finance and Accounting*, April, pp. 359–75.

Pattillo, J. W. (1975) 'Materiality: the elusive standard', *Financial Executive*, August, pp. 20–27.

Peters, J. M. (1990) 'A cognitive computational model of risk; hypothesis generation', *Journal of Accounting Research* 28 (Supplement): 83–103.

Porter, B. A. (1988) *Towards a Theory of the Role of the External Auditor in Society*, Research Monograph no. 1, Accountancy Department, Massey University, Palmerston North (New Zealand).

—— (1992) 'An empirical study of the audit expectation-performance gap', *Proceedings of Conference on Auditing*, Bristol, 3–4 April.

Power, M. (1992) 'From common sense to expertise: reflections on the pre-history of audit sampling', *Accounting, Organizations, and Society* 17(5): 437–54.

Reininga, W. (1968) 'The unknown materiality concept', *Journal of Accountancy*, February, pp. 31–5.

Robson, K. and Cooper, D. J. (1989) 'Understanding the development of the accountancy profession in the United Kingdom', in D. J. Cooper, and T. M. Hooper, (eds) *Critical Accounts*, Basingstoke, UK: Macmillan.

Rose, J. W., Becker, W., Becker, S. and Sorter, G. (1970) 'Towards an empirical measure of materiality', *Empirical Research in Accounting: Selected Studies*, pp. 139–56.

Russell, P. (1991) 'Department of Trade and Industry investigations', in M. Sherer and S. Turley (eds) *Current Issues in Auditing*, London: Paul Chapman Publishing, pp. 76–98.

Sherwood, K. (1993) 'Are going concern reports required by statute?', *Accountancy*, March, p. 84.

Shuo, W. and Yam, S. C. (1987) 'Audit profile: People's Republic of China', *International Journal of Government Auditing* 14(4): 11–12.

Sikka, P., Puxty, A., Willmott, H. and Cooper, C. (1992) 'The expectation gap', *Certified Accountant*, September, pp. 33–5.

Sikka, P., Willmott, H. C. and Lowe, E. A. (1989) 'Guardians of knowledge and public interest: evidence and issues of accountability in the UK accountancy profession', *Accounting, Auditing and Accountability Journal* 2(2): 47–72.

Singleton-Green, B. (1990) 'The new auditing guideline on fraud', *Accountancy*, April, pp. 33–4.

Skerratt, L. C. L. and Woodhead, A. (1992) 'Modelling audit risk', *British Accounting Review* 24(2): 119–37.

Skousen, C. R. and Yang, J. L. (1988) 'Western management accounting and the economic reforms of China', *Accounting, Organizations, and Society* 13(2): 201–6.

Skousen, C. R., Yang, J. L. and Dai, X. M. (1990) 'Auditing in China' in R. S. O. Wallace, J. M. Samuels and R. J. Briston (eds) *Research in Third World Accounting*, vol. 1, London: JAI Press, pp. 157–69.

South African Institute of Chartered Accountants (1984) *Audit Risk and Materiality*, Auditing Standards Committee, Discussion Paper 6, Johannesburg: SAICA.

Strawser, J. R. (1990) 'Human information processing and the consistency of audit risk judgements', *Accounting and Business Research* 21(18): 67–75.

—— (1991) 'Examination of the effect of risk model components on perceived audit risk', *Auditing: A Journal of Practice and Theory* 10(1): 126–35.

Study Group on Audit Technique (1965) *Materiality in Auditing: an Audit Technique*, Toronto: Canadian Institute of Chartered Accountants.

Swinson, C. (1991) 'Time to take the bull by the horns', *Accountancy*, February, pp. 21–2.

—— (1992) 'Duty and definition', *Accountancy*, November, pp. 112–13.

Synder, M. and Woolf, E. (1993) 'The McFarlane report: reflections on a failed mission', *Accountancy*, April, pp. 80–82.

Tai, B. Y. and Yang, D.-Z. (1988) 'Recent developments in auditing education in the People's Republic of China', in K. Someya (ed.) *Accounting Education and Research to Promote International Understanding*, New York: Quorum Books, pp. 226–30.

Tang, Y. W., Chow, L. and Cooper, B. J. (1992) 'State auditing', in *Accounting and Finance in China: A Review of Current Practice*, Hong Kong: Longman, pp. 180–94.

Tombs, A. (1993) 'The auditor and fraud', *Internal Auditing*, September, p. 33.

Turley, S. (1985) 'Empirical research in auditing', in D. Kent, M. J. Sherer and S. Turley (eds) *Current Issues in Auditing*, London: Harper & Row, pp. 248–66.

Vinten, G. (1988) 'Behaviourial aspects of accountancy', *Managerial Auditing Journal* 3(2): 28–31.

—— (1992a) 'Rottweiler or poodle? The internal auditor in action', *Leadership and Organisation Development Journal* 13(4): i–iv.

—— (1992b) 'Internal audit after Maxwell and BCCI: public responsibility versus loyalty to the organisation', *Managerial Auditing Journal* 7(4): 3–5.

Walker, T. (1993) 'China acts to curb corruption', *Financial Times*, 26 August, p. 4.

Walsh, J. (1993) 'Turning down the voltage', *Times Magazine*, 16 August, pp. 32–7.

Walton, P. (1991) *The True and Fair View: a Shifting Concept*, Occasional Paper no. 7, London: Chartered Association of Certified Accountants.

—— (1993) 'Introduction: the true and fair view in British accounting', *European Accounting Review* 2(1): 49–58.

Wang, S. N. and Qian, J. F. (1987) 'Education and training of accounting and auditing personnel', in Shanghai University of Finance and Economics and the University of Texas at Dallas (E.-Y. Lou, S. N.

Wang and A. J. H. Enthoven [eds]), *Accounting and Auditing in the People's Republic of China: A Review of its Practice, System, Education and Development*, Dallas: Centre for International Accounting Development, University of Texas, pp. 127–37.

Warman, A. (1993) 'Accountants as detectives', *Certified Accountant*, January, pp. 29–30.

Willmott, H. (1989) 'Serving the public interest? A critical analysis of a professional claim', in D. J. Cooper and T. M. Hooper (eds) *Critical Accounts*, London: Macmillian.

—— (1991) 'The auditing game: a question of ownership and control', *Critical Perspectives on Accounting* 2(1): 109–21.

Zhang, C. H. X. (1993) Personal letter from him (International Relations Officer, Chinese Institute of Certified Public Accountants) to the present authors, 17 August.

Zhao, Y. L. (1987) 'A brief history of accounting and auditing in China', in Shanghai University of Finance and Economics and the University of Texas at Dallas (E.-Y. Lou, S. N. Wang and A. J. H. Enthoven [eds]), *Accounting and Auditing in the People's Republic of China: A Review of its Practice, System, Education and Development*, Dallas: Centre for International Accounting Development, University of Texas, pp. 165–91.

Zhou, Z. H. (1988) 'Chinese accounting systems and practices', *Accounting, Organizations, and Society* 13(2): 207–24.

Part VI

An overview

In Chapter 19, van Hoepen places the key themes of this book in the context of a review of significant aspects of Chinese culture. His identification of the clash between current developments and a Chinese tradition that stretches back long before the time of the centrally directed economy is thought provoking.

An overview

Chapter 19

Accounting in China
A case of vanishing cultural influence

M. A. van Hoepen

INTRODUCTION

An investigation of the cultural influences on accounting is part
of what may be called the environmental determinism theory.
Even at first glance it is not hard to conclude that China, given
its long history and its unique culture, is a splendid case for both
the investigation and explanation of the ties between culture and
accounting. Historically Chinese accounting is primarily consti-
tuted by the principles and ideologies based on Confucianism,
Buddhism and other philosophies.

For the purposes of this study we can distinguish four periods:

Till 1949   Traditional China.
1949–1978   Socialist centrally controlled/planned economy.
1978–1992   Socialist centrally planned commodity economy.
1992–present   Socialist market economy.

I do no justice to China's long history before 1949 when I describe
'traditional China' as only one period. I do so mainly because it
is not my intention to give a historical overview. Moreover, I think
that cultural influences, as far as they are still of influence on
modern Chinese accounting, stem from the influence of religion
and traditional Chinese philosophies and a certain degree of
conservatism related thereto.
   I referred in the subtitle to 'vanishing cultural influence'.[1] I hope
to explain that cultural influences on accounting diminished in
China in the three periods after 1949, the while (quite different)
economic influences gained importance.

RELATIONSHIP BETWEEN ACCOUNTING AND CULTURE

Before going into more detail about the relationship between accounting and culture in China, it is helpful to give a short overview of the type of research that is relevant in this context. Research in this field is quite recent or, as Gray (1988:4) says, is 'only just beginning to be recognized'.

The growing interest in cultural influences on accounting systems is a result of the growing interest in comparative financial accounting research, which Nobes and Parker (1991) think can be explained by:

1 A historical reason.
2 A multinational reason.
3 A comparative reason (that is, changes in external financial reporting and its changing institutions have increased interest in research into what has been done in other countries).
4 The harmonization reason (increasing harmonization of external financial reporting, especially within the European Union and by the International Accounting Standards Committee).

The historical reason, however, until now did not prove to have a distinct explanatory value. Even Nobes and Parker, although they mention it first, do little more than point at the growing hegemony of the 'British system' over the 'Italian system' of some time ago. The last three reasons seem to provide adequate explanation.

The growing interest in comparative accounting research has resulted in numerous country studies, showing many differences between accounting practices. It is in the attempt to explain these differences that culture comes in.

CULTURAL INFLUENCES AND THEIR EXPLANATORY VALUE

Although several accounting researchers and practitioners maintain that accounting is culturally neutral, most researchers nowadays argue that, since accounting was invented (and thus influenced) by humans, it cannot be completely culturally neutral. Therefore, culture might give us at least some explanations of differences. Only a few researchers go as far as Belkaoui (1990) by stating that: 'Culture dictates accounting.'

The context for the investigation of the relationship between accounting and culture was undoubtedly laid by Hofstede (1980) in his book, *Culture's Consequences: International Differences in Work-Related Values*. Culture is defined in this study as 'the collective programming of the mind, which distinguishes the member of one group from another'.

In 1980 Hofstede developed a 'Value Survey Model' to quantify the effect of national cultures on organizations. In this model Hofstede (1980:25) used four cultural dimensions:

1 Individualism ('individualism v. collectivism').
2 Power distance ('large v. small power distance').
3 Uncertainty avoidance (strong v. weak uncertainty avoidance).
4 Gender ('masculinity v. femininity').

Although it is not possible, given the constraints of space, to elaborate here on these cultural dimensions, it is important to note that Hofstede's work did not emerge from a vacuum, as far as accounting research is concerned. Mueller (1967) had already provided a classification of four stages of development of accounting systems:

1 'Macro-economic framework'.
2 'Micro-economic approach'.
3 'Independent discipline' (of accounting).
4 'Uniform accounting'.

It is clear that this classification was strongly influenced by cultural factors. Such influence is even more obvious in Mueller's (1968) classification of development into ten groups, in which he uses criteria such as business complexity and social climate (see also Choi and Mueller 1992).

ACCOUNTING AND ITS SOCIETAL CONTEXT

Hofstede's work prompted a fair amount of research in which the relationship between societal/cultural influences on the one hand and accounting practice on the other hand is more or less implicit. However, Gray (1985) has made this relationship much more explicit in the development of a model in which societal values are related directly to accounting values or accounting subculture.

As a starting point Gray takes Hofstede's four cultural dimensions and develops four accounting values which are directly related to them. These accounting values, or values of accounting sub-culture, are:

1 'Professionalism'.
2 'Uniformity'.
3 'Conservatism'.
4 'secrecy'.

Gray also distinguishes four dimensions to accounting practice:

1 'Authority of accounting systems' (by which, it seems, 'accounting principles' is meant).
2 'The force of application'.
3 'Measurement practices used'.
4 'The extent of information disclosed'.

The relationship between societal values, or cultural dimensions, on the one hand and accounting values, or accounting sub-culture, on the other can be condensed as shown in Table 19.1. Only individualism and uncertainty avoidance seem to play an interpretative role, whereas power distance and gender are not even mentioned. The reason for this is perhaps that these last two dimensions are more on a micro-level (enterprise level) than on a macro-level (country level).

The relationship between societal values and accounting practice may be summarized, as shown in Table 19.2.

From Gray's study it is evident that the revealed relationships are far from unique and linear, which is a major drawback if we

Table 19.1   Direct associations between societal and accounting values

Values of accounting sub-culture	Relationship with societal values	
	Positive	*Negative*
Professionalism	Individualism	Uncertainty avoidance
Uniformity	Uncertainty avoidance	Individualism
Conservatism	Uncertainty	Individualism
Secrecy	Uncertainty avoidance	Individualism

Source: Perera 1989: 47

Table 19.2 Societal values and accounting practice

Societal values/managerial work-related values	Accounting values	Accounting practice
Individualism	Professionalism	Authority
Large v. small power distance	Uniformity	Application
Strong v. weak uncertainty avoidance	Conservatism	Measurement
Masculinity v. femininity	Secrecy	Disclosure

Source: Perera 1989: 47

try to apply the research in a practical situation. Indeed, if we look to empirical research in this area, be it that which tries to explain national practice from environmental/societal factors or that which tries to discover spheres of influence (whether or not on a statistical basis), we can only be disappointed. Disappointment arises not so much from the small number of publications but from the lack of hard, verifiable and objective conclusions and the degree of explanatory value.

The explanation of 'national practices' is little more than a handful of unverifiable statements on the influence of mainly individualism and uncertainty avoidance, but it is doubtful if this is sufficient to explain the differences in accounting practices between, for example, Sweden and The Netherlands. Cultural differences may have a greater explanatory value when it comes to a comparison between countries which are not so similar, such as the UK and China.

With regard to spheres of influence, the ultimate wisdom amounts to no more than a division between the 'Anglo-American' and the 'Continental-European' spheres or the division between 'macro uniform systems' and 'micro business practice.' Only a few researchers pay any attention to developing countries and countries with a centrally planned economy, but in this area it seems to be that historical and economic reasons rather than cultural values explain the differences in accounting systems and practices. Moreover, it is doubtful whether these explanatory factors (which are far from being direct cultural factors) still hold their explanatory power nowadays in the 'Western' hemisphere (that is, North America, Europe, Australia and New Zealand). Is there still much difference within the European Union between 'common law' countries and 'codified Roman law' countries, at least to the extent that it can explain differences in accounting practice? Also, the influence of the stock exchange authorities in France and Italy is very much 'American', despite the fact that these countries have relatively few quoted companies. Perhaps, here again, the causes of differences (although in my opinion these are far from cultural factors) have a greater explanatory value when it comes to a comparison between countries which are not so similar. Let us therefore turn to accounting in the People's Republic of China during the different periods that were distinguished at the beginning of this chapter.

CULTURE AND ACCOUNTING IN TRADITIONAL CHINA (–1949)

Historically, China is one of the oldest countries using an accounting system (together with Phoenicia, Babylon and ancient Israel). Well over two thousand years ago, China was already applying a highly developed accounting and auditing system for financial and economic activities. According to historical reports, the first forms of accounting emerged during the *Shang* Dynasty (1500 BC–1000 BC). Before the revolution at the beginning of this century, when feudalism comprised the social system of China, peasants had to pay part of their harvest to the feudal lords. These dues were collected by local officers who kept records and prepared accounting records of their collections. Six major traditional cultural elements originate from this period.

Theory of opposing *Yi* (justice) and *Li* (profit)

In traditional Chinese philosophy, *Yi* (justice) and *Li* (profit) are opposed. Confucius never talked about *Li*. Taoism also warned people not to think about *Li*. After the *Qin* Dynasty (221 BC–207 BC) and the *Han* Dynasty (206 BC–AD 220), some neo-Confucians strongly advocated the theory of 'seeking justice (*Yi*) and not pursuing profit (*Li*)'. Consequently, the saying, 'nobles think about *Yi*, while common people think about *Li*',[2] has been an integral part of Chinese traditional culture. The culture of opposition between *Yi* and *Li* resulted accordingly in discrimination against merchants and accountants in Chinese history. For example, merchants and private accountants were stipulated by law to be the lowest social class. The laws in the *Qin* and *Han* Dynasties even forbade merchants to wear silk clothes, to ride a horse or to take a carriage. These legal provisions were in fact a humiliation for merchants as well as for accountants. After the Middle Ages, there was an unprecedented boom in commercial activities in the West, and attitudes towards accounting and reporting changed rapidly there. At the same time, many merchants and accountants in China threw away their account books and returned to farming.

Accounting is defined as a means towards the maximization of owners' profits or shareholders' wealth. Thus, according to the Chinese tradition, accounting activities are naturally categorized as *Li*, since accounting serves either the profits of other individuals (e.g. landlords, mill-owners) by whom accountants are employed or the profit of accountants themselves.

No doubt, any recognition of and emphasis on the importance of profits in the accounting world would be criticized publicly according to the theory of opposing *Yi* and *Li*. As a result, both accounting and accountants have long been detested by the Chinese and this culture still has an impact on today's accounting theory and practice in China. At present most Chinese accountants are still reluctant to use the word 'profit' let alone discuss the profits of an enterprise. In Chinese accounting theory, serving the masses, rather than maximizing profits or wealth, is usually considered to be the most important objective of accounting. Establishing profit centres is criticized by many accountants and managers in China. During the Cultural Revolution especially, enterprises were never created as profit centres. Even today, the use of cost centres in enterprises is more popular than the use of profit centres. Promotion for accountants in China is more difficult than that for other professionals, partially because of the public scorn for accounting.

Opposition of trust and contracts

Business transactions in the West depend largely on (legal) contracts signed by the parties concerned. Legal contracts are the basis of accounting measurement and they constitute events to be reported. In today's business world, accounting reports and business contracts play complementary roles in providing information.

In Chinese culture, however, ethical principles and moral standards play a predominant role in the world of business and accounting. In Chinese business habits, there is much more emphasis on mutual faith and understanding. The Chinese believe that the basic nature of human beings is good, so to write everything down in black and white is considered to be a demonstration of distrust and to be against the nature of human beings. In Chinese philosophy, a good understanding and relationship based on mutual trust does not require legal provisions in order to stipulate the responsibilities and obligations. Accordingly, trust and contracts are opposed to each other. Based on this belief, the rigid relationship between accounting and business contracts is not so evident in China as in the West. Sometimes the events referred to are not legal contracts but customers' oral requests or managers' oral promises.

Dogmatic attitude

The Chinese are sometimes criticized for their dogmatic and conservative attitudes, which dominate their way of thinking in many cases. In the development of accounting, the Chinese behaved dogmatically. For example, as early as the *Zhou* Dynasty (1100 BC–771 BC) and the *Qin* Dynasty (221 BC–207 BC), government accounting offices already had a three-account reporting system, comprising the *Cao Liu* Account, the *Xi Liu* Account and the *Zong Qin* Account.[3] Such a system was very advanced at the time. However, the same three-account system continued to be handed down for about two thousand years, until the beginning of the twentieth century. During this long period of time, no one changed the system significantly, let alone created a new one. This dogmatism has long limited any show of imagination and creativity in the development of accounting by the accounting profession. As a result, the Chinese traditional accounting system remained at the 'single-entry' stage for centuries. Even nowadays, some agricultural departments or private firms still use the 'single-entry' bookkeeping system.

Following political propaganda, some accountants and academicians dogmatically considered that accounting should serve political institutions and should be developed under the guidance of politicians. It is interesting that, not long ago, Chinese academic papers and textbooks on accounting used the same method for citing classics as for quoting political slogans. In some accounting research papers, the authors used quotations from their leaders (mostly political leaders) to demonstrate their theories. Accounting theory was arbitrarily pushed towards slogans and quotations.

Conservative thought

China is one of the most ancient nations in the world. Its cultural tradition goes back thousands of years, and its cultural structure is well established. As a result, people hold to their traditional habits and refuse to change.[4] This mentality results in a reluctance to accept foreign accounting techniques, and in the upholding of Chinese national accounting theories and approaches, even when they are completely out of date. As noted earlier, traditional Chinese accounting practice used a single-entry system and was seldom affected by the evolution of accounting techniques outside China over the past two thousand years. Today's Chinese accounting practice still retains a strong national style. For example, the journal account is still called the 'water-flow account' as it was named under the Chinese single-entry system hundreds of years ago; older accounting personnel still prefer the abacus to modern instruments (such as electronic calculators and computers); amounts of money in accounting documents used to be written in Chinese numerals which are far more complicated than the Arabic numerals used elsewhere.

Until July 1993, the Chinese accounting recording system permitted the use of three different approaches. Industrial enterprises used the debit credit method, which was introduced from the West. Commercial enterprises used the increase decrease method,[5] created by some Chinese commercial people and accountants in the 1960s. Agricultural departments used the receipt payment method, which is an improved version of the traditional Chinese 'single-entry' system, and is cash based. The question as to which method (Chinese or Western) is the more advanced generated a fierce debate in the Chinese accounting literature of the 1980s, but no consensus has been reached. Another illustration of the prevailing conservative attitude is that accountants in China are always averse to risk in their decision-making; they usually prefer a lower return on investments under conditions of certainty to higher returns under conditions of uncertainty.[6]

Collectivism

By studying Hong Kong, Singapore and Taiwan, where the great majority of inhabitants are Chinese, Hofstede (1980) discovered that the Chinese there belong to what he described as the group of low individualism or high collectivism. The same characteristic undoubtedly prevails also in the mainland of China. In short, Chinese culture is essentially characterized by collectivism; that is, China as a society is very much group or mass oriented whereas the West is individually oriented. The characteristic of collectivism has its impact on Chinese accounting as well. For example, the orientation of users of accounting information is different between China and the West: in China the users are, or used to be, mainly economic and administrative bodies with macro-economic interests while in the West the users of information are largely shareholders, creditors and others with private interests. Also, the accounting principles in China up till 1992 explicitly revealed collectivism. The Chinese accounting principles used to be entirely embodied in the national uniform accounting system and the main principles differed from those in the West. Four unique principles were specified in Chinese accounting and all of them showed the influence of collectivism:

1 The principle of serving the national economic plan.
2 The principle of serving the state's general and specific economic and social policies.
3 The principle of the national interest as a whole.
4 The principle of the labouring masses (i.e. accounting must rely on the masses to reach the objectives).

Religion

Religion has always been an important part of a country's culture. China has traditionally been characterized as a country of Buddhism. The Chinese Buddhists say that people's desires are the roots of evil. Buddhism preaches that if one wants to be rid of miseries and distresses, one must give up all of one's earthly desires and try to escape from reality. That is, people should divorce themselves from the material world (including money and personal values). Some commandments of Buddhism also stipulate that Buddhists can neither accumulate wealth nor incur any debts. Buddhists detest being preoccupied by profits in daily life. The creed of Buddhism has considerable impact not only on the Chinese economy but also on Chinese accounting.

Generally speaking, Buddhism and other Chinese religions (e.g. Confucianism and Taoism) lead the public to comprehend accounting primarily from the spiritual point of view. Although China has many splendid temples and innumerable religious classics, it is difficult to find some valuable accounting material. In China, the religious arena was traditionally considered as a 'sacred place' where monetary transactions were forbidden. By contrast the religious arena in the West was also the site of economic activities, or even the centre of commerce and finance (for instance, Italy in the Middle Ages and later Flanders and The Netherlands). The difference in religions between China and the West may explain why the development of accounting in China is still a little way behind the West. Currently, although the impact of religion on accounting has diminished, religion still influences the Chinese accountant's thought and behaviour. In fact, all the above areas including the theory of opposing *Yi* and *Li*, the opposition of trust and contracts, the dogmatic attitude, collectivism, and particularly conservatism, are entirely or partially related to the Chinese religions. However, as discussion of the next stages will reveal, the purely cultural dimensions (culture in the sense of a 'collective programming of the mind') which were described under the heading of 'Traditional China' have lost their importance very rapidly over time. While these might explain why Chinese accounting is in a less developed state than Western accounting, they can hardly be seen any more as basic elements in the explanation of differences.

CHINESE CULTURE AND ACCOUNTING (1949–78)

Chinese accounting is shaped not only by traditional culture but also by modern culture and national economic development. Following the Founding of the PRC, the Chinese economy was under Soviet influence until 1957. Then there was the Great Leap Forward till the early 1960s. After the Great Leap Forward, there were three years of economic crisis and three years of economic adjustment. The Cultural Revolution followed. Finally, a New Economic Order began in 1978 under the leadership of Deng

Xiaoping. In accordance with the development of the different economic systems, the accounting system in China also changed from the early Soviet model to today's structure, which is more or less the Western stylized system with some Chinese characteristics. Before the Great Leap Forward began in 1958, the accounting system in China was almost a copy of the former Soviet system, although the Chinese hesitated in those days to admit this. The modified Soviet system was called 'State Accounting'. Accounting served the state with accounting information which was mainly related to the implementation by enterprises of the state's production quota and government budgets. During the Great Leap Forward (1958–60), although Soviet influence still existed, accounting nationwide was characterized as 'manager personal accounting'. Accounting was used as a tool towards promotion by the enterprises. Managers personally selected an accounting approach and decided on the content of accounting statements, and even on the amounts of profits, costs and income. From 1960 to 1966, accounting in China was redeveloped, with a combination of the Western system, the Soviet System, and of the characteristics of the Chinese. The accounting system during this period was a type of compound accounting. However, during the Cultural Revolution, this compound accounting was destroyed. Accounting simply did not exist any more. After 1978 a nationwide accounting system was resumed. This new system may be described as a semi-Westernized system with Chinese characteristics. There were four predominant influences on accounting during this period.

State theory

China is a nation with a socialist structure. Central to the concept of socialism is the principle of social ownership of the means of production (sometimes called state ownership). Accordingly, the accounting system under the socialist structure follows this tenet. State ownership of the enterprises in China leads naturally to the conception of a unified accounting system embracing all of these enterprises. In effect, the national economy, or its industrialized sectors, becomes the accounting entity and the individual enterprise is represented as an accounting sub-entity. All accounting control systems, methodologies and financial reporting standards are prescribed by the central government, and all levels of government departments and all enterprises must follow this system. The accounting system of each enterprise is interconnected through the implementation of a national chart of accounts. Thus, accounting in the enterprise is converted into an instrument of national economic administration for the realization of control over the activities of the enterprise.

In fact, under socialist economic theory (i.e. state theory), accounting is the 'administrator' and representative of people's properties. Thus accounting objectives and functions are different from those in the West owing to different socio-economic conditions and objectives. In setting accounting principles or norms, for example, Western countries are initially motivated by profit-maximizing prospects. In China the focus is much more on physical production to serve public requirements. As a result of this, the accounting function in China is, or used to be, to review and supervise the economic activities of different units, to examine the execution of the State Plan and the State Budget, to strengthen accounting control over the micro as well as the macro economy, and to satisfy the management needs of the different economic units.

In accordance with state theory, the Chinese accounting theories always emphasized the necessity of providing the country's macro-administration with accounting data. According to the Accountancy Law of the People's Republic of China, adopted on 21 January 1985, the duties of accountants were to 'uphold the State public finance system and the enterprise financial system, and protect the socialist public assets' (Article 1). The National Auditing Office, which is directly under the State Council, commands national auditing practice and develops auditing standards. The main objective of auditing is to prevent violations of the state public finance system and the enterprise financial system. The public finance department of the State Council regulates accounting for the entire country and formulates the state's uniform accounting system which is a model for all of the enterprises. Accountants employed by the enterprise must exercise accounting supervision over business transactions in the enterprise on behalf of the state. However, when a conflict of interest between the enterprise and the state occurs, the accounting office and its staff would certainly be in a difficult position. How to solve this problem has recently been a topic of debate in the Chinese accounting literature (see among others,

Wu 1985, 1986; Hou 1987; Zhao 1990; Li 1990).

Although the influence of state theory does have some cultural dimension, it is doubtful whether this can be regarded as a purely, cultural influence. It is more likely to be a consequence of existing economic conditions.

Class theory

Marxism presumes the existence of conflict among the social classes of a society, and the result of the class struggle is one class ruling over another. Using this idea, some Chinese authors created a theory associated with the class struggle, called the class theory. The class theory has been summarized as 'take the class struggle as the guiding principle' and by 'handling the class struggle well, everything will be well'. This theory is regarded in socialist China as one of the most important Marxist theories. According to the class theory, the struggle of different classes will exist in China for a long time. To discuss and analyse social issues from the standpoint of class has been another cultural tendency in China since 1949, and particularly in the 1960s and 1970s. Accordingly, this class view has considerably shaped the people's understanding of and attitude towards accounting. For example, some authors in the 1970s proposed that the establishment of the Chinese accounting system should be under the guiding ideology of the class struggle theory. This proposal was refuted in the 1980s. In the late 1970s and early 1980s, a debate began in the accounting literature on whether or not accounting has a class characteristic. Proponents argued that accounting could be done by different classes in a given society, and thus it could serve the interests of different classes (e.g. the proletarians and the capitalists). They argued that accounting, as one of the social sciences, has a class character. Opponents argued that the fact that accounting could be used by different classes simply proved the non-class character of accounting. Instead, accounting had only a technical character. The compromiser considered that accounting had not only a class character but also a technical character and that neither should be overemphasized at the expense of the other (e.g. Wong 1981, Tian 1983, Hu 1984). This is currently the predominant view in the literature.

Marxism

Although Marxist theory originated in the West, it has not been a part of the Western culture. However, since Marxism was introduced to China from the Soviet Union in 1917, it has been an important and inseparable part of modern Chinese culture. Marxism has had profound influence upon Chinese society in the spheres of the economy, politics, culture, education, and so on. In particular, since 1949 it has significantly affected Chinese accounting, including accounting concepts and principles, the development of accounting, as well as accountants' attitudes and behaviour. Today Chinese accounting theories are entirely associated with Marxist theory. For example, basic concepts, such as interest and interest rates, wages, costs, fixed assets, funds, profits, and depreciation, defined solely according to Marxist theory. However, common concepts which are used in the West, such as return on investment (ROI), debt/equity ratio, earnings per share (EPS), residual income, and capitalization, are little known to many Chinese accountants and even to many accounting professors.

The Cultural Revolution

The Cultural Revolution was a period of cultural retrogression in recent Chinese history. Some radicals (e.g. the 'Gang of Four') hoped to build a non-monetary economic system in China. They believed that the accounting system, which took monetary units as the means of measurement was the shield for the currency in circulation, and thus it should be eliminated from all economic activities. The Gang of Four asserted that, 'even if we do not perform accounting for ten years, money (i.e. resources, or wealth) can never go to foreign hands.' In fact, the Gang of Four succeeded in putting their words into effect. During the ten years of the Cultural Revolution (1966–76), accounting in all state and collective enterprises was terminated, the accounting people were dismissed, and the accounting departments in universities were closed. The Cultural Revolution was the most dangerous expression of discrimination against accountancy in Chinese modern history. Propaganda (e.g. movies, drama, and novels) during the Cultural Revolution denounced accounting personnel. This not only resulted in public prejudice against accounting and accounting personnel but also led to the ruin of accountants both physically and mentally. It seriously disrupted the development of accounting established after 1949.

To summarize, the theory, system and institutions of Chinese accounting have been built around the frameworks of both traditional and modern culture. Although culture continues to have an impact on Chinese accounting, it is a rapidly vanishing influence. Indeed, for the second period (1949–78) discussed here, one could seriously question whether the influences as mentioned are actually of a cultural nature (as a collective programming of the mind) or whether they are the consequences of prevailing economic conditions. The open-door policy pursued since 1978 (the third period to be discussed) has changed the Chinese accounting system remarkably, both theoretically and practically.

CHINESE CULTURE AND ACCOUNTING (1978–92)

Since 1978 China has followed an open-door policy. This policy has inevitably brought Chinese culture into collision with the Western world, resulting in a mutual exchange of ideas and people:

1 Learning English or other Western languages has been taken up nationwide; as a result, many foreign accounting standards (GAAPs), as well as books and articles, have been circulated in China or translated into Chinese;
2 Many Chinese, including accountants and accounting educators, have gone to countries throughout the Western world for study (e.g. for higher degrees) or for training. Many who have returned have themselves started to contribute to the establishment and development of a new Chinese accounting system;
3 Many foreign accounting professors have been invited to give lectures, to carry out research at Chinese universities or to conduct training programmes for Chinese accountants;
4 Many Chinese accounting professors have attended international conferences, seminars, symposia, and workshops on accounting, and some have been invited by foreigners to give lectures on Chinese accounting.
5 Foreign joint ventures in China have been set up, and the Chinese have learned a lot from these firms about accounting and business administration. As a result, a number of

accounting regulations, such as 'Accounting Regulations for Joint Ventures Using Chinese and Foreign Investment in the People's Republic of China', have been issued.

6 Many joint research projects relating to accounting have been or soon will be completed. These research projects have benefited both China and the West in striving for a better understanding of accounting systems.

Chinese accounting has benefited a great deal from this cultural and accounting exchange. In particular, the Chinese have learned much from the accounting theory and practice of the West. Since China opened the door to the West in 1978, China has tried to develop its accounting system more or less in the Western style, and the accounting gap between China and the West has gradually been narrowed. The changes in the accounting system may be summarized as follows:

1 Chinese accounting professionals began to consider that the establishment of a new Chinese accounting system should be based on both deductive and inductive approaches.
2 The public gained a new understanding of the functions of accounting.
3 The social status of the accounting profession improved.
4 The state government registered a number of accounting professionals as CPAs for the first time since the founding of the PRC.
5 Accounting firms and agencies were set up and started to provide accounting services.
6 Many universities either restored or set up accounting departments for training and education. Meanwhile, accounting associations nationwide were established, and a number of accounting journals emerged.
7 Top students at universities became eager to pursue accountancy as a career.

CHINESE CULTURE AND ACCOUNTING (1992–PRESENT)

The fourth period starting in 1992 has been described as the period of the socialist market economy. The fact that purely cultural influences on accounting are now melting away in China cannot be illustrated any more clearly than by looking at the objectives of accounting as stated by the new accounting legislation:

1 To provide information for macro-economic management.
2 To provide information about the financial position and operating results for relevant parties.
3 To provide for the information needs of business management.

These objectives are no different from the accounting objectives that can be stated for any more or less centralized economy (for instance, France). The present state of the art of accounting in China is perfectly reflected by the list of causes of differences in accounting practice as discerned by Nobes and Parker (1991: 11–20):

1 Legal systems.
2 Providers of finance.
3 Taxation.
4 Accountancy profession.
5 Inflation.
6 Theory.
7 Accidents of history.

There is no notion whatsoever of cultural influences (defined as the collective programming of the mind, which distinguishes the member of one group from another).

CONCLUSION

Cultural studies of the former state of the art of accounting in China, which can prove exciting for accounting historians and anthropologists, might also put some of the peculiarities and national characteristics of the present state of the art of accounting in China into proper perspective. Most of these peculiarities, however, are much better explained by historic and economic reasons than by (direct) cultural influences.

Present day Chinese accounting fits perfectly into different classification studies, whether these are stage-of-development studies, morphological studies or mixed classifications. China no longer demands a separate category.

Country studies (either parochial or xenophile) on the present state of the art of accounting in China can be very useful for those confronted with Chinese accounting, but China is not exceptional in that.

NOTES

1 This chapter is derived extensively from two other publications: van Hoepen M. A., (1992) Culture and External Financial Reporting, monthly periodical for accountancy and business economies, September, pp. 390–9 (in Dutch); Zhang, T. X. Gao, S. S. and van Hoepen, M. A. (1992) Accounting and Culture: the Chinese Case Study, Centre for Research in Business Economics, Department of Financial and Management Accounting, Erasmus University, Rotterdam, Report 9202/Acc, January.
2 The Chinese people in those days were categorized into two classes: nobles, who comprised the educated people and the officers, and the common people.
3 The *Cao Liu* Account is similar to today's 'journal'; the *Xi Liu* Account is a kind of detailed account; while the *Zong Qin* Account is more or less similar to the 'general ledger'.
4 The impact of conservatism on accounting, in particular on accounting measurement practices, has been demonstrated empirically with some Western cases (Choi and Mueller, 1992). The accounting principle of conservatism has been criticized by the Chinese ever since the establishment of socialist China. Conservatism as used here is conservatism as a cultural factor and has no direct relationship with the principle of conservatism in accounting.
5 This approach is a revised version of the debit credit approach, using the Chinese characters '*Zeng*' (Increase) and '*Jian*' (Decrease), and some other adjustments. This approach requires that the sources of funds are strictly separated from the use of funds. A transaction associated only with a source of funds or with a use of funds is entered on either the *Zeng* side or the *Jian* side whereas a transaction associated with both a source and a use of funds is entered on the *Zeng* side and the *Jian* side and the amount of *Zeng* is equal to that of *Jian*. The major advantage of this approach is that it can easily be learned and applied by the Chinese, because the words 'debit' and 'credit' translated into Chinese are difficult to use to explain economic transactions if their real accounting meaning is not mastered.
6 This tends to confirm that conservatism is linked most closely and positively with uncertainty avoidance (Gray 1988).
7 Eclecticism is also regarded as one of China's cultural characteristics.

REFERENCES

Belkaoui, A. (1990) *Judgment in International Accounting: A Theory of Cognition, Cultures, Language and Contracts*, New York: Quorum Books.
Choi, F. D. S. and Mueller, G. G. (1992) *International Accounting* (2nd edn.), Englewood Cliffs, NJ: Prentice Hall.
Gray, S. J. (1985) 'Cultural influences and international classification of accounting systems', Paper presented to European Institute of

Advanced Studies in Management (Brussels) workshop on accounting and culture, Amsterdam, June.

—— (1988) 'Towards a theory of cultural influence on the development of accounting systems internationally', London: Abacus, pp. 1–15.

Hofstede, G. (1980) *Culture's Consequences: International Differences in Work-Related Values*, Beverly Hills, Calif: Sage.

Hou, B. L. (1987) 'Restructuring accounting management systems from a macro perspective', *Zhonggue Jingji Wenti (Chinese Economic Issues)*, November, pp. 29–32 (in Chinese).

Hu, W. Y. (1984) *Modern Accounting* (in Chinese), Shanghai: Fudan University Press.

Li, B. Q. (1990) 'Accounting supervision weakness and its reform strategy', *Contemporary Economic Science*, December, pp. 80–4 (in Chinese).

Mueller, G. G. (1967) *International Accounting*, New York: Macmillan.

—— (1968) 'Accounting principles generally accepted in the United States versus those generally accepted elsewhere', *International Journal of Accounting Education and Research* 3(2): 91–103.

Nobes, C. W. and Parker, R. H. (1991) 'Introduction, and causes of differences' in C. W. Nobes and R. H. Parker (eds) *Comparative International Accounting* (3rd edn), Englewood Cliffs, NJ: Prentice Hall, pp. 3–22.

Perera, M. H. B. (1989) 'Towards a framework to analyse the impact of culture on accounting', *International Journal of Accounting* 24(1): 47.

Tian, J. (1983) *The Basis of Accounting* (in Chinese), Beijing: Central Television and Broadcasting University Press.

Wong, W. Y. (1981) *A Fundamental Course of Accounting* (in Chinese), Liaoning: People's Publishers.

Wu, T. C. (1985) 'The system of accountants appointed by the state', *Jingji Ribao (Economic Daily)*, 21 December (in Chinese).

—— (1986) 'The view of accounting independence and the State supervising enterprises', *People's Daily*, 7 February (in Chinese).

Zhao, D. W. (1990) 'Study on the reform of our accounting management system', *Journal of Yunnan Institute of Finance and Trade*, Autumn, pp. 1–3 (in Chinese).

Index

a priori research 241–2
A shares 77, 119, 281; indices 108–10
academic exchanges 230, 270, 310, 364–5
accounting curriculum 303–9
accounting development 23–37, 200, 202–13; accounting profession 30–2; before 1949 202–3; classification of stages 351; co–operation between Chinese and foreign CPA firms 32–4; and economic objectives 225; 1949–78 140–3, 204–6; 1978–93 207–11; phases of reform 25–9; risks of foreign investment 34–6; standards setting process 29–30; traditional economic system 24–5
accounting education 17, 206, 259, 299–318; accounting reform 145–6, 270; and computerization 234; Cultural Revolution 16, 142–3, 206; curriculum 303–9; link with accounting profession 307–11; phases 301; political accounting 311–12; students' expectations of prospective employers 311–15
accounting equation 161, 185, 254, 254–5
accounting functions 140; reforms and 143–9
Accounting Law of the People's Republic of China 1985 24, 145, 174, 207, 211, 361
accounting practices: Accounting Standards and changes in 161–7; categories 272; Cultural Revolution 16; national differences 353–4; see also accounting reform, computerization
accounting principles: Accounting Standards for Business Enterprises 155, 160, 180, 213–14; auditing system 328; collectivism 358; international harmonization 185, 255–6
accounting profession 30–2, 287–8, 288–9; links with accounting education 309–11; personnel shortage 259–60; role and the state 361–2; status 258, 308; in traditional China 354–5; see also accounting education, certified public accountants
accounting reform 140–9, 157, 246–84; academic research and education 268–70; analysis of reasons 261–73; economic reform and 140–9, 246–9, 262–8; effects 274–80; enterprise management function 140, 143–6; external market decision function 140, 147–9; financial reporting 274–5; internationalization 254–6, 278–80; legal system 256–7, 270–3; management control 275–8; phases

For Product Safety Concerns and Information please contact our
EU representative GPSR@taylorandfrancis.com Taylor & Francis
Verlag GmbH, Kaufingerstraße 24, 80331 München, Germany